INFORMATION IN

THE ENTERPRISE

— it's more than technology

Re-issue of the original edition, re-formatted.

This version of the book has been created to re-issue the book originally published in 1992. This has been done following many requests to make the book available again after it went out of print several years ago. It has been re-typeset with pages re-formatted accordingly, but the original text remains the same. There have been obvious changes to publisher and copyright information. The References have been changed to be presented in an author-date form. Almost all the original word hyphenation has been removed so the text is much easier to edit and use for other purposes such as training materials.

The original book was used in many companies, some of which adopted the Information Architecture model described. Thousands of copies of the book were sold around the world. Before re-issuing the book, the contents were reviewed for content and currency. The experience and advice in the book have remained remarkably current with the passage of time. The most significant change is that Digital Equipment Corporation no longer exists following takeover. Many problems and solutions discussed in the book remain problems for many companies who would benefit today from the information contained herein.

Some key messages when the book was first issues remain as valid today as then: enterprises pay insufficient attention to overall information, focussing primarily on computer-supported or computer-assisted applications—thus there remain fundamental misconceptions of information systems and failure to manage information; we predicted Individual Information Systems—that has happened including the prolific use of social media; many key problems we identified, remain—history is repeating itself, and many are not learning from it.

A new edition of the book is planned for 2019-2020, when it is expected the text will be changed substantially, with much new material.

Geoffrey Darnton
April 2018

INFORMATION IN THE ENTERPRISE

It's More Than Technology

Geoffrey Darnton
Sergio Giacoletto

DUROTRIGES
PRESS®

The following are trademarks of Digital Equipment Corporation:
DEC, DEC/CMS, DEC/MMS, DECnet, DECsystem-IO,
DECSYSTEM-20, DECUS, DECwriter, DIBOL, Digital logo,
EduSystem, IAS, MASSBUS, PDP, PDT, RSTS, RSX, UNIBUS, VAX,
VAXcluster, VMS, and VT.
The trademarks of other organizations are acknowledged and
nothing in this book is intended to detract from those trademarks.

Views expressed in this book are those of the authors, not of the
publisher. Durotriges Press is not responsible for any errors that
may appear in this book.

This book was published originally with ISBN 1-55558-091-2
(Digital Press), ISBN 0-13-176173-0 (Prentice-Hall), and ISBN
0-87692-789-4 (Prentice-Hall of India).

Originally published in 1992, re-issued in 2018.

This re-issued edition published by Durotriges Press, Bournemouth,
England, with the following ISBNs:

978-1-912359-03-5 (hardback)
978-1-912359-04-2 (paperback)
978-1-912359-05-9 (ebook)

*It must be remembered that there is
nothing more difficult to plan, more
doubtful of success, nor more dangerous
to manage than the creation of a new
system. For the initiator has the enmity
of the old institution and merely
lukewarm defenders
in those who would gain by the new
ones.*

*Machiavelli
The Prince, 1513*

*We trained hard ... but it seemed that
everytime we were beginning to form up
into teams, we would be reorganized.
I was to learn later in life that we tend
to meet any new situation by
reorganizing; and a wonderful method
it can be for creating the illusion
ofprogress while producing confusion,
inefficiency, and demoralization.*

*Petronius Arbiter
Greek Navy, 210 B.C.*

Contents

Chapter 6

Organizational Impact

Part 3

Chapter 7

Information Technology and Systems

Chapter 8

The Information Management Challenges

Information, Systems, and Architecture

Chapter 10

Information and IT Infrastructures

Chapter 11

Epilogue

Appendix A

Appendix A:

List of Figures

List of Tables

[page left blank intentionally]

Preface

The evolution of human endeavor is frequently characterized as a sequence of transitions from an agricultural to an industrial to a service economy. It is often asserted that society today is becoming an information society, and indeed that many companies are becoming information based. We believe that in practice this is only partly true; in recent decades most of the emphasis has really been on information technology rather than information. We are about to see a fundamental shift to a wider consideration of information, knowledge, and wisdom, with IT positioned as an enabling factor. As a paradigm shift, this applies to society, enterprises, and individuals.

In the last few years an enormous amount of literature has been written about information systems and the enterprise, but very little about the information itself. As a result, many considerations of the information needs of enterprises are implicit, or dispersed, rather than handled in a disciplined manner. We believe that the time has come for enterprises (as well as societies and individuals) to address this issue.

The previous major paradigm shift to an industrial economy required the development of massive manufacturing infrastructure. Similarly, a paradigm shift to an information economy requires the development of a massive information infrastructure which must be designed and constructed, that is "architected", carefully.

This book, therefore, addresses the creation of information architecture supported by IT infrastructure and the architectural principles behind them. The discussion is grouped into three parts.

Part I—Executive Brief

Part I presents the book's key themes.

- The information needs of the enterprise are far too extensive to

be handled only by its computerized systems.
- Information technology encompasses much more than computers and networks.
- One of the greatest weaknesses in enterprise organization is the failure to assign responsibility for managing the overall information and knowledge assets of the enterprise independently of the technology.
- Information, information technology, and organization interact in many crucial ways presenting to the enterprise both substantial opportunities and substantial threats.

Chapter 1 gives the summary of the key themes of the book and presents our high-level vision for the future based on key objectives of information infrastructures. Chapter 2 provides a set of recommendations for building an enterprise-wide information infrastructure that are addressed to different levels of enterprise management.

Part II—Digital's Experience

Part II gives practical explanations of information and IT infrastructures (by way of case study), indicating their relationship with applications of information.

In Chapter 3 we describe our personal experience in developing an enterprise information management model for Digital Europe. This experience spans nearly a decade and is offered to help readers who have similar goals of creating enterprise-wide information infrastructures. We use internal as well as customer experience to generalize an overall model, which we then describe in the subsequent chapters.

Chapter 4 provides a model for building a systems architecture covering both applications and data in computerized and non-computerized systems. This systems architecture represents a departure from traditional business systems planning methods. It offers opportunities for a better fit between modern organizational forms and information systems.

Chapter 5 explains how to build a business architecture that identifies the relevance of information to an enterprise's mission, objectives, and strategies. We add value to more traditional business analysis methods by focusing on information needs and IT opportunities. We show why we do not advocate that anyone try to decide enterprise strategy before defining information or IT strategies or planning the information systems. These tasks must be done together.

In Chapter 6 we focus on some of the organizational impacts of technology we have observed during the evolution and implementation of information architectures. We give a practical example of how IT can be used to build flexible organizations—for example, through the use of virtual project teams. We then comment on the impact on management styles and the changes in roles and responsibilities brought on by the extensive use of IT.

Part III—Enterprise-Wide Information Infrastructures

Part III gives our personal view of the theory and literature underlying the issues we address.

In Chapter 7 we define information technology and its importance to the global economy, the enterprise, and the individual. We then analyze IT opportunities as well as threats and look briefly at various classes of information systems.

Chapter 8 discusses the distinction between information and IT. Here we present various challenges that enterprises face in managing information, among them, knowledge, integration, technology, interpersonal communication, and organizational management and direction. We also look at the evolving role of the Information Services (IS) function and suggest a model for information and information technology management.

Chapter 9 presents different analogies used in the information world. We look at the theoretical foundations of some of the key ideas behind information management and applied information and systems theory, and dwell on some key metaphors that link information with the architectural and biological worlds. We discuss information in its roles as a major enterprise asset.

In Chapter 10 we describe the components of both an information and an IT infrastructure and provide some basic guidelines for building them. We also explore the most recent developments in product architectures, such as client/server and open multi-vendor systems.

Added Value

Finally, we believe this book adds value to existing knowledge in several important ways:

- Many organizations are either constructing or thinking about constructing extensively integrated systems of computer applications; we give concrete suggestions on how to go about doing that.
- We present the experience of a large multinational company (Digital) in constructing an enterprise-wide information infrastructure.
- The use of information technology involves both opportunities and risks, some of which we describe and explore.
- Traditional approaches to strategic planning are biased toward top-down definitions and de-composition. We do not share that bias but instead propose parallel activities at several levels in an enterprise.
- We propose several roles that an information management and technology executive should undertake in order that information and IT are managed satisfactorily.
- Our book is unconventional and controversial in places. This is because we question certain conventional wisdoms and represent many of the directions for change that can be found today. Change occurs in part because of differences between the past and present, and we are very much concerned with current directions of change.

Our book is not a scientific or systematic study, yet it departs from a strictly practitioner approach in its exploration of many of the theoretical foundations of information technology. It offers ideas and approaches to which the reader may respond with either indifference or enthusiasm. Some of these approaches have been successful, whereas others have not yet been implemented fully.

The danger that faces a book written by two people working for the same company is that it may be perceived as a statement of corporate policy or intention. Our work is our own and should not be construed in any sense as an official statement of Digital Equipment Corporation. We accept full responsibility for errors of commission and omission. Throughout we identify many shortcomings that we believe exist in current approaches and literature and, in some cases, propose alternatives. Thus the book serves as a manifesto for much more rigorous research and advanced development in the management, organization, and application of information theory and principles.

Geoffrey Darnton, Titchfield, England
Sergio Giacoletto, Geneva, Switzerland
July, 1992

Acknowledgements

This book would not have been possible without ongoing support within our own company, for which we thank both management and colleagues. It is the essence of a book such as this that it draws upon a tradition of ideas from many different sources.

The ideas we present have developed as a result of work with many colleagues over the past few years. It is impossible to name everyone involved. We thank all of them, and feel that especially we should note Alfonso Di Ianni, Radu Eftimie, Glen Gage, Ken Gordon, Werner Kasel, Jan Koolhas, Jean-Claude Nikles, Graham Scott, and David Stone. Obviously, as authors we have added our own views, and accept complete responsibility for the ideas as finally presented.

Special thanks are due to Pier Carlo Falotti, the President of Digital Europe, for his continuing support for almost a decade and for sponsoring our early architectural work.

We appreciate the helpful advice we have received from Leslie Berkes, Steven Dekany, Kathleen Suchan, and Norman Ward, who had the very difficult task of reviewing early drafts of the manuscript and providing helpful suggestions, which we have been able to incorporate.

Finally, we would like to express our gratitude to Chase Duffy and George Horesta of Digital Press who put so much work into making this book a successful publication.

[page left blank intentionally]

PART 1

Executive Brief

The table below lists the themes we outline in Chapter 1.

Theme	*Messages*
Information Opportunities and threats	Information and IT[1] present enterprises with very different ways of doing things; significant opportunities are available, but so are threats-these are contrasted.
IT and organization	IT can be used to support all organizational forms, and it is an enabler for some new emerging and very different kinds of organization. Enterprises must organize to use all the information, not just what is computerized.
Scope and value of information	Information is an asset for every enterprise; the information available to an enterprise is much greater than just what is computerized; some key principles govern information systems; information technology is much broader than just computer-related technology.
Infrastructure and architecture	Information and IT infrastructure radically alter an enterprise's cost structures and economic feasibility; something like an information architecture effort is needed at several levels in the enterprise.
Informate[2]	Use information and information technology to enhance people's skills and make it possible to organize with adaptable objective-oriented teams.
Powershift[3]	There is a change in paradigm—from gaining power by controlling information, to gaining it by giving and using information; in order to survive, middle managers must be expert at something and be capable of adding value to the work of their teams; traditional chains of command and authority are breaking down.
The shape of things to come	Levels of human consciousness and awareness are being changed by knowledge and information.

Chapter 2 presents our recommendations for different management levels regarding the definition and implementation of corporate and global information systems. Enterprise strategy should not be separated from information, organization, or overall technical strategies. Work on all must proceed in parallel and with a high degree of synergy and integration.

1. This book uses the terms "information technology" and IT differently as explained n Chapter 7.
2. The term "informate" comes from Zuboff (1988).
3. The term "powershift" comes from Toffler (1990).

Themes and Visions

The use of information is revolutionizing our professional and personal lives. We see now and will continue to see a shift in social and technological paradigms of a magnitude far greater than that caused by the Industrial Revolution. Paradoxically, although information technology has helped create many of the world's problems, it may also hold the key to solving those problems.

We are going through massive change in which information and information technology are deeply implicated. To understand information technology, it is no longer sufficient only to know the many ways computers can be used; it is also necessary to understand how computers are coordinated to meet a whole set of integrated enterprise objectives. Many enterprises are creating "global villages" of people and partners all around the world pursuing their objectives; they are making use of information and deploying information technology in ways that make both the information and the technology critical components of the enterprise, its products, and its services.

Information technology can be used both successfully and unsuccessfully. What does this mean? The successful use of information technology gives an enterprise appropriate systems that provide optimum resource allocation and competitive advantages, and that make possible totally different styles of enterprise organization. Well-deployed, flexible systems can be extended easily to support new goals and reconfigured quickly as both business needs and the environment change. The unsuccessful use of information technology results in systems that require a very long time to alter, or adapt, have high maintenance costs, reduce the flexibility of the enterprise to adapt as necessary, and fail to keep the enterprise effectively "in control".

The dangers in viewing mere investment in computers as a panacea are noted by Strassman (1990):

> "There is no relationship between expenses for computers and business profitability .... You will find that similar computer technologies can lead either to monumental successes or to dismal failures .... Measuring managerial productivity is the key to knowing

how to invest in information technologies .... The lack of correlation between information technology spending and profitability is contrary to advertised claims. "

It defies the common belief that investing in electronic processing of information somehow leads to lower costs and results in competitive advantage .... My way to understand this diversity is to attribute business performance not to computers but to *Management Value added.*

Despite these cautions, however, Strassman presents overall an optimistic view of investing in computers.

In short, information can be used to enhance productivity and creativity, or to inhibit individual freedom and lock people into bureaucratic structures and procedures.

Much of our discussion is about information technology, but we know that information technology supports only part of an enterprise's information needs. We develop this theme further in the book, and we address both information infrastructure and IT infrastructure.

Information Opportunities and Threats

Information can be organized in support of all kinds of enterprises: profit making, nonprofit, government, international, and individual (throughout we will use "enterprise" to mean any of these). Such support should realize opportunities and counter threats. However, it can amplify threats as well. Some examples of information's dual nature are shown in Table 1. The term "information system" here means the systematic organization of information for a particular purpose.

Chapter 5 discusses information opportunities more deeply within the realm of information technology.

IT and Organization

The application of information technology is neutral; it can be used to unlock corporate and personal productivity and creativity or to freeze existing structures and inhibit individual freedom. What may not be so neutral is an underlying set of ethics from within technological cultures that considers technological needs more urgent and of higher priority than non-technological needs. Chapter 7 discusses this issue in more detail.

More enterprises are coming to realize the value of their intellectual assets. In this regard, the greatest challenge to an enterprise is to create organizational structures that will maximize the sharing and use of knowledge.

Table 1.1 Information System Properties: Opportunities and Threats

Property	Opportunity	Threat
Flexibility	Easy adaptation to new situations and needs	Easier to put unnecessary effort into low-priority systems with lower (or negative) added value
Interoperability	Easy to connect with trading partners	Easier to be taken over, or combined by merger
Distributed	Supports more responsibility at different levels in the enterprise	Loss of effective control; not knowing what people are doing with their installed computing base
Open systems and standard formats	More readily available building blocks	Security of information; more difficult to achieve differentiation; making a commodity of components results in a need for alternative sources of added value
Integrated business processes	Rapid matching of information systems and organizational structures	Highly complex systems with no overall organizational ownership of complete processes
Low and decreasing price-performance ratios	Rapid expansion of installed computing capacity	Little documentation of processing being done, less coordinated decision making, and increasing support costs; IT budgets expanding faster than corporate profitability.
Low cost of information access and transmission	Everyone can have the information they need when they need it	Information pollution
Highly integrated systems	More mechanisms are available to control the enterprise	Less innovation; becomes more difficult to change structure
Easily produced, highly aggregated information for the whole enterprise	Information becomes a demonstrable asset with an estimate of its whole enterprise value	Security; GIGO (garbage in/ garbage out, and the garbage produced becomes "sanitized")
Ubiquity	Processing power is readily available when needed	The greater the investment in current systems, the greater the potential cost of change; change avoidance and acceptance of status quo

IT can support any organizational structure. The question is, which is better—centralized or distributed? This is a concern of many people setting the strategic direction for their activities, and, generally, the answer to the question is Yes. This means there is no absolute answer-in some cases it is better to centralize; in others it is better to distribute. What we can say, however, is that it is better to design information systems so that they are *distributable;* that is, they may start centralized but they have the flexibility to be distributed if that becomes more appropriate.

One of IT's key opportunities is to support the decentralization of activities while maintaining the ability to coordinate and control. Also likely to become increasingly important is IT's ability to adapt to a declining concentration of people in urban areas-to take advantage of the expertise increasingly available in remote areas offered by people who want to live and work in less-congested surroundings.

The decision to centralize or distribute depends on the information application, the available technology, the culture of the enterprise, and the skill of the designers. Because of strong relationships between information systems and enterprise culture, some ways of organizing the enterprise will be exceptionally difficult without information technology (for example, supporting flexible entrepreneurial teams, virtual teams[1], and telecommuting). Also, there are some technologies, such as distributed databases, that will not be of much use if computer applications have been centralized.

As shown in Table 1.2, IT can provide substantial opportunities for flexibility.

But, as Table 1.3 shows, IT can also produce inflexibility in several ways if used incorrectly.

The key for any enterprise is to avoid the pitfalls and obtain the bene-fits from information generally and IT specifically.

One of the most important reasons so many enterprises do not benefit from IT is that they have allowed themselves to be organized along strictly departmental or functional lines-for example, sales, marketing, or manufacturing—with no provision for cross-functional[2] responsibilities. 2 *Moreover the individual departments have been permitted to commission their own information systems without coordinating their work with other departments.* In other words, if an enterprise has 20 different departments, all of which have direct contact with customers, there should be no surprise that within that enterprise there will be at least 20 different definitions of what a customer is.

1 For a detailed discussion of virtual teams, see Savage (1990).
2 The term "cross-functional" is used increasingly to mean cross- or interdepartmental.

Table 1.2 IT as an Enabler of Flexibility

Activity	*Enhanced Flexibility*
Downsizing	The ability to minimize and optimize factor inputs required for output goods and services. The 1970s and 1980s saw some dramatic savings in areas such as inventory control, where substantial downsizing of working capital needs was achieved; in other areas, by separating service activities, core manufacturing has downsized labor inputs substantially. The ability to distribute system components.
Rightsizing	The ability to optimize the mix of skills and resources in order to respond to changing market demands, and to take advantage of new IT opportunities.
Merging	Mergers between companies with compatible systems are much easier. Group operations can be set up with the members of the group retaining identity through separate information systems.
Moving into new markets	IT supports a more rapid deployment of resources in identifying and satisfying new market needs.
Improving time to market	IT moves the support for time to market from minimum inventory through just-in-time to mass customization.
Globalization	IT enables large complex companies to work across geographies as a network of entrepreneurs (small units).
Mass customization	IT enables companies to build products to a specific order while keeping the applied benefits of JIT (just-in-time) manufacturing.
Significant powershift	Information is changing many traditional power relationships in and between enterprises.

IS departments (information services, and so forth) are beginning to realize that what is still missing is an overall enterprise view of information needs, which have nothing to do with the enterprise's organization into departments. In many enterprises IS recognizes this problem and responds by offering data management and some kind of enterprise modeling service.

Up to now there has been little systematic computerization of integrated cross-functional requirements; instead, arbitrary sets of activities have been automated piecemeal, depending on technological feasibility, negotiated budgets, and the technological prejudices of the people doing the work. Often, bridging structures are created to optimize cross-functional business processes, but such structures still almost inevitably refer back to the organization of the enterprise because their designers come from the different departments. Thus, systems and solutions usually remain tied to rigid

8

organizational and departmental requirements. A glaring omission from the organizational charts of most enterprises is responsibility for the enterprise's overall information needs. Yet it is critical to look at the information flows of the enterprise, together with its business processes, *independently of the enterprise's organization and its automated systems.* The fact that almost all processes have some automated support does not mean they should not be examined on their own. We discuss this in more detail in Chapter 8 and provide some suggestions for organizing responsibility.

Table 1.3 IT as an Inhibitor of Flexibility

Activity	*Reduced Flexibility*
Implementing enterprise strategy	IT planning and the implementation of effective cross-functional business processes are delegated to the existing organizational structure of the enterprise.
Implementing data definitions	Data inconsistency arises between different applications for the same enterprise (e.g., many different definitions of trading partners have been implemented in different computer systems).
Merging	Companies fail to merge because of incompatible information systems.
Understanding key business processes	Nobody knows how some of the old processes work because they are embedded in computer-based applications.
Managing effectively	IT is sometimes used as an excuse for managers who don't understand what they should and so blame the computer program.
Choosing methods of developing computer applications	The selection of development methods, or the choice of a single consistent method, is frequently advocated as a solution to what are essentially management problems.
Optimizing enterprise activities	Most MIS-type systems are department oriented and as such inhibit organizational change.
Implementing effective cross-functional activity	Information systems may be used to "protect turf".
Inertia and fears of change	Perhaps the greatest brake on change is the existing installed base. Radically changed ways of doing things involve moving into the unknown.

Because knowledge and information are key assets in any enterprise, each business unit is responsible for their correct use, just as it is for other enterprise assets such as cash, people, and facilities.

The Scope, Management, and Value of Information

Since the beginning of civilization, one of society's major problems has been how to share and preserve information and, sometimes, how to keep it secret. Power can come from controlling information; power can also come from providing information. In today's world enterprises do not attempt to classify and manage all of the information they use or that is available to them. Indeed, such an exercise would be impossible given all the information in the brains of employees and in the external environment. Nevertheless, people tend to think that computerized information is all planned and structured, and that all information used by the enterprise can be identified.

Often the goal as well as the belief is that the "meta-data" at least will be put into some kind of data dictionary. Yet all attempts to do so that we know about have reached only part of the available information, and the reality as we see it is that the identified, documented, and understood information is generally some arbitrary subset of all the information the enterprise needs-and a small subset at that.

Scope

A common assumption in many discussions of IT is that

"information"= computerized information

and that this represents the total or at least a significant portion of the enterprise's information needs[3]. *It is disturbing to note how few examples there are of data and information modeling attempting to identify key information needs for a data dictionary, regardless of whether or not the data is in a computerized information system.*

We address this point in more detail in Chapter 9, but observe here that in purely financial terms, most enterprises spend considerably more on information than on information technology.

Figure 1.1 summarizes some of the main categories of information used by every enterprise. It identifies structured, semi-structured, and unstructured or unrecognized information.

---

3 Usually the focus on computerized information arises not as a result of a careful consideration of all an enterprise's information resources, or even those that enable the enterprise to exercise the most effective control; frequently it arises because it is the easiest approach or because it can involve the use of exciting technological tools.

Management

We argue that there is as yet no centralized and consistent way to manage all the information available to an enterprise. The trick is to manage the processes that use the information. However, just controlling the structured data stored in an electronic form is a challenge few enterprises have yet overcome. Information management is complex enough even after all of the interconnectivity and data definition issues have been solved. We understand why many enterprises still install hundreds of stand-alone personal computers, but in in our view, this is likely to increase information management problems. The need for many independent PCs in an organization should be taken as a symptom of an immature IT infrastructure that cannot provide the necessary end user services.

The management of information becomes even more complex when information from the external environment is included.

Figure 1.1 Information Available to the Enterprise

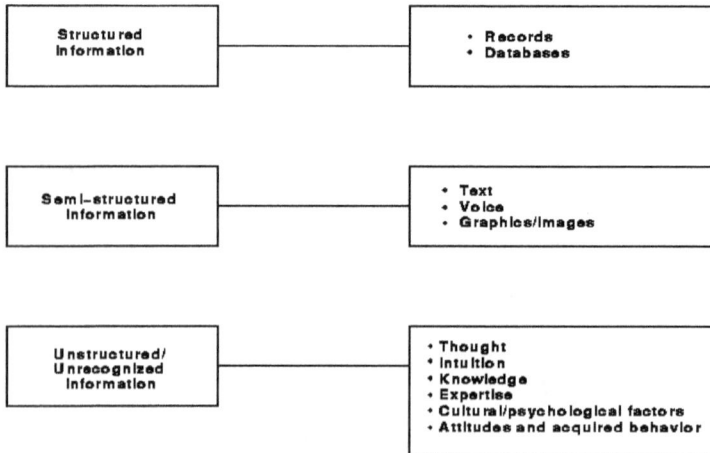

The following scenario describes many large enterprises:

- Many computers are linked together; many more remain disconnected.
- There is a vast amount of data stored in ubiquitous and dispersed databases, all very different and implemented with very different

technologies.
- The computer-based information is mostly well structured in the centrally managed computers and is fragmented in the standalone PCs and workstations.
- The needs of the enterprise require the use of unstructured information, the volume of which is many magnitudes greater than the volume of structured information.
- There are many ways of understanding and using the available information.
- The interaction between the enterprise and its environment creates highly complex information requirements.

We suggest that traditional information management, in which the enterprise's information resources are managed centrally and in a top-down fashion, is a potentially dangerous illusion and essentially irrelevant. Even at the level of structured data, it is surprising how many enterprises believe their main information needs are handled by a coordinated or centralized system, even though they still use many unintegrated PCs. Imagine the challenge of "managing" all of an enterprise's information.

What does such management mean? What are the real goals of information management in such a context? Once these questions have been answered, how is information management to be achieved? Clearly, the conventional wisdom on information management must be rewritten.

Value

In simple terms, the value of information to an enterprise can be measured by the difference in the market value of the enterprise with and without the information. It is a measure of how far information adds value.

As information becomes an increasingly important asset for many enterprises, certain key principles begin to govern the definition and use of information systems. Chapter 9 treats the foundations on which these principles are based. Here we simply summarize the principles.

- Information should only be supplied if it will affect a decision.
- The cost of providing information should not exceed its added value to the enterprise.
- Information systems must consolidate available information

to maximize the benefit of using knowledge.

- Information systems must make available all the information people need to perform their tasks when they need it.
- Information systems must provide the enterprise with enough control to adapt to changing needs and environment.
- Information systems must support effective two-way communication with all partners.
- Information systems should filter available information, making available only what is needed in a form that maximizes its usefulness.

Obtaining value from information involves performing various operations on it. Information technology provides mechanisms to do this. Just as information is commonly mistaken as computerized information, so information technology is often thought of as primarily computers. Table 1.4 lists the basic operations on information and gives examples of both computer-based and noncomputer-based IT that can support them.

Infrastructure and Architecture

The term "Infrastructure" means the provision of facilities in a standard way to satisfy the common needs of individuals, enterprises, and even entire economies. Infrastructure usually has a dramatic economic impact on both those who use it and those who do not. It enables a much higher level of cooperation and interdependency in the achievement of goals than would be possible without it. Some monumental examples of infrastructure are roads, railways, air traffic control, educational institutions, libraries, telecommunications facilities, legal systems, and services such as water, electricity, sewerage, garbage collection, and garbage disposal. Just consider the economic impact for the individual, the enterprise, and the economy without such infrastructures.

Information and information technology infrastructures affect profoundly the economics and feasibility of information use. An important benefit of high level infrastructure integration and implementation is that changes in the enterprise's organization, or the addition of new activity, can be achieved at significantly lower cost. We only need to look at the ubiquity of inconsistent stand-alone computer systems (which arose because of an absence of infrastructure and particular enterprise organizational forms)-and the substantial cost to deal with their short-comings—to understand the huge costs of not having well-developed infrastructures.

Many enterprises are finding that some information technology devices (for example, photocopiers and telephones) can be considered almost as commodities, reducing the discussion of infrastructure to economics and performance rather than mode of usage. Some computer-based technology (such as word processing and spreadsheet packages) is also moving in that direction. Nevertheless, most enterprises face major questions about their computer-based information technology infrastructure needs.

Table 1.4 IT: Computer and Noncomputer examples

Operation	Computer	Noncomputer
Knowledge	Text databases and retrieval, processing, artificial intelligence, and expert systems	Libraries (printed and microform), equipment to support experts and knowledge workers (e.g., measurement instruments)
Origination	Computer terminals, EDI	Forms, documents, instruments
Collection	Document scanners	Files, control devices (e.g. thermostats), dictaphones, binding, photographs
Organization	Document indexes, knowledge and rule bases	Bibliographies, indexes, abstracts, typewriters
Storage	Databases, magnetic media, CDROMs	Filing cabinets, microform, libraries, video recorders
Processing	Computers	Photocopiers, faxes, automatic coffee makers, alarm clocks
Interpretation	Data conversion	Dictionaries, dials and gauges, diagrams, charts, and graphs
Application	Data processing systems	Documentation for meetings and operations, valves and switches
Retrieval	Database management systems, data manipulation languages	Microfiche, microform, instrumentation
Communication	Communications hardware and software	Telephones, faxes, pipes, wires, information display boards, TV and radio

Operation	Computer	Noncomputer
Dissemination	Electronic mail, reports	Books, newspapers, overhead projectors, printing and print handling
Decision Making	Spreadsheets, simulation, statistical and mathematical calculations	Formulae, models, support for meetings, theories, case studies

We advocate what we call an information architectural approach, which recognizes that several levels of abstraction are needed within any enterprise, because different groups in a given company have different needs and languages. Our architectural approach is based on four levels: business, systems, technical, and product.

A business architecture is concerned with the enterprise's mission, objectives, and strategy; its links with other partners; its information needs; and the information technology opportunities for effective resource usage and competitive advantage. A systems architecture comprises the complete set of information systems needed to support the enterprise. A technical architecture is a product-independent taxonomy of types of information system and the design principles that apply to each generic system type. Finally, a product architecture is the computing platform on which the computerized information systems operate (that is, all the components needed by the different systems provided within a common operational environment).

The different architectures address very different audiences, as shown in Table 1.5.

Table 1.5 Information Architecture: Components and Audiences

Architecture	Audiences
Business	CEOs; CIOs; department heads; cross-functional business process teams; business, industry, and technology consultants; engineering and marketing managers (who want to understand what customers want and need)
Systems	CIOs (Information Management and Technology executives, as we describe them here), department heads, information officers, information system portfolio managers, system development account managers, industry and technology consultants, development managers
Technical	Information system development managers and project leaders, technical consultants, industry strategists, chief designers, senior analysts, IT managers, hardware and software engineering managers

Architecture	*Audiences*
Product	Technical strategists, designers and analysts, IT managers, operations managers, applications support

Of course, infrastructure issues are not confined to the enterprise level. Public and global infrastructures have a strong influence on what enterprises can achieve both on their own, and working together. For example, satellite and optical fiber capacity provides opportunities for different economies of scale with enterprise network and application infrastructures.

There are many efforts to define and implement standards. Enterprises can adopt standards as they evolve or can participate in the definition of standards. We are seeing growth in global information systems, with more and more connections between information providers, information consumers, and trading networks. This is creating different challenges from those of "merely" integrating the enterprise.

One point we will reinforce throughout the book is that it is neither possible nor desirable to define an information architecture in a top-down, linear fashion. The various architectural activities must be carried out together, with appropriate synergy between them. We often encounter the definition of business strategy before any definition of the necessary information systems. To make matters worse, the definition of needed information systems in such a scenario is frequently tied to the organizational structure of the enterprise. We believe that the business, information, and organizational strategies must be developed together, inseparably from the technical strategy. Thus, our architectural approach requires parallel activity with a high degree of vertical and horizontal integration between architectural layers and enterprise activities.

Informate

We use the term "informate" coined by Zuboff (1988), who demonstrates eloquently that computers need not be used merely to automate certain tasks, but can instead enhance skills and "empower" people. Her careful study of several cases in which computers have been introduced, identified the many levels at which effects are felt, from the individual to the company to the information revolution taking place in society as a whole. "Informate" seems a reasonable word to describe a major aspect of this information revolution.

The key benefits of information technology do not arise primarily from the automation of tasks performed previously by other means. Rather, they arise from a redefinition of fundamental processes and how they are performed, along with the use of IT as a means to increase the skills of people in the enterprise. In other words "Informate, don't just automate".

There has been some fear that the automation of many tasks by information technology will lead to significantly greater unemployment, and undoubtedly there have been cases where this has happened. However, as we will demonstrate later with some reliance on OECD sources, the real long-term change will be more in the quality and nature of work, with far greater opportunities for people to use technology to enhance their skills and level of effort.

Information technology adds value in some fundamental ways. These are summarized in Table 1.6. The use of the properties described there helps to "informate" those affected by the inexorable march of information technology. Enterprises alter their organizational structures to make increasing use of these properties. (For example, virtual teams do not need to be in the same place because IT mitigates many of the effects of time and space; key enterprise processes can be redesigned because of the possibility of linking tightly interdependent sequences of event.)

Table 1.6 IT Added Value

Property	*Added Value*
Space	The effect of space can be reduced dramatically so that many activities can be performed in spite of the geographical distance between them.
Time	Barriers of time can be reduced dramatically, and many activities can be performed with very small time gaps between their different components.
Event sequences	Partly as a result of reduced need for time and space, it is possible to put together tightly dependent sequences of events.
Complexity	Some calculations are simply not an option without computer support.
Knowledge	The knowledge of several experts can be combined to provide an accessible pool of knowledge beyond the scope of any individual.

Powershift

"Powershift"like "informate"is an apt description of another important aspect of the information revolution. The word was coined by Toffler (1990) in the third book of his trilogy, which "focuses on the rise of a new power system replacing that of the industrial past".

Every employee in an enterprise, as well as every employee of trading partners, can be considered an information processor. Some of the information processes can be very simple; others can be very complex. In the past, with the traditional division of labor, only a very few people in a company, the managers, had complicated tasks. By definition, they were information processors, since their job was to gather information, collate it, analyze it, and use it to give direction. The traditional view is that as companies evolve, the simple tasks (simple in terms of economic and technical feasibility) are automated and middle management is squeezed out. A less traditional view is that complete business processes are overhauled or redesigned, resulting in different ways of organizing enterprises in which traditional management roles are no longer needed.

In the latter view, alternative styles of working, along with a greater information component in all jobs, shifts the means of gaining power from controlling information to using it for added-value activities. More and more professionals make autonomous decisions based on information they receive directly. Eventually an enterprise will comprise a network of professionals using sophisticated information technology to enhance their own information-processing capability.

In such an environment traditional management control no longer works. Pure top-down, central planning is not effective because of the increasing complexity and size of the information processing task. This is analogous to the failure of centrally planned economies, which cannot overcome the enormity of controlling everything.

For any particular enterprise the extent of an observable powershift depends on the questions of how far managers manage and how much autonomy the individual has in achieving enterprise objectives. If managers do "manage", then they must be able to make some decisions others cannot make, and these decisions must be based upon additional information. Such decision making needs the support of information processing facilities.

Much broader than simply empowering managers is empowering all employees. Individuals, in order to have more autonomy, must have

18

access to the kind of information that supports their activities.

The evolution of autonomous entrepreneurial teams, and the increased informating of the people performing different tasks, requires new ways of organizing. Organization is independent of management, since it brings added value that is unobtainable without it. This is shown in Table 1.7. It is interesting to note that in this table for every "added value" there may well exist specific disadvantages as well.

We can conclude that any IT that comes to depend on any of the properties of organization described in Table 1.7, will support an enterprise, with additional properties derived from the interactions between IT and organization.

Table 1.7 Organization Added Value

Property	Added Value
Cohesiveness[1]	An enterprise probably could not survive and achieve its objectives if its components simply interacted in random ways.
Specialization	Organization enables different people to specialize in different skills and activities.
Interdependence	Almost a corollary of specialization; when people are specialized, interdependencies build up and organization provides a mechanism to implement these interdependencies.
Mechanization	Organization brings together specialized parts, and so is a way of achieving the mechanization of certain tasks and activities.
Rationalism	Planning and organization to implement planning are very powerful paradigms. They lead to a rationalized view of achieving objectives.
Implemented determinism	Organization arises as part of a process to achieve an objective; hence, it is a way of implementing a deterministic approach to goals and objectives.
Power	Power generally arises from organizing specialists and by manipulating the resulting interdependencies.

[1] This is offered by Beer (1979) who states that "Cohesiveness is the primary characteristic of organization. This fact derives from the very purpose of organization which . . . exists to contain the variety proliferation that arises from the uninhibited interaction of the elements of a system".

Individuals, too, benefit from the resulting changes in the underlying distribution of power. *There is a major shift in paradigms of power away from achieving power by keeping information, toward achieving power by making information available. It will become increasingly difficult to rely on authority by position, as more and more people obtain authority by knowledge.* Authority no longer comes exclusively from the number of people controlled or from budget size, but more and more from the leadership provided, from personal value added, and from the manager's ability to set the direction for a team of professionals. As Zuboff (1988) states,

> "Managers who must prove and defend their own legitimacy do not easily share knowledge or engage in inquiry. Workers who feel the requirements of subordination are not enthusiastic learners".

Traditionally, many middle managers have been information processors, creating and passing on summaries of information, passing on policies and decisions further down the enterprise, or attempting to handle unexpected events[4]. Layers of management can now be skipped for both communication and decision making; there is much horizontal and vertical communication across many layers. As a result, the piece of value added that was provided by pure information gathering and distribution is no longer needed. The middle manager can only survive in the future by providing personal added value, and to do that, the manager must be an expert at something. More managers must "coach" people, not merely direct and coordinate them. They cannot afford to be independent of the technical requirements of what is being managed.

All of this takes away even more power from line managers, who simply no longer have the ability to understand what is going on but must trust professionals such as project managers, account managers, engineers, and team leaders to do the work. Thus, the impacts on the enterprise include changes to the traditional chain of command and traditional lines of authority.

Toffler's essential thesis, that knowledge now provides the key raw material for creating wealth, is echoed with increasing frequency[5]. One of the enterprise's greatest challenges is to move away from being driven by the interests of its organizational units, toward taking direction from customer needs and the entrepreneurial realization of new opportunities[6]. It is very important to note that these shifts in power and traditional organization are inextricably linked with

---

4 In more formal terms discussed later in the book, we say that traditional middle management performs the roles of information attenuation, information amplification, and variety attenuation-tasks that information technology often performs very well.

5 See, for example, Stewart (1991).

6 See, for example, Dumaine (1991), who explores ways in which traditional organization charts are replaced by ever-changing flexible teams.

the application of information technology and the existence of both information and IT infrastructures. Toffler makes the point that "Just as owners became dependent on managers for knowledge, managers are becoming dependent on their employees for knowledge". Solutions to needs and problems rely increasingly on knowledge. It is becoming irrelevant to know only what a product will do, but it is critical to know the kinds of situations in which products can add some value, when to use them, and when not to use them.

The Shape of Things to Come

Our vision of the future from an information perspective is a world in which:

- Everyone has access to the information they need, when they need it, and in a form in which it is most useful.
- Information is used within a context of ethical objectives.
- There are multiple and competing sources of high-quality information.
- There are multiple and competing sources of models for the interpretation of information.
- Information systems are flexible enough to adapt quickly to changing enterprise and environmental needs.
- Information, information systems, and information technology are harmonized in controlled and known ways.
- Problems can be addressed quickly and efficiently by the creation of cross-functional teams or other appropriate organizational forms.
- A complex network of information flow connects the world.
- Network organizations have the flexibility to maximize effort from entrepreneurial activity.

Our practical experience comes from being part of the development, operation, and use, first, of the internal global network of Digital and, second, of a much broader information and information technology infrastructure. Our experience is in an environment that is typically three to five years ahead of the industry average in using networks and two to five years ahead of the cost curve in terms of cost per unit of processing. We are able to take advantage of our internal costs and therefore can use more technology than most at the same cost.

Digital's global technical infrastructure has influenced profoundly the way its employees behave and organize, to the point where the interaction between IT and organization is inseparable. We no longer know what comes first!

Traditional hierarchically based decision processes do not give the flexibility to respond to market changes and customer demands quickly enough. We need to give more power to cross-functional entrepreneurial teams in all stages of value chains and value networks: in the design and manufacture of products and services; in the design and selling of solutions; and in the support of customers.

As we break the organization into smaller entities, we use the information and IT infrastructures to connect the entities, enabling them to share information. A traditional matrix organization is no longer adequate because we need to communicate across customer, industry, product, and department dimensions. Here again, IT provides the underlying technology to manage across those different dimensions, although the skills of management must also change and adapt. Managers and employees must learn to "think globally, act locally", as well as "think locally, act globally". They need to be responsive to local needs and close to their customers, while tapping into global resources of the company itself.

Our organization vision is that every employee and every team can act as independently as possible to satisfy customer needs while operating within the context of a global mission and objectives. We believe that on a world scale this vision can only be achieved in a large company if the information and IT infrastructures are managed as enablers for organizational change and as support for every employee and partner.

With information becoming a major enterprise asset, it is necessary for every individual to learn how to manage it. More of the value added that individuals provide is in the form of increases to the enterprise's information resource. More of the value added enterprises provide is in the form of information embedded in services and products.

The Technological Shape of Things to Come

Here, for technically oriented people, we present a more technological vision of the future.

We started our network in 1979, and now we have a worldwide network of over 60,000 computer nodes providing access to all employees and external connections to customers, suppliers, and partners. We have also increased exponentially the per-person computing power.

By the late nineties most employees will have a workstation, with power in the range of 50 to 100 MIPS and with the availability of large disk capacity (local or remote). Through FDDI technology this workstation will be connected to the local metropolitan area network at 100 Mbits per second. Those metropolitan area networks will be connected to a globe-wide area network, which will provide a number of services, typically transnational, such as database servers, information servers, mail servers, and external gateways. The computing power of these server centers will be in the order of 1,000 to 10,000 MIPS. All of this will run basically unattended, with four of five command centers maintained over the network, all the backups being automatic, and the end user taking care of the local workstation.

Through this vision we will marry the independent worlds of stand-alone PCs, departmental minis, and corporate data centers. No data centers exist in our vision of the future; there are end-user environments, server centers, and command centers. Already in our company, every employee can access all the on-line information from any Digital location, from home, possibly from a customer site, and soon from mobile locations. Our global information system connects all parts of our enterprise and its environment, and it is an integral part of the enterprise, used by every employee and available to many customers, suppliers and partners.

In the next few years there will be continuing dramatic increases in computing power for constant cost. The cost of storing information directly accessible and processable by computers will continue to fall rapidly. There will be many improvements in the ways people interact with computers, adding many alternatives to today's terminals and work-stations. The availability of communications capacity for sharing information will continue to increase.

What will people be doing with all of this computing and communications power? As we showed earlier, information technology has focused primarily on supporting the use of structured data. We are now seeing much more semi- and unstructured information use, which requires much greater computing power. Thus, we see a very fast increase in the ability to handle voice, graphics, images, rules, and knowledge. The more information and knowledge people possess, the more they will want to be in control of their destinies by working in consensus with others.

In a very short time, it will be technologically feasible to have all the world's printed books available on-line at a realistic cost. It is our experience that once people pass a certain threshold of information technology (and this applies to books as much as to computers), there is an unpredictable explosion in applications of information. As the end of the century approaches, such an explosion will occur as it becomes possible to reexamine and combine so many aspects of knowledge. We are about to see not only huge amounts of knowledge available for processing and use simultaneously, but also technological developments that will deliver massive increases in available computing power. Nobody can predict the outcome of this scenario, but knowledge and the ability to apply knowledge seem likely to go through a transformation previously unknown in the history of humanity. Levels of human consciousness and awareness are about to be changed; so is the ability to set and monitor ethics and objectives.

[page left blank intentionally]

Recommendations for Management

We are often asked to prescribe what management and others should do in order to identify and implement information and IT infrastructures. Clearly, there are dangers in presenting too brief a prescription, because every enterprise is unique. However, there are some things we believe would benefit many enterprises, and we state these in this chapter in summary form. Despite the risks from generalization, we hope this summary will provide a useful starting point, even if it appears initially as somewhat perfunctory.

The enterprise can exploit information appropriately only by managing business, organizational, and technical issues holistically. There is no direct correlation between extensive use of IT and enterprise success—a sound information strategy is a necessary but not sufficient condition. Our view is optimistic; we believe IT can make a significant, positive impact in any enterprise. In this chapter we offer a number of brief recommendations (discussed in detail later in the book) and issue a call for action to user, information, and technology managers.

Top-Down, Bottom-Up, in Parallel

Activities and processes needed to implement an information architecture must be performed in parallel. The ultimate goal is to make all of those activities and processes an integral part of the overall enterprise management system. This will eliminate any remaining antagonism between the systems department and any other departments or organizational units. Organizational structures that will bridge the gap between information and information technology must also be in place. In our experience, most enterprises address information technology needs in some way or other, but very few address the information needs of the entire enterprise. Figure 2.1 shows a few key parallel activities. These parallel activities involve

26

action to:

- Develop a vision, mission, objectives, strategies, and critical factors for the enterprise (strategizing).
- Review organizational structure and behavior in light of the information architecture.
- Initiate an effort to define an overall enterprise information model.
- Ensure appropriate management of the application portfolio.
- Rationalize the existing information and IT infrastructures, and define a strategy for the future.

Figure 2.1 Parallel Activities

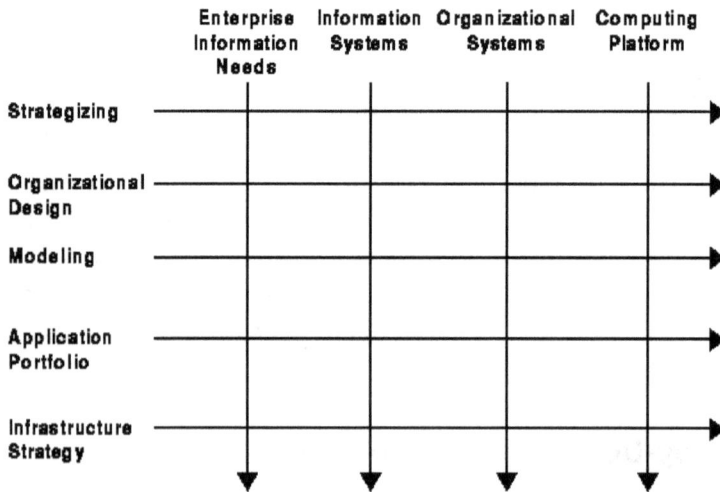

Some people will argue that these activities must be performed in sequence and from the top down. We do not agree; we strongly believe in a parallel approach because in today's environment the rate of change is too rapid for a sequential approach. In fact, we believe the parallel approach is nearer to the reality of enterprise behavior.

Strategic Actions for Top Management

It is not necessary (and not feasible in any event) to develop a detailed business plan in order to define an information architecture. Business plans change too quickly to provide a stable enough base for the information plan, which needs time for implementation. In many cases, enterprise needs change significantly before traditional business planning can be completed. We advocate, therefore, a flexible approach that enables a parallel definition of information, IT, and business architecture.

From an enterprise point of view, it is necessary to define a few key elements, which then become the foundation of the information architecture. To do this we advocate a systematic identification of information needs and a consideration of IT opportunities (both computer and non-computer-based), in addition to defining the more traditional strategy elements (such as those we identify in Chapter 5).

Figure 2.2 lists the specific actions we recommend for the top management of the enterprise. However, bear in mind the following points:

- Increasingly, the successful enterprise is making maximum use of its information and knowledge assets.
- It is necessary to know the available information and knowledge assets, along with enterprise needs and opportunities.
- An information infrastructure must be identified, developed, and managed across the enterprise in the same way as are other infrastructures.
- Where information technology is used in products and services, such use must be included in the overall information and IT strategies.
- It must be understood how information and information technology can be used to the greatest advantage for products, services, and enterprise functioning.
- It is essential to know how information and information technology may be used by competitors and opponents.
- It is not appropriate to define an enterprise strategy and then follow it with an information systems strategy predicated on the enterprise organizational structure. The enterprise, information, organization, and technical strategies must be developed together.
- Information technology is one of the greatest enablers for the recognition and optimization of key enterprise processes that cross traditional business departmental lines.

Figure 2.2 Strategizing Actions for Top Management

- Review the purpose of the enterprise in light of opportunities for taking full advantage of information assets available to the enterprise—what information is available and what it could be used for.
- Determine what additional information should be available to improve or enhance the current enterprise purpose.
- Identify possible and actual threats from existing and new competition based on use of information.
- Review IT trends to assess what kinds of technology can be embedded in the products and services of the enterprise, to enhance existing offerings, or to create new ones.
- Review the mission, strategy, objectives and goals, and critical factors.
- Identify the core competencies and core processes of the enterprise necessary to fulfill the purposes of the enterprise.
- Consider new organizational forms made possible by information technology (such as networks, orchestras, spider-webs).
- Assess the impact of changes to the existing information architecture, and ensure appropriate resources are allocated to adjust it.

Organizational Recommendations

Most enterprises should review the roles and responsibilities related to information management, as well as the existing organizational structures and behaviors (described in Chapter 8). It is equally important that they manage both information and information technology (IT) at all levels. We advocate that at the top level one person can own both roles, in a position we call Information Management and Technology (IM&T) executive, or one person can manage information and one, IT.

Every manager, and eventually every user, must be aware of and responsible for managing relevant information assets and making effective use of IT. Figure 2.3 shows a set of actions for the management of the enterprise.

Increasingly, enterprises need to make effective use of their knowledge and information assets. The challenge they face is to implement organizational forms that will allow them to maximize the added value from knowledge and information assets. There are many forms of organization, and large enterprises should have the strategic capability to consider and apply the forms most likely to achieve their objectives.

Figure 2.3 Organizational Actions for Management

- Define clearly roles and responsibilities to manage information and IT at different organizational levels (corporate, division, function, department, team, etc.).
- Institute education programs on the value of information through the enterprise.
- Embed in each person's terms of reference the necessary responsibilities and measures with regard to management of information.
- Consider rewarding people for the value they add to the information assets of the company.
- Institute education on the value and appropriate use of information technology (including an understanding of its limits).
- Provide education about essential organizational principles (particularly about the possibilities of information-based and IT-supported enterprises).
- Understand the many options available for organizational form supported by IT (e.g., virtual teams, moving the work to the people, flat organizations, flexible terms of working).
- Establish formal change management processes to implement new systems holistically, integrating changes to business, organization, and IT.

Every enterprise also has a fund of creativity locked away in the people working for its objectives. It should organize itself to release and benefit from that creativity, and to help meet the different goals of its people and partners.

Models and Architecture

Strategizing and organizational design activities should be based on appropriate modeling and architectural work. In other words, a compromise is needed between theory and practice. Summary recommendations for IM&T management are shown in Figure 2.4. Very few enterprises engage in rigorous modeling, in the belief that more general strategizing and needs identification are sufficient. We believe that overall models and architectures should be checked for completeness and consistency. Modeling is not a trivial activity, but good models help to make the whole picture clear and make changes and impact analysis easier.

There is an uneasy alliance between formal, theoretical rigor and short-term practical decisions. The "right" balance between them is needed, and the neglect or overemphasis of either causes serious difficulty.

Many system development organizations spend a great deal of effort seeking the "silver bullet" (after Brooks, 1976) — often in the form of a single, consistent system development method. The industry has not yet found one appropriate development method, because of the major differences in computing cultures, problems to be solved, application areas, organizational and contractual issues, and styles of development. We advocate ·a flexible system development method, one that can be adapted to the range of problems and development styles the enterprise is likely to encounter. This is another area where good consultants can help.

Figure 2.4 Recommendations for IM&T Management

- Create a strategic capability for modeling and architectural work as permanent activities.
- Educate the IT organization on the benefits and pitfalls of formal approaches (i.e., don't overdo it).
- Educate the business world on the benefits and pitfalls of informal approaches (i.e., don't under-do it).
- Don't waste time or conduct religious wars trying to enforce a single "methodology" (any approach is good if it fits the organizational culture; integrates business, information, and IT requirements; and solves problems).
- As the enterprise's environment continually changes, be ready for the underlying models to change continually also.

Application Portfolio Management

The existing and planned applications portfolio should be reviewed regularly to ensure good fit with business priorities and architectures. It is also important to look continuously for functionality that can be moved from the application portfolio into the infrastructure—for example, messaging systems, reference databases, information warehouses, and common transaction controllers. Some recommendations for business, IM&T, and departmental management are shown in Figure 2.5.

Many information systems fail, not because of "technical" issues, but because the target part of the enterprise is unable or unwilling to make use of it. For every proposed system, be sure to identify all groups likely to be affected by it in some way. Is the impact understood, and is there enough consensus to ensure that the system will add value to the enterprise in some demonstrable way? The fact that someone has the budget to sponsor the development of a new system does not mean that everyone who will be affected knows about it or is convinced that it will actually help.

Figure 2.5 Application Portfolio Recommendations for Business, IM&T, and Management

- Incorporate an ongoing review of information needs in all business and departmental plans.
- Integrate planning and review of application portfolios within business and departmental plans (IS planning does not exist as a separate process!).
- Establish an IM&T management project office that knows about all applications.
- Identify application portfolio managers matrixed between the business and user community and the IM&T department (the role of business and user management is to provide priorities; the role of IM&T is to provide modeling and architectural direction and to deliver infrastructure).
- Create a separate budget to support cross-functional applications and ensure the appropriate sponsorship for cross-functional programs.
- Identify applications that belong to the information infrastructure, and secure sponsorship and funding.
- Business and departmental management must accept responsibility for its own specific applications.
- Consider carefully the consequences of adjusting the process to use an existing package, vis-a-vis developing a new application to automate an existing process.

Infrastructure

All enterprises should probably undertake infrastructure projects in order to take advantage of the IT opportunities of the 1990s and beyond. We have listed recommendations for IM&T infrastructure management in Figure 2.6.

Infrastructure implementation will not be easy in many cases.

Different parts of the enterprise may have to give up certain activities. There must be sufficient enterprise commitment to sponsor and guarantee the success and availability of infrastructure. (Consider, for example, changing from separate departmental networks to enterprise-wide networks.)

Figure 2.6 Infrastructure Recommendations for IM&T Management

- Identify information needs, and ensure that the information and IT infrastructures provide the right support.
- Build and manage a global communications infrastructure to serve the enterprise. Connect to customers, partners, and suppliers (integrating data, voice, and image; handling structured and unstructured information).
- Adopt an IT architecture compliant with open standards.
- Define, implement, and manage the application components of the infrastructure (e.g., messaging, videotext, reference services, information center services, directory services).
- Develop a strategic capability to apply different styles of development (e.g., prototyping, package acquisition, subcontracting, spiral).
- Reconsider the balance between in-house IT personnel and subcontracting, both in systems development and operations; in-house work should be done only if it can provide a competitive edge and meet industry quality and productivity standards.

Managing Information and IT in the 1990s and Beyond

The world of the 1990s and beyond is one of interconnected enterprises creating global information systems. Each enterprise must meet the challenge of managing information as a vital asset and creating a corporate information system now. If it does not, it runs a risk of being disconnected and excluded from future opportunities brought by global inter-connectivity.

People must learn to live in an information-dense world and use information and IT as necessary tools of their professional and personal lives.

PART I I

Digital's Experience

Here we present what is essentially in the nature of a case study summarizing our experiences and many of our reflections on those experiences. It is not a formal statement; nor is it a collection of materials used internally by Digital. Rather, it represents our own experiences and thoughts, based on many but not all aspects of Digital's experience.

Our experience is mainly in MIS-type applications and in the development of enterprise-wide information and information technology infrastructures. Thus, we do not talk about producing operating systems or office management systems for sale; nor do we talk about controlling robots or other machines. However, we are concerned with integrating all of these activities to aid key business processes. Moreover, our experience encompasses much more than Digital; we have worked with many of world's largest corporations and many government bodies, and we have incorporated the fruits of this experience where appropriate.

We start by describing the evolution of an enterprise information management model, identifying essential considerations as we go. Historically, the evolution of IT infrastructure came first, along with the earliest implicit product architectures. These product architectures were followed by explicit and documented technical and product architectures. As price-performance ratios fell and much higher levels of integration between computer applications became possible, matters of portfolio management became more important and feasible. Hence, systems architectures emerged.

Enterprises are, to an increasing extent, embedding IT in products and services, and the use of IT is becoming an integral component of enterprise strategy. Technology has evolved sufficiently to support higher levels of enterprise and global integration; rational integration can now be achieved between top-level enterprise mission and objectives and information technology operational environments. Redesigning business processes is no longer a relatively academic exercise; the processes can be redesigned and implemented, taking full advantage of available technology and new organizational forms. Against this background we see the emergence of mature business architectures.

Finally, along with the revolution in information and IT infrastructures, have come equally substantial changes in work organization, management patterns, and individual behavior. We bring together many observations about these nontechnical dimensions of change by looking at organizational impact. Our enterprise information management model started in the technical arena, but it has evolved to recognize the equal or greater importance of associated organizational and behavioral changes.

Evolution of a Model: 1983—1990

The late 1970s seem a long time ago now—at least in terms of corporate organization, global interconnectivity, and the use of information technology.

Remember that time? There were no masses of PCs. Faxes had yet to become a major communications tool. Computers were expensive and relatively small (in processing speed and storage capacity). In the MIS world, computers were used for some central departments like accounting and departmental uses such as word processing and administration. Many management structures were hierarchical, with a large middle management layer in place to handle all the information. Computers were being introduced to perform relatively isolated, specific functions such as accounting, machine control, research and development, large-scale computation, administrative activities and the beginnings of word processing. Computers and related information technology were generally sponsored and paid for from the budgets of separate departments that could justify the expense based on their own activities.

Global networks were not yet a commercial reality. Telephone exchanges were generally old, and communications required much manual intervention. Punched tape machines and telexes were common.

Ten Years Ago

Ten years ago networking was very limited. Services such as electronic mail were used only on an experimental scale, and telex style communication carried most corporate traffic. There was some limited synchronous communication between computers, such as file transfers taking place between some applications, particularly financial.

It was not realistic then to implement office automation systems. Some database management systems existed but only for specific specialized applications. Nor was it realistic to identify and rationalize key business processes and then make extensive use of information technology to support them.

On the organizational side, the technology to support organizational forms such as virtual teams was not available, and teleconferencing was highly experimental. Matrix structures existed for higher levels of management, but it was not easy for the employee to take part in multiple networked teams. Travel was necessary to overcome many restrictions of time and space.

Different business departments installed and ran their own data processing centers, their own networks, and they commissioned their own computer applications. Historically, managers were rewarded for running their own departments well, not for cooperating with other departments by looking for economies of scale, sharing the use of resources, or sponsoring the common implementation of common tasks.

Moving On

We have come a very long way in the last ten years or so. We are now witnessing just the beginnings of a major revolution. Experience with telecommunications switching systems and exchanges, circuits that carry either voice or data, file and data transfer activities, and initial communications software led to recognition of the strategic value of a pervasive infrastructure.

Simple economies of scale were obtained through the construction of a common network connecting as many offices as possible by what appeared to users as an internal telephone system and an internal computer interconnection system. This required establishing overall ownership for the development and deployment of the common communications infrastructure.

This all required organizational changes, without which the benefits from the technology would not have been obtained. Individual departments had to give up control over their own networks. One unified network emerged with single departmental responsibility for identifying and providing the service levels required by all the other departments. Service reliability was of paramount importance. The change in departmental responsibilities made it possible to maximize economies of scale and build exceptional reliability.

At the same time, different departments were running their own computers for all purposes, including such core business activities as selling and fulfilling orders. This led to much redundancy in equipment, inconsistent computing platforms, and problems of integrating applications that needed to cooperate. Thus, another contribution to the overall infrastructure was made. Individual departments relinquished control over the computers used for the core business activities. These computers became the responsibility of one department, which was then able to take responsibility to provide a common operational environment and provide essential services such as the protection of key data.

The reliability of the infrastructure was put to an extreme test in 1990 when fire destroyed a major Digital facility in less than two hours, displacing 400 people and destroying the computer equipment. Activities affected were a major customer support facility and a support facility for computer applications running in several countries. The fire started at around 10.30 A.M. on a normal working day but support operations resumed that afternoon.

There are many ways of performing word processing, handling graphics, processing documents, storing and retrieving information, and integrating individual professional needs. Because this diversity can lead to the emergence of different and incompatible cultures, we extended the infrastructure to provide a common office environment. Doing so involved changes in traditional departmental responsibilities. Nevertheless, it achieved substantial economies of scale from common cultures of end use, the provision of services to secure information, and standard ways of integrating disparate professional requirements.

There is no room for the many more examples of Digital's early infrastructure construction. We will simply note here that *the application of technology beyond a certain threshold leads to unpredicted uses of the technology, significant behavioral changes, irreversible organizational changes, and new sets of expectations.* There has been a dramatic increase in computer application integration (both horizontal and vertical) and a widening of the "horizons of expectation" for the application of IT. Moreover, fundamental changes are taking place in traditional patterns of power and control, and the information and knowledge components of many tasks are growing. We now enjoy substantial economies of scale as a result of our pervasive integrated infrastructure.

Figure 3.1 shows what we believe to be some of the factors at work in the development of infrastructure. It illustrates our speculation of a model going through different generations, each of which has at least four stages.

Figure 3.1 Model Evolution

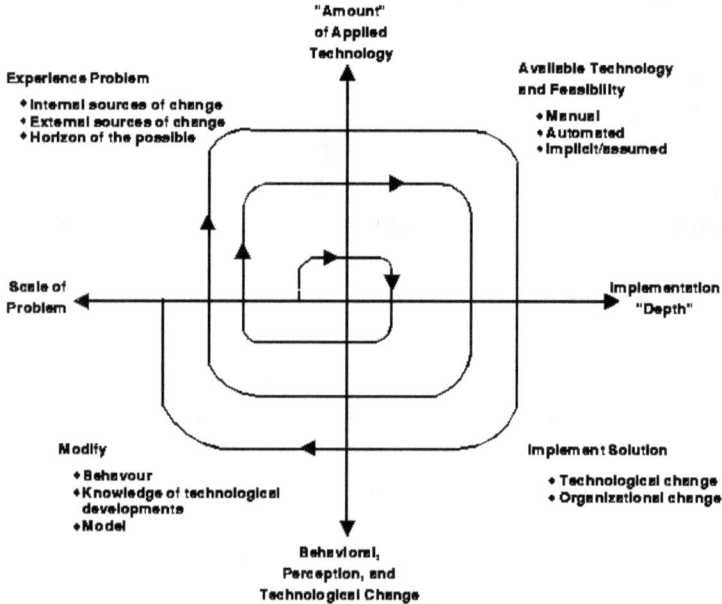

First, the enterprise experiences some kind of "problem" fundamental to the enterprise, which can be an external or internal source of change or simply a change in the horizon of the possible for an individual or a group that can influence direction.

Second, the enterprise investigates needs and then decides on a solution combining computerized and non-computerized information systems. This involves judgments about what is technically, economically, and organizationally feasible.

Third, the enterprise implements the selected solution, which involves technical and organizational change. The implementation can happen at different depths of technology.

Fourth, behavior changes, and what was originally new or innovative becomes normal or even mundane. There is a shift in awareness of what technology can do, combined with a greater understanding of technological developments.

New "problems" arise, which may be real or, because of a changed awareness of technological and organizational possibilities, may produce symptoms resembling problems. The spiral[1] is repeated (and, of course, some activity in all four quadrants is happening at the same time).

Significantly, not only are the implemented IT-based applications evolving, but also *the underlying model of what is wanted is evolving.* This is very relevant in the evolution of our architectural, or Enterprise Information Management Model; as technological, organizational, behavioral, and depth-of-implementation changes have taken place, the focus of the model has evolved as well. Ten years ago we were putting in place network and other infrastructure components, so the emphasis was on product architecture. Now we are engaged in vertical integration—from enterprise goals and objectives, to operational systems, horizontal integration of core business processes, and interactions with different partners. Thus, there is more emphasis on defining and implementing business architectures. We are now at a point where many people understand and accept the need for an architecture aimed at technology. Not so many people understand and can apply a business architecture, but this is where we now expect substantial added value in the next few years. We see this already happening in many large companies.

Our Digital Experience

During the past eight years, we and many others have been involved in the development of information strategy for Digital Europe. The evolution of the model we describe has progressed from point solutions to specific departmental problems, through early integration and architectural work, to a business architecture and an Enterprise Information Management Model.

Like any enterprise embarking on a new use for computers, we started by providing support for isolated applications in specific technical domains such as process control, research and development, accounting applications, or early general-purpose tools such as word processing packages. Unlike many enterprises that retained, and extended, a centralized mainframe approach, however, we had distributed our applications by the mid-1970s. We had also distributed

---

1 We have shown a "neat and tidy " spiral to help conceptualization; reality is not likely to be so neat.

much responsibility and decision making.

Early on, we established integration by developing infrastructure tools such as time-sharing operating systems and shared computing resources. The integration of applications was achieved by feeders, where the output of one application is used as the input to another. This was suitable for applications that had been developed by different departments. Common databases and files followed quickly to provide mechanisms for the "common coupling" of applications.

In 1983 we produced an early architectural model (explained in more detail below) to provide:

- Vertical integration from business needs to implemented computer-based applications
- Horizontal integration at the business and systems level to ensure the definition of cooperating cross-functional processes
- Horizontal integration at technical and product levels to define and put in place a common operational infrastructure

Organizationally, it was early in the integration of "islands of automation". Different departments and groups had various application development programs under way, different departments owned different applications, and in some cases different groups ran their own operational environments.

Infrastructure is often equated with network, which, although not correct, is understandable. Even before abstract thinking about information architectures matured, the first significant networking developments were taking place. We were dealing with a multibillion-dollar operation, in multiple geographies, with different departments, but without mainframes. There were many computers in many different locations, and they needed to talk to each other. It has been quite a culture shock to many business and technical managers that not only is it feasible to run a multibillion dollar business without mainframes, but from an organizational point of view it can be extremely desirable. (Many managers we have talked to, start to think in terms of needing mainframes after only a few million—let alone billion-dollars of turnover.) Thus, the first architectures were simple product architectures that provided the enterprise with a network of computers capable of communicating easily with each other and sharing information. The use of computers to communicate was not restricted to files of structured data or individual transactions; it was also made available for unstructured information such as electronic mail, documents, and graphics.

Decreasing price-performance ratios, decreasing real costs for computing power, and an earlier unbundling of hardware and software made it realistic to integrate more and more applications. It also made computer support for more applications technically and economically feasible. Those who could obtain the budgets spent increasing amounts on applications, but this was generally happening at the department level.

The proliferation of computer applications among different departments generated a need for a more consistent approach. There were economies of scale to be obtained from sharing computing resources, networks, and operational facilities. Between 1983 and 1985 an independent IS department was born, with the charter to provide common computing and communication services and common application development services. At this time the PC had been born but was not yet ubiquitous, and workstations had been conceived but could not really be considered born yet. A lot of work was put into defining more complete and more formal technical and product architectures.

At around 1985-1986, as we were implementing the first technical and product architectures, we realized the need for more comprehensive work at the European-company level to define an information system strategy. We started a program called an "Information Architecture for the 90s", which was intended to raise senior management awareness and develop a four- to five-year strategy. There were many ideas from management schools at the time, but generally we were on our own with the organization of distributed computing to support distributed management and business goals, and with the use of IT to support genuine cross-functional business processes.

One external idea we used to start the program was called the "5 Zeros Concept" (from Archier, 1984), which appears in diagrammatic form in Figure 3.2. The 5 Zeros Concept suggests that in order to be competitive in the 1990s, every company must strive for five zeros:

- Zero faults in product design
- Zero production delay
- Zero stock
- Zero paper
- Zero breakdowns

We took this very powerful concept and adapted it. We saw that in order to achieve these five zeros, we would have to integrate business processes across different departments. Zero design faults meant that design had to be connected to production. Zero stock meant that order processing had to be connected to manufacturing. Zero delay meant that manufacturing had to be connected with forecasting, and so on.

All this supported our architectural work, which indicated the need for cross-functional business processes and cross-functional systems. Ideas such as the 5 Zeros Concept supported the earlier idea of having an integrated business architecture and systems architecture, which is now built into the critical success factors of the company. At this point we also realized that having an integrated business architecture and systems architecture was not possible without making fundamental organizational changes within the company. There are many inter-dependencies involved in the structure of an enterprise. By definition, the formalities of such interdependencies are highly complex, and it often helps communication and focus to create a schematic diagram to use as metaphor. Figure 3.3 shows the schematic used extensively in Digital Europe as a planning framework. [2]

Figure 3.2 The Five Zeros Concept and Information Architecture

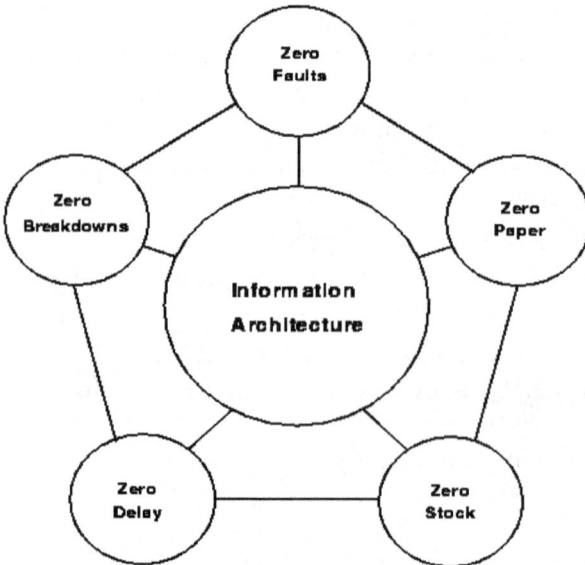

We use this framework at the corporate and departmental levels

2 This model was developed by Pier Carlo-Falotti (CEO and president of Digital Equipment Corporation in Europe), as an extension of the seven-s model presented in Pascale and Athos (1981) and originated by Waterman, Peters, and Phillips. (1980).

to plan enterprise evolution. In the diagram, "systems" is intended in a broad sense and includes both automated and non-automated systems. The original information architecture model was basically technologically driven. It paid lip service to organizational factors, but in reality failed to address them very well. Nevertheless, even though it was a simple model, it was still useful as a focus for discussion across different departments and geographies.

Figure 3.3 Enterprise Planning Framework (EPF)

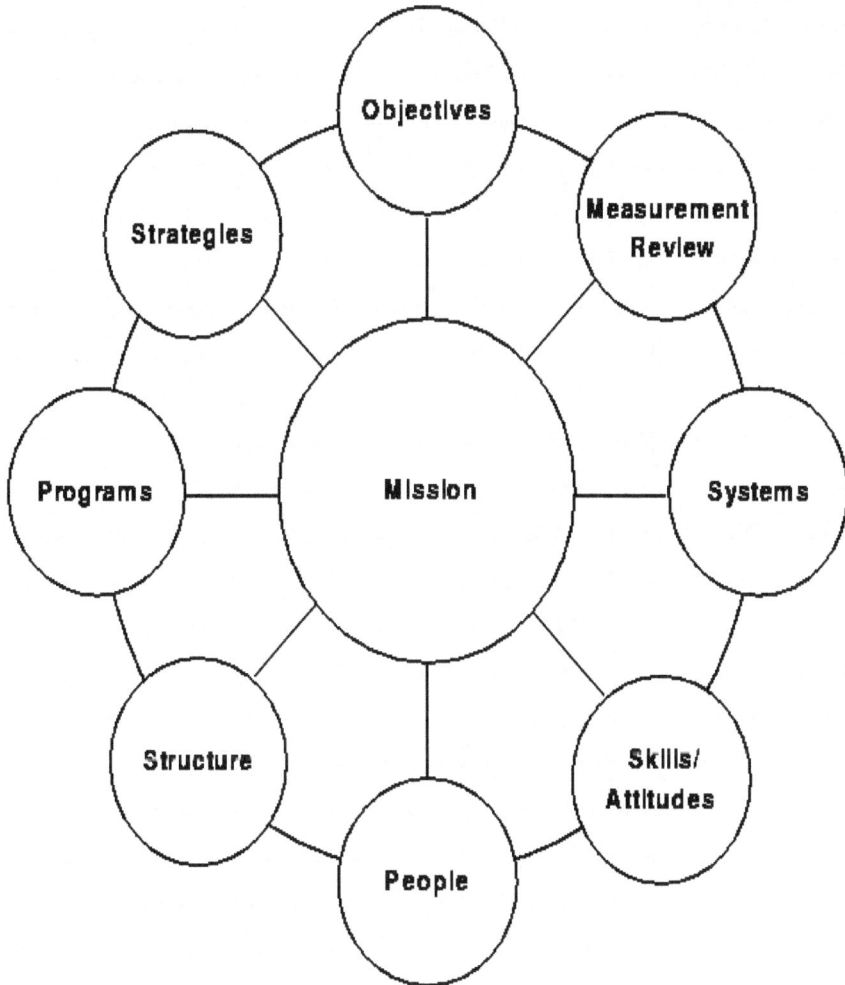

The planning framework can be supported by a set of critical success factors, which are illustrated in Figure 3.4 as a simple model, symmetric to the Enterprise Planning Framework

In order to take account of organizational critical success factors, the original information architecture model has been extended into a more comprehensive version, which we call the Enterprise Information Management model. It is shown in Figure 3.7 (page 65). The behavioral implications of the extended version are considerable. To produce an enterprise-wide information model independent of organization and technology requires major adjustment to business and organizational planning and technology deployment. IT becomes increasingly pervasive, and stronger mutual dependencies arise between IT and the organization[3].

Figure 3.4 Critical Success Factors for the EPF

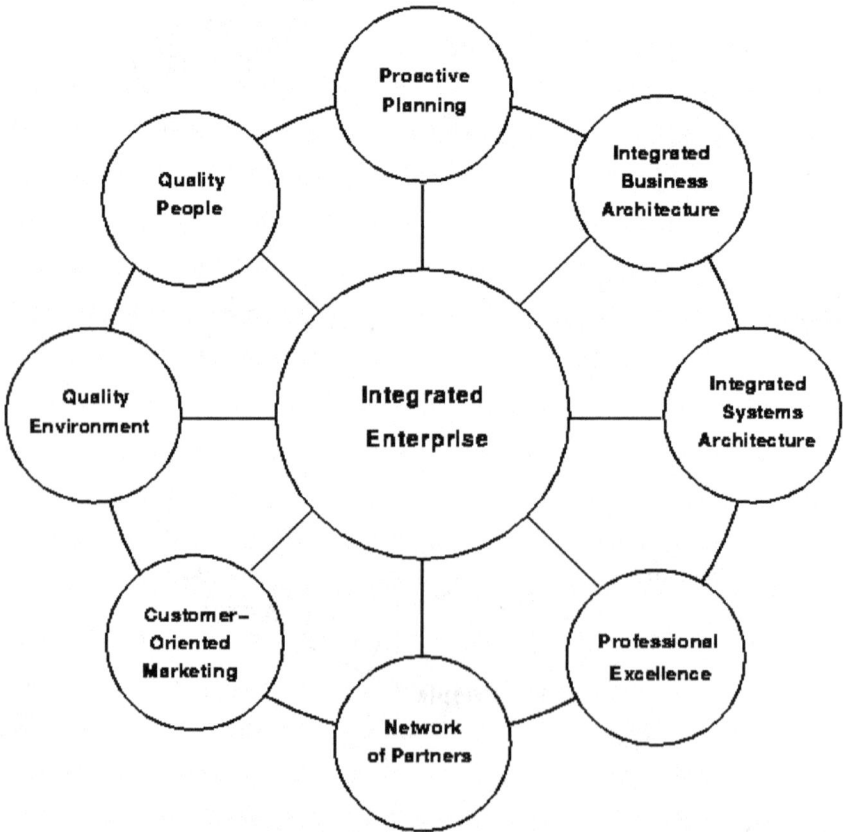

---

3 Consensus in establishing a true enterprise-wide model requires the participation of senior managers or technical people within established departments. This makes it difficult to achieve a view of the enterprise not predicated on the existing enterprise structure.

Early Product Architectures

The introduction of the VAX family of computers and the VMS operating system enabled us to start developing product architectures to bring together previously incompatible hardware and software platforms. Then networking—the interconnection of separate computers—helped make basic computing platforms more available. The creation of protocols and the provision of access layers to make it easier to use network services was a natural extension of the separation between hardware and operating systems.

These developments were followed quickly by database and forms products, along with a data dictionary, simple 4GLs, and an overall office environment.

Our earliest product architectures were based on common computing platforms that provided a range of functionality. Thus, for Digital in Europe this meant:

- VAX (with VMS) architecture
- DECnet and associated communications equipment
- VAX Information Architecture for databases, dictionaries, forms, query Languages, and transaction processing
- ALL-IN-1 for integrated office environments

For noncomputer-based IT, the product architecture included libraries, manuals, photocopiers, telephones, mail, meeting aids, telexes, and faxes. The economic and organizational issues involved deciding the points at which economies of scale and other factors will justify substituting computer-based for non-computer-based IT (for example, replacing regular mail with electronic mail, putting libraries and documents onto CDROMs and moving toward a paperless office, and using electronic conferencing aids to change the fundamental structure and dynamics of meetings). At Digital, obviously, there were systems that fell outside this architecture, and they remained until replacing them became a high enough priority to justify the resources required to do so. In general, as an enterprise becomes more dependent on information technology, a standard operational environment becomes important in order to provide business users with a reliable and consistent computing and networking service at a reasonable cost to the enterprise. The creation of a product architecture involves a difficult balance between standardization and variety—what will be computerized and what will not. Perhaps the most important economic principle behind a product architecture is that the range of available products must provide enough variety for the systems to be implemented—neither too few products, nor too many. This balance is at the heart of technical and product architecture design.

Application Integration and Distribution

There are several ways in which applications can be integrated, some more obvious than others. Here are a few examples:

- Transactional integration
- End-user environment integration
- Management integration
- Planning integration
- Operational integration

Transactional integration can be summarized in the following way:

- Vertical integration within one department to bring together the department's information system needs. Mature examples can be found in accounting and manufacturing departments.
- Horizontal integration between departments. This requires a degree of cooperation among people usually appointed by the departments to represent their separate interests. One example is the integration of sales and manufacturing.

Horizontal integration can be exemplified by the system that supports a sale. Different enterprises define transactions in different ways. For example, some consider a sale completed when the goods have been delivered; others consider the sale incomplete until the goods have been paid for. In either case, an architectural approach identifies the key state transitions and then defines business process integration independently of the enterprise's organizational structure. Some unit needs to do order entry, and from a technical point of view it does not matter whether that unit is sales or general administration. However, it may matter if the order entry system was designed by one department with very strong cultural typing. If another department takes over, it may want to rewrite the application. It is this kind of problem that makes IT an inhibitor rather than a supporter of organizational change.

Vertical integration usually links the activities of the same department. For example, accounting will link all processing related to accounts payable, accounts receivable, inventory, payroll, and general ledger. Manufacturing may try to link its scheduling and inventory applications or its scheduling and project management.

Another kind of departmental integration provides a common culture, such as an interface to many different applications, even if those applications do not exchange data. Typically, this takes the form of an office automation environment. The goal is to provide common features to a disparate range of applications, including screen and keyboard standards. One department may embark on a program for making all sorts of different applications available to users within a common interface environment.

Management integration is more difficult to visualize and implement. It involves creating information systems that can provide both information attenuation and information amplification[4]. A very common example of such integration, involving information attenuation, is where management information from certain business units is aggregated and passed to a level of management above the units themselves.

Planning integration is the least common type found in practice. It involves defining appropriate measures of overall enterprise performance, which can then be used for planning and goal setting. Information amplification systems are necessary so that objectives are propagated throughout the enterprise and appropriate commitments to achieve these objectives are obtained from different business units. Sub-sequent performance can then be measured against these commitments. Operational integration involves building a common operational platform capable of doing the work of many departments with a much simplified set of products.

Proposal for an Information Architecture Model

Our experience, along with that of other groups, led us in 1983-1985 to an overall information architecture comprising four "architectures":

- Business
- Systems
- Technical
- Product

These architectures interact with each other. In some sense they provide a method for the development of an enterprise-wide portfolio

---

4   Chapter 9 explains information attenuation and amplification.

of information systems that make appropriate use of information technology at each particular point in time.

The basic information architecture model appears in Figure 3.5. It has provided a valuable focus for the specification and deployment of information systems, and it will continue to do so for some time.

Figure 3.5 Information Architecture Model

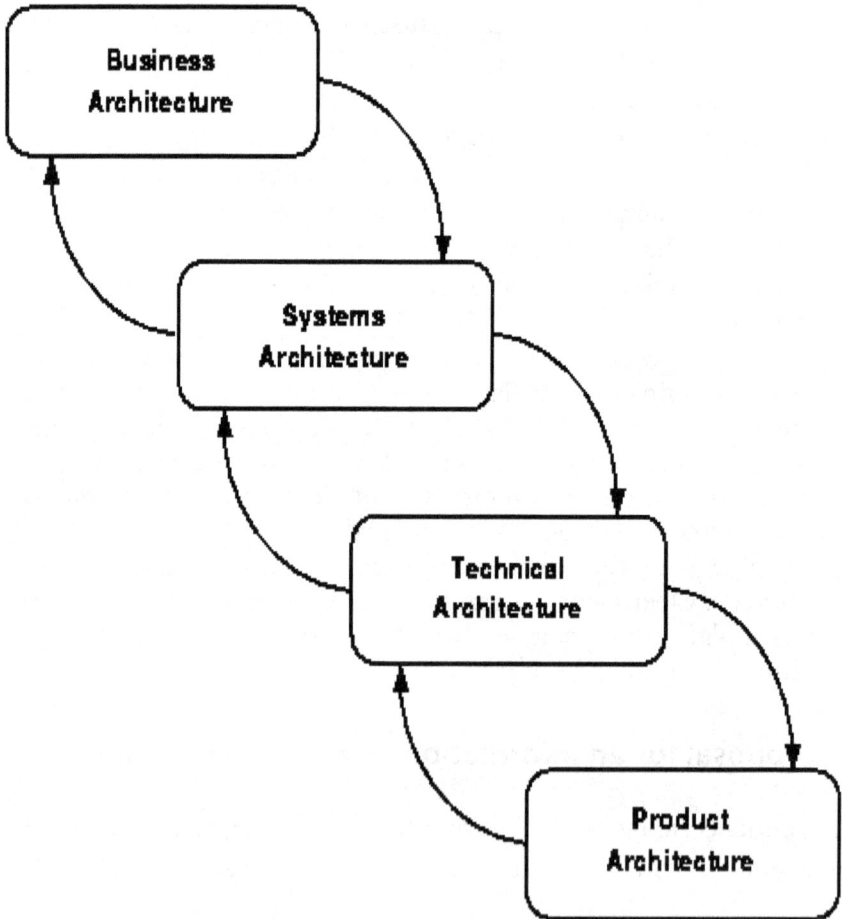

The value of the model, is that it broadly represents different audiences and different views of an enterprise's information processing needs. Here is a quick summary matching architecture to audience and domain:

- **Business architecture**—the overall information needs of the enterprise (or in some cases a specific "strategic business unit")
- **Systems architecture**—an identification of an interrelated set

of required information processing systems, along with priorities and organizational critical success factors
- **Technical architecture**—a product-independent identification of processing environments and the design principles to apply to them
- **Product architecture**—an integrated set of hardware and software products to provide an enterprise infrastructure

It is easy (and quite common) to interpret this diagram prescriptively. That is, first there should be a business architecture for the enterprise, then a systems architecture, after that a technical architecture, and finally, when products are selected, a product architecture.

The reality was not like that. First, a product architecture just "happened" because hardware and software products were brought in and used. A technical architecture was the earliest to be articulated. At about the same time, the first systems integration efforts began to define application portfolios in practice before a more formal articulation. Then came the first systems architecture, and after that came articulation of a product architecture, and finally definition of the first version of a business architecture. Clearly, a neat linear sequence remains an artificial construct.

Figure 3.6 shows these architectures in a spiral. If there is to be emphasis at any point in time, it ca be on any of the architectures; and work can also proceed in parallel, on more than one architecture.

Figure 3.6 The Information Architecture Model as a Spiral

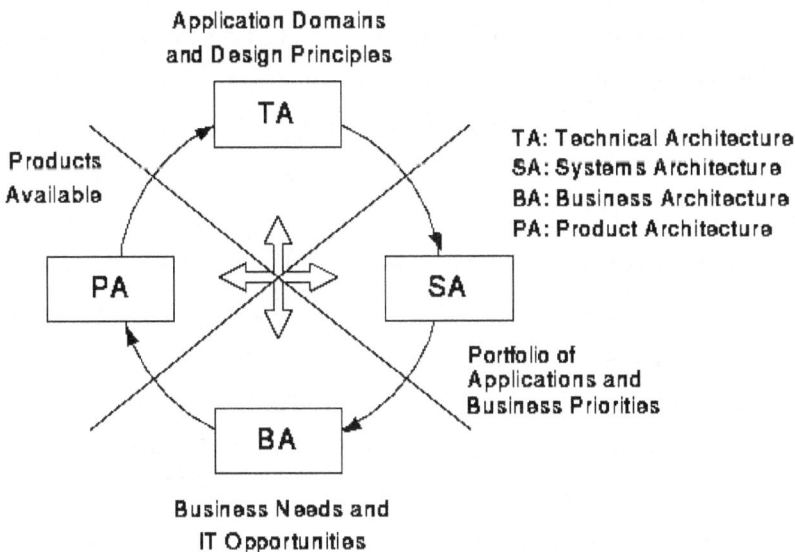

TA: Technical Architecture
SA: Systems Architecture
BA: Business Architecture
PA: Product Architecture

If architecture development is being driven in an IS department such as we describe in Chapter 8, we recommend that some work be done on all the architectures at the same time to ensure a reasonable degree of vertical and horizontal integration—that is, vertical between the different architectures and horizontal between the different departments. Top down, by itself, is too expensive; bottom up, by itself, is too fragmented. We also recommend ensuring that the overall enterprise architecture addresses *the total information needs of the enterprise* and not just the computerized systems.

An information architecture is a mechanism for creating a greater degree of independence between business, organization, applications, and IT. The aim is to recognize change as a reality, establish mechanisms to manage it, and use it to advantage where possible. For example, when business needs change, any impact on applications should be minimized but the support from IT maximized. Likewise, when organization changes, the applications should be adjustable with minimum effort. One goal of an information architecture is to provide support for a much higher degree of flexibility.

Technical Architectures

Creating a technical architecture involves a taxonomy of systems within the scope of the architecture. Our initial taxonomy included processing environments for:

- **Reference**—the information used to support key business activity. Reference database subjects include customer, price, and employee.
- **Transactional**—the key transactions of the business such as sale, purchase, hiring, and making a contract.
- **Management reporting**—reporting with different levels of aggregation to support different kinds of decision making.
- **Personal productivity systems**—all the functionality required in the office, such as document processing, electronic mail, and profession-specific support. This also included the dissemination of company information to the employees' electronic workplace.
- **Infrastructure**—such as operations and development.

This taxonomy is biased in terms of computing culture—that is, the departments and systems out of which the technical architecture was created. Another group within Digital from a different computing culture produced a technical architecture similar to the one here, but its environments were data access, data capture, end-user, reference and dictionary, and infrastructure.

Each enterprise will have an unique technical architecture, and there may be good reasons for an enterprise to have more than one. A technical architecture is not expressed in terms of known products; it is technologically and organizationally based because it requires an understanding of technology and of the kinds of problems it is to solve.

Our technical architecture was founded on our views and experience about information flows and approaches to design. If we were asked to help produce one for a bank, supermarket chain, oil company, factory, or chemical manufacturer, the results would likely be different for organizational, application, and technical reasons. Indeed, we have helped in such diverse environments.

A technical architecture is basically a statement of fundamental design principles. There are many such principles. Here are a few examples:

- A technical architecture is an "insulating layer" separating enterprise requirements for information systems expressed through systems architectures, and a set of products and software components expressed through a product architecture.
- A technical architecture should define an environment and infrastructure for the integration and cooperation of different applications:
  — Different users need different combinations of functionality from a particular machine.
  — Applications need to cooperate in sharing data and information.
- A technical architecture provides a taxonomy of application types relevant for the particular enterprise.
- However the business is organized, there are certain data subjects and basic operations performed on them that will always be required, whichever department performs the various roles.
- Certain key business processes, often performed by more than one department, when de-composed, converge on a common set of information processing activities.
- A technical architecture should assist in building systems flexible enough to:
  — Run on small or large machines.
  — Ease the migration to larger systems as the enterprise expands.
  — Run applications in either distributed or non-distributed modes.
  — Provide any local language requirements.

— Change implementation products as performance needs change.

When a taxonomy of product-independent applications has been produced, each type of computing environment should be described in detail. In our case, for example, there are detailed definitions of reference and transactional environments, which help enormously in these ways:

- In the creation of a product architecture, there will always be a mix of products bought in and used as they are, products bought in and altered, and applications commissioned (either in-house or externally). A technical architecture provides a framework for positioning available products.
- Resources for investment in developed software systems (or hybrid hardware and systems software) are limited, and once available products can be matched with the technical architecture, it is easier to prioritize investment opportunities.
- The technical architecture provides a technology—rather than a product-based expression of how best to support the information needs of the enterprise.

In our experience, the greatest danger is the temptation to shop for a range of products and then define the technical architecture based on an installed product base, thus justifying the product mix *ex post facto*.

We have also found that the technical architecture can be a source of frustration. It is an expression of technological requirements, not all of which are likely to have been realized by the product architecture. Since it can be used to drive investment decisions, it may produce some dissonance within the enterprise.

It is important to realize that a technical architecture may never be fully implemented because of continuous change; but even incomplete it can be used to manage some of the dynamics of a continually changing information architecture. It can enable broad technological developments and changes in business needs to be incorporated in a more controlled way.

Systems and Business Architectures

Historically, product architectures preceded technical architectures. Then came formal portfolio management to identify and integrate applications both within and across departments. This was the first step toward a systems architecture.

Systems architecture work is now reasonably mature, having evolved well beyond early portfolio management approaches. "Systems architects" work throughout the enterprise. Their work coordinates the definition of architectural approaches and the application of a systems architecture in different departments. Chapter 4 discusses systems architecture in detail.

Business architecture was the last information architecture component to be developed formally. As with the other components, we started with a collection of established practice, taken largely from management literature and business school approaches. However, we found little theoretically sound, concrete advice on taking a set of enterprise objectives and identifying formally the "associated" information needs. We also found little to help with demonstrating (also on the basis of sound theory) the interconnections between enterprise, overall information needs, organization, and information technology. Our experiences and thoughts on these matters are summarized in Chapter 5.

Payback

We believe that our information architecture work over the past few years has provided Digital Europe with substantial quantitative and qualitative benefits. Many of the organizational changes we have done over the past couple of years would not have been achieved in such a short period of time without the available information and IT infrastructure. Financially, the benefit from our infrastructure can be valued at the equivalent of many millions of dollars per year, since current alternatives to some of the ways we use the infrastructure would involve demonstrably greater cost and lower efficiency.

The economics of infrastructure require a study in its own right. However, some concrete examples of quantitative and qualitative benefits here will be enlightening.

As we pointed out earlier, the development of an infrastructure involved establishing an integrated communications network throughout Europe that provides voice, video, and data transmission services. All departments gave up responsibility for their own networks, and the IS department assumed responsibility to provide networking to everyone. Integrating services on specific links has provided savings of 30 to 50 percent of cost, and the cost savings for the whole network have been about 15 to 20 percent of what the costs would be without the integration of the services. The cost saving is much more substantial when measured against the likely costs of separate departments continuing to acquire their own communications services. These savings are attributable to simple integration of departmental needs and the services that utilize the network.

What are we doing with all the installed network capacity? Many people assume that electronic mail represents the highest volume of network traffic. In fact, however, the highest-volume network users are the different levels of application integration, ranging from batch file transfers between applications to individual messages for high-performance, distributed transactional systems. Other high-volume users of the available bandwidth are electronic conferencing, videotex services, and document transfer.

Interestingly, electronic mail accounts for well below 10 percent of bandwidth used. The trends for electronic mail are that the size and volume of messages is increasing, the cost per message is falling, and the percentage of bandwidth utilization is falling.

We started our infrastructure development well before PCs and faxes were ubiquitous. Thus, the installed infrastructure had a significant impact on the economics of both PCs and faxes. The cost of providing incremental computing power via PCs would have been much more expensive than providing it from incremental utilization of the infrastructure when all costs are taken into account (such as hardware and software acquisition, configuration maintenance, training, support, and basic services such as backups of essential data). It would also have been significantly more difficult to model what everyone was doing with their PCs, and of course there would have been the increased risks of loss of critical information.

The economies of scale are such that we cannot identify a realistic alternative to electronic mail which would save us money. Ranked from cheapest to most expensive in aggregate terms, the communications alternatives are electronic mail, paper, fax, telex, telephone, and travel for face-to-face meetings. Electronic mail costs around 80 percent less than paper and about 70 to 90 percent less than fax. Generally fax is a bit more expensive than paper, so presumably speed and convenience are worth the extra cost.

As electronic mail utilizes only a small part of available bandwidth and inter-application communication utilizes the highest proportion, our greatest savings on communications costs come about through optimization of applications distribution. Hence, the product, technical, and systems architectures are interconnected and must be designed in conjunction with the design of the organization.

Stand-alone PCs and faxes may be the cheapest ways of adding incremental functionality to small (and perhaps medium-sized) enterprises, but beyond a certain point, far greater economies of scale will be obtained from information infrastructures.

Application areas that would be much more expensive to operate without the infrastructure include software maintenance and update, software licensing, automated logistics, financial data warehousing, human resources management, and transatlantic data center management, just to name a few. The costs of defining and maintaining our information architecture are only a fraction of the quantifiable cost savings, let alone the total benefit to the company.

Overall Enterprise Information Management Model

The original information architecture model shown in Figure 3.5 included organizational and skill-related issues by implication only; but as we worked with it, we found that these issues—the general organizational critical success factors—needed greater emphasis. We developed an extended model, called an *Enterprise Information Management Model*, which appears in Figure 3.7[5]. It shows additional boxes for organization, tasks, and skills.

An enterprise needs to be "in balance" with the information technology it uses and with the organization structure implemented. So the Enterprise Information Management Model can be considered a network of components, many of which have their own "architecture". We say "network", because organizations are shown traditionally as hierarchical structures. Of course, hierarchical structures are inappropriate for showing multidimensional and multidirectional interaction between components.

We have an Enterprise Information Management Model with these key components: business, organization, systems, tasks, skills, data, technical, applications portfolio, and product. It is important to understand that we have not attempted to model the whole enterprise but primarily those aspects we consider important from an information

---

5 The original diagram was developed in 1987 in conjunction with Jan Koolhaas, at that time a consultant with Digital.

point of view. There are many ways of conceptualizing an enterprise, or one aspect of it, such as, in our case, information. Our view is in no way "superior" to other possible views, but it does represent our experience and our particular organizational approach to defining and deploying information systems. Most enterprises will want to produce their own conceptualizations.

Figure 3.7 The Enterprise Information Management Model and IT

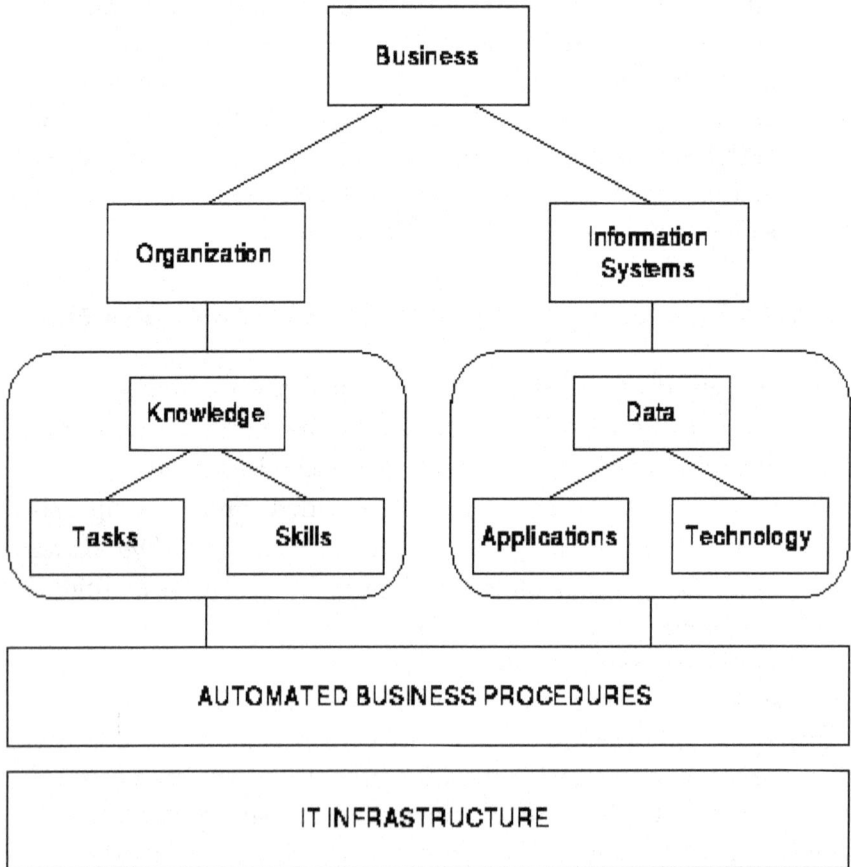

We have found that a simple conceptualization (or metaphor) is essential for communication between the IS department and the various users, and for helping the user community understand the need to look at the total picture of organizational dimension, business, and technology. Hence, the diagram shown in Figure 3.7 clearly emphasizes computer applications because its development was sponsored primarily for IT activity.

Using the Diagram

We start from the center, the applications, and ask "What, after all, is a computer application?" Well, it is nothing other than an automation of some of the enterprise's activities. (One hopes that automation occurs after a careful evaluation of how the activity should be performed, and that the application is not merely the automation of a previously existing task.) In order to automate certain activities, we need access to certain data and we need to comply with a certain set of technical criteria, such as the design of the user interface.

These applications have a dual link with the skills of the individual— they will change the skill of the individual in performing roles but need new skills to use the application. All applications lie on top of a particular infrastructure. We help the project managers and users to understand that when they plan and design an application they must take many different aspects into account:

- Traditional analysis to determine what tasks are to be automated
- What the data needs are
- Data model construction
- Compliance with the overall technical architecture
- The contribution made by the application infrastructure
- The capacity and type of communications network with the set of applications required to plan the infrastructure
- The methods and tools (such as those provided by CASE environments) needed to build the infrastructure

Our Enterprise Information Management model is not mathematically proven, nor do we present it as "more correct" than others available. Rather, it is a way to convey a set of messages. Since, by definition, the model is a partial conceptualization, it is possibly missing components and relationships. Nevertheless, it represents a helpful way to achieve consensus within a group, even though it may later prove difficult to convey some of the related ideas to others not part of the original consensus.

It makes sense to have an "architecture" for some of these components. One important part of an architecture definition is the set of principles behind it. Subsequent chapters treat briefly the key principles underlying different architecture components.

Concluding Comments

This chapter has painted a broad-brush picture of the evolution of our model for handling enterprise information needs at several levels of abstraction. These levels help insulate different layers of the enterprise model from change in other layers.

Historically, enterprises have focused on automating manual tasks. Over the years, economic, organizational, and technical feasibility have led to tasks being automated somewhat incoherently, usually in the context of an established enterprise structure of departments. Moreover, individual processes have been automated without overall organization or business process design. The result has been duplicated data entry, multiple definitions and usage of data, inconsistent data definitions, and no systematic flow to represent the real information needs of the enterprise. For these reasons it has been difficult to obtain substantial benefit from IT through time saved in overall enterprise processes. Much expensive management and development effort is expended on managing inconsistency and dealing with the consequences of inconsistent and inefficient, partially automated business processes.

Most enterprises have succeeded in assembling a very mixed collection of applications, technology, and computing platforms. Because every large enterprise is multi-vendor, there must be a systematic architectural (or whatever term others may prefer to use) approach to achieve effective and economic integration of the pieces.

All enterprises are faced with continual change of business needs, organization, information needs, and technology. As a result, many enterprises are striving to identify and integrate key business processes. This involves a rethinking of organizational structures and a fundamental reexamination of the way of doing business. These enterprises are seeking to integrate what they have in support of enterprise needs, while preserving as much of their investment as possible.

As a matter of fact, the best course for many of them may well be "Don't Automate, Obliterate"[6].

We suggest that rather than place emphasis on either top-down or bottom-up enterprises or approaches, enterprises should coordinate

---

6 This phrase is from Hammer (1990), who proposes that before computer assistance is applied to a problem, the underlying processes should be rationalized. Hammer describes some of Ford Motors' experiences with this approach and, intriguingly, mentions that Mazda achieved more spectacular results with it, but does not discuss Mazda's experiences. The key message is to redesign processes and eliminate some tasks (that is, "obliterate") before applying automation.

activity simultaneously at multiple levels. (This is a better representation of the reality of organizational behavior, than a theoretical sequential process.) Although sequential top-down methods are common in the literature, we believe that spiral development, and models with a lot of positive and negative feedback, are better.

The multidimensional model we have introduced has seen much evolution, and that evolution is continuing. Most enterprises will end up with their own models, which will probably be somewhat different from ours.

To sum up, a well-designed and implemented information infrastructure, with all its architectural components, offers an opportunity for substantial cost savings and competitive advantage.

[page left blank intentionally]

Chapter 4

Systems Architecture

Information Systems Planning in the Literature

Martin (1989) explains that "The term *information engineering* refers to the set of interrelated disciplines that are needed to build a computerized enterprise *based on information systems*". He goes on to describe the characteristics and high-level objectives of information engineering, which lean heavily toward the computerized aspects, along with the development, use, and control of data processing resources.

Martin identifies the following methods to be used in an information strategy planning study:

- Linkage analysis planning
- Entity-relationship modeling
- Technology impact analysis
- Critical success factor analysis
- Goal and problem analysis
- Business area identification

He suggests carrying out a study in the sequence listed, but points out that this should be varied if necessary. The entity-relationship modeling and business area identification are of primary interest to information systems planners, whereas the other methods are of direct interest to top management. He advocates that this kind of study should not be conditioned by the existing enterprise organizational structure: "The information architecture should therefore be designed independently of the current corporate organization. Implementation of the architecture will reflect the current organization and its concerns". According to Martin, a careful analysis of the critical success factors reveals some of the information needs of the enterprise. He suggests that a strategic data model is required to support the relationships between critical success factors, business strategy, and management goals.

62

Cash, McFarlan, and McKenney (1988), write about "Corporate Information Systems Management", and in their opening paragraphs clearly express their bias toward IT: "Over the past 30 years, a major new set of managerial challenges has been created by the rapid evolution and spread of information systems technology (IT), which in this book will include the technologies of computers, telecommunications, and office automation". Their book quite explicitly does not claim to address the overall information needs of an enterprise when asserting that "This new edition of *Corporate Information Systems Management* focuses on the overall information system function within a corporation", and that "Previous chapters laid out a series of frameworks for viewing the information technology activity and each function of IT management ... We have chosen to view an organization's IT activity as a stand-alone *business within a business*".

Cash, McFarlan, and McKenney are undoubtedly correct in their assertions that IT can have a profound impact on enterprises and can be used to leverage competitive advantage in many important ways[1] (and used in ways that may diminish an enterprise's competitive position). They raise many of the important organizational issues facing the IS department.

QED (1989) discuss what they call strategic information systems and lean toward the systems' computerized aspects in their remarks, "Strategic information systems are those computer systems that implement business strategies". It is, of course, a moot point whether or not a non-computerized information system, such as a marketing knowledge base or a set of new product plans, can be considered a strategic information system. The QED book (the authors are not identified) gives a very useful summary of several approaches to information systems planning and thinking about strategic information systems.

Vincent (1990) emphasizes IT, stating "*The Information-Based Corporation* provides a unique approach to applying the right information technology by viewing the company as a whole rather than many separate parts". He states that "Corporate relationships provide the context in which information technology can improve corporate performance, add value, and realize advantages. This book focuses first and foremost on corporate relationships. These are the corporate leverage points. Information technology is the lever".

---

1 For example, Cash et al. (1988) identify potential uses of IT to counter forces such as threat of new entrants, buyers' bargaining power, suppliers' bargaining power, threat of substitute products or services, and traditional intra-industry rivals.

Vincent proceeds with a very interesting discussion about the use of information technology for the improvement of corporate financial performance.

Blokdijk and Blokdijk (1989) present a useful discussion of methodology before discussing information systems planning. They distinguish between systems thinking and functional thinking, stating that they "adopt the systems thinking approach because it is the most fundamental, flexible, teachable, and so portable approach", and that in the systems approach "planning and design is executed by looking at the real world as if it is a system". Their approach hints at issues broader than the computerized aspects of information systems, but they do state their intention explicitly: "This book is intended to give a theoretical base and a practical method of executing the planning of organization supporting computerized information systems, and the planning and design of individual applications, of which the boundaries and priorities are defined in the information systems plan".

An extensive review and comparison has been conducted by Olle et al. (1982, 1983, 1986, and 1988) under the auspices of the IFIP Comparative Review of Information Systems conferences. In the introduction Olle (1982) states that "Being in the business of designing information systems in this second half of the 20th century, one tends to forget that this has been an age-old activity ... the fact remains that even today a large part of decision making in organizations is supported more by informal (or "soft") than by formal (or "hard") information". It is not surprising that an enterprise such as IFIP would look only at computer-assisted information systems. Olle explains the scope of work of the IFIP working group, entitled "Design and Evaluation of Information Systems", as "the development of approaches for the analysis, design, specification and evaluation of computer assisted information systems". The group's published papers give the impression that the target system is a computerized information system. Thus, the problems encountered are not the same as those that arise in the design of corporate or global information systems.

Maddison et al. (1989) present a framework of information systems development for managers. As part of that framework, business strategic planning is followed by information systems strategic planning. The authors state that "The purpose of ISSP is to produce an overall strategy that co-ordinates all information systems of the organization ... Long-term plans for what is to be computerized, what should be manual i.e.

not computerized—what has potential for future development, and broad estimates of resources and manpower are reviewed, coordinated and agreed". In discussing a hypothetical need for salespeople to have better access to information, they say, "This clearly leaves the technical detail of whether the salesman is provided with a set of manuals, or a portable terminal ... out of the objectives at this stage".

Most of the subsequent discussion presumes computerized systems are the target, but not necessarily so—many subsequent activities could be applied to non-computerized systems as well.

Remenyi (1991) provides a very useful summary of several established methods of strategic information systems planning. Although he emphasizes computers and IT heavily, many of the approaches he describes would be used before or in conjunction with the development of IS and IT strategies.

The problem for the information system designer is the dearth of literature about handling and designing non-IT-based, or manual components of information systems.

It is our view that this absence of guidelines for identifying and handling the overall information needs of the enterprise independently of implementation, combined with the strong bias in the literature and established practices for moving quickly from enterprise strategy and planning to IT, is probably the greatest single weakness in approaches available to the practitioner today. In the coming years this weakness will pose a substantial challenge to information workers, business schools, and information system practitioners.

Computerized information systems are tremendous enablers; this is apparent in much of the literature we have been discussing. However, the use of IT may also limit information management, particularly where strategies focus only on the computerized aspects of information needs. IT can facilitate overall information management, and it will do so more and more as its part within the overall information system is understood and implemented. An over-narrow use of IT through emphasis on corporate databases and related applications can result in very rigid approaches to information system design. In such cases the developers may not even be aware of their own limitations. This is indeed a great pity because such an approach fails to utilize IT's full potential.

Beer (1979, 1981) proposes an interesting way to identify certain information needs as a consequence of planning and strategy activity. He introduces the ideas of *actuality*—what an enterprise is able to do now; *capability*—what an enterprise could be doing now within existing constraints but with additional effort; and *potentiality*—what an enterprise ought to be doing and what is feasible by dealing appropriately with constraints and available resources. He describes programming as actuality planning, planning by objectives as capability planning, and, normative planning as potentiality planning. He then proposes three specific measures: measuring productivity by the ratio of actuality and capability; measuring latency by the ratio of capability and potentiality; and then measuring enterprise performance by either the product of productivity and latency or the ratio of actuality and potentiality. This approach provides an interesting identification of ratios that can be used for control. It enables the underlying information systems to be designed to provide the appropriate information, which has the effect of summarizing a great deal of detailed information.

Espejo and Watt (1978) also discuss developing control systems by combining management by objectives with developing a set of operational indices (such as those offered by Beer). Martin (1989), in discussing critical success factors, hints at a similar approach.

In Chapter 5 we identify the need for a stage between enterprise strategizing studies and information systems planning, one that addresses explicitly the information needs of the enterprise before a complete portfolio of information systems is identified and designed. In some cases there may be direct linkages with computerized information systems, but many indices and control mechanisms can be calculated and operated without extensive computer assistance, although in most enterprises, undoubtedly, computers make the tasks easier. Nevertheless, normative and strategic planning, in the sense used by Beer and others, cannot be performed by computer, so the design of the planning information systems must ensure a careful synergy between the people involved and the computerized information systems that support them.

Hence, non-computerized information systems (that is, systems for the recognition, capture, processing, presentation, or use of information) are at the core of strategizing studies for business or information systems planning, even though the results of the studies may lead to major computerized or computer-aided systems. Frequently, the most likely computerized support for strategy studies will be word and document processors and perhaps graphical editors. Other tools are emerging to provide more systematic foundations for enterprise, information, and organization strategy work. The results of a strategy study include very valuable information, and enterprises may go to extraordinary lengths to protect the information so generated.

How far is it reasonable to consider the organization and conduct of a strategy workshop as an information system? Strategic planning information systems are undoubtedly socio-technical systems, and because of their extensive normative, intuitive, and entrepreneurial content are likely to remain so. Artificial intelligence in this kind of situation can provide considerable assistance, but for the foreseeable future it can be nothing more than an aid to human intelligence. Roles, responsibilities, communication, and decision making need to be defined very carefully when humans are left in an information system's loop.

IT and computer systems lie at the heart of many enterprises now. Since such systems are of vital importance, understanding them and using them appropriately are essential for the senior managers of most enterprises today. Computers and IT are fascinating, and the achievements from their applications have helped broaden and even create new life styles. However, this does not mean that the computerized parts of information systems are so important that discussion of information needs that have not yet been computerized can be relegated to the bottom of the pile or not even discussed at all. The computerized parts of enterprise information systems are accidents of history, and every enterprise must deal with those aspects that have not yet been computerized. This neglect may well lie at the core of many senior management knowledge and control issues. One challenge for the 1990s will be to argue against the idea that an information system must be computerized to be considered strategic.

Setting the Scene

Our Information Architecture Model contains a systems architecture that includes data, technology, and applications. An enterprise's information assets and knowledge reside in computerized and non-computerized information processing and usage. A systems architecture complements a business architecture and identifies the information systems required to support the enterprise's information needs.

It is somewhat difficult to determine the scope of information systems planning and constructs such as information systems architectures. This is because most of the information needed and used by an enterprise is likely to be unstructured and not computerized, even though most of the literature and practice refer only to the computerized information systems.

Figure 4.1 illustrates this dilemma, which is one every enterprise will deal with either by explicit decisions or by simply allowing things to happen (or not to happen, as the case may be). The problem, of course, is what happens with the non-computerized information system needs and who is responsible for doing something about them. The total knowledge available to an enterprise is a combination of what can be classified as automated and non-automated systems. What is automated at any point in time is only a (partly arbitrary) subset of the enterprise's information and knowledge requirements based on a combination of technological, economic, and organizational feasibility.

Figure 4.1 Systems Architecture

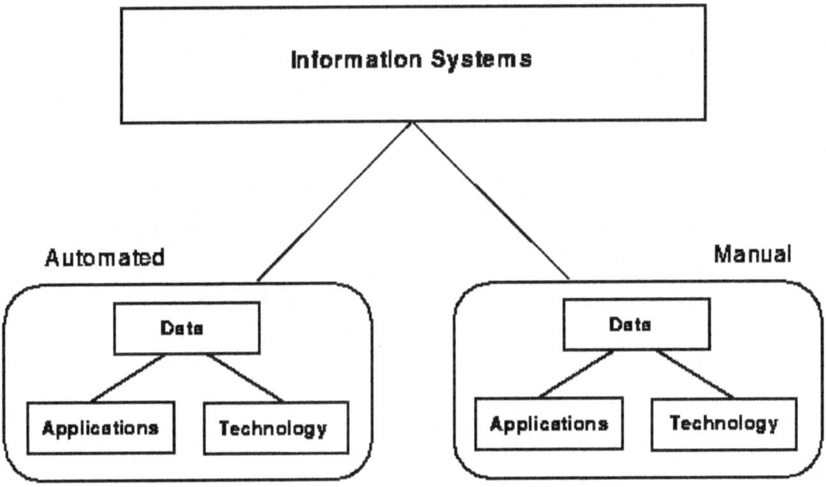

There is a great deal of non-computerized information technology, some of which is IT-based, some non-IT-based, and some IT-assisted. The significance here of much of the non-IT-based technology is that it is not perceived or classified as computer-based. In the case, say, of smart telephone exchanges, embedded computer chips give computers a role to play; but for many enterprises contemplating a corporate data model or similar construct, it is likely that the role of computer chips in the telephone exchanges will not be included either in the model or in the systems planning. The telephones and exchanges may appear in systems planning, but most of the literature on information systems planning ignores such essential IT as telephones and faxes.

We emphasize very strongly that a full systems architecture should identify all information systems needed by the enterprise, and decide which are non-IT-based and which are IT-based. The IT-based systems will use both computer and noncomputer IT. Examples of computer and noncomputer IT are shown in Table 1.4.

We can play with the earlier enterprise information model a little and place systems architecture in the middle, as in Figure 4.2. This scheme presents a different view of some of the interactions between systems, organization, and infrastructure.

Figure 4.2 Systems Architecture Related to Information Architecture Components

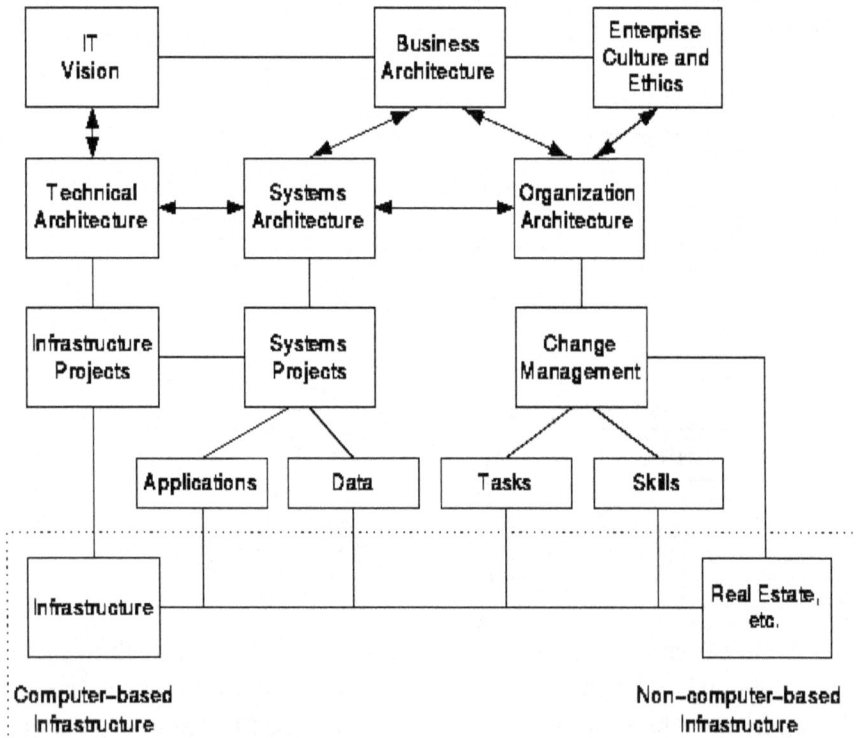

An IT vision is developed along with a business architecture. The enterprise cannot ignore its culture and ethics, as these will be major drivers of organizational structure and behavior. If part of the information executive's role is to own the infrastructure, then the IT vision will lead to a technical architecture. The technical architecture will interact with the systems and organization architecture to help decide which pieces of what needs are to be met from infrastructure or applications. It can also decide the technological mix of IT, IT-based, and non-IT technology.

One of the outcomes of a systems architecture is the identification of system projects. The types of projects will be heavily conditioned by the existing infrastructure.

On the organizational side, implementation and changes will need to be handled by some change management processes. These will have an impact on defined tasks, skills, and non-IT infrastructure such as real estate and facility planning. It is increasingly unwise to embark upon real estate and facility planning independently of computer-based infrastructure development. It is much cheaper to include cabling infrastructure at the building design stage than it is to modify a new or occupied completed building to provide extensive information and computer-based infrastructure.

Of course, there is a direct analogy between constructing a building and developing computer applications: extensive and deep modification of an existing package is often much more expensive than is designing flexibility into the applications at the beginning. In many cases, we have found that it pays to provide every workplace with multiple communications facilities such as twisted wire pair, coaxial cable, Ethernet, and optical fiber, even if there are no immediate plans for everyone to use all of them. Architects have learned this expensive lesson from modifying existing buildings. They have also learned the benefits of providing new buildings with suspended floors and ceilings as a matter of course. Like building architects, software specifiers and developers often need to take more care to build flexibility into their software constructions.

Practical Systems Architectures

One can paint a broad picture of the emergence and maturing of a systems architecture approach. This emergence has occurred in parallel with technological developments and with the evolution of approaches to enterprise and organizational planning.

The historical sequence of thinking and practice can be set down as:

- Linking of stand-alone applications
- Portfolio planning within an enterprise business department
- Cross-functional information system specification and development
- Feedback to business architecture work and feed-forward to technical and product architecture definitions
- Synergistic integration of computerized and non-computerized aspects of information systems

Many different enterprise departments evolved computer applications, and it became increasingly possible and desirable to link them together. This provided some bottom-up push for departmental information systems planning. At the same time there was an emergence of more literature (for example, Anthony, 1965) proposing categories for management and control that began to treat the need for planning. This provided a top-down push to identify information systems for the different levels and activities.

In terms that we would expect today to find associated with a call to install CASE tools and environments, Cash et al. (1983; 1988)[2] discuss a portfolio approach to IS development. They present the same symptoms as have many present-day CASE industry commentators (for example, system development failure, development times well beyond estimates, budgets well above initial estimates, inability to meet performance needs, and unused installed applications), and they offer as their diagnosis "three serious deficiencies in practice that involve both general management and IS management. The first two are the failure to assess the individual project risk and the failure to consider the aggregate risk of the portfolio of projects. The third is the lack of recognition that different projects require different managerial approaches". They prescribe a set of project management tools, showing how each contributes to ensuring the success of a project. These are interesting ideas, and we hope that at some stage data may be produced, after the prescribed tools have been tested in practice, to know the conditions under which the recommendations can be considered sound.

McFarlan, followed by Cash et al., present the IS portfolio and show how the risk profiles of different enterprises could be legitimately different. They look at portfolios on a company-wide basis, although in reality, company-wide portfolios can only be achieved if there is some enterprise-wide mechanism for their development. If there is none, then the development of enterprise departmental portfolios is the best that can be expected.

Many commentators have pointed out the lost opportunities, even the misfortune, created by simply applying computers to automate manual tasks and overlooking the fact that the effective use of IT involves organizational change. One way to initiate an examination of possibilities is to find key enterprise processes whose activities cross departments, and then apply some rationalization process to modify

---

2 The initial idea of a portfolio approach is found in McFarlan (1981), which starts with three examples of major computer system development projects in 1980 Fortune 500 companies.

enterprise practices as well as implement IT and organizational change in parallel.

The first systems architecture we produced was not for a complete enterprise but for a key business process—order fulfillment. Figure 4.3 shows a de-composition of the sales order fulfillment business process. The diagram is not identical to the one actually developed, but it does show how many activities have been brought together and integrated so that IT can play a maximum role in providing feasible support. It should be noted that within this overall sales order fulfillment model there are both manual and automated activities. For example, within "recognition" there is "receive", which is sometimes manual because an order arrives through the mail, someone opens the envelope and recognizes that it is a sales order; alternatively, an order may be received electronically from a customer, in which case the recognition of the order is also performed electronically.

Figure 4.3 Order Fulfilment Systems

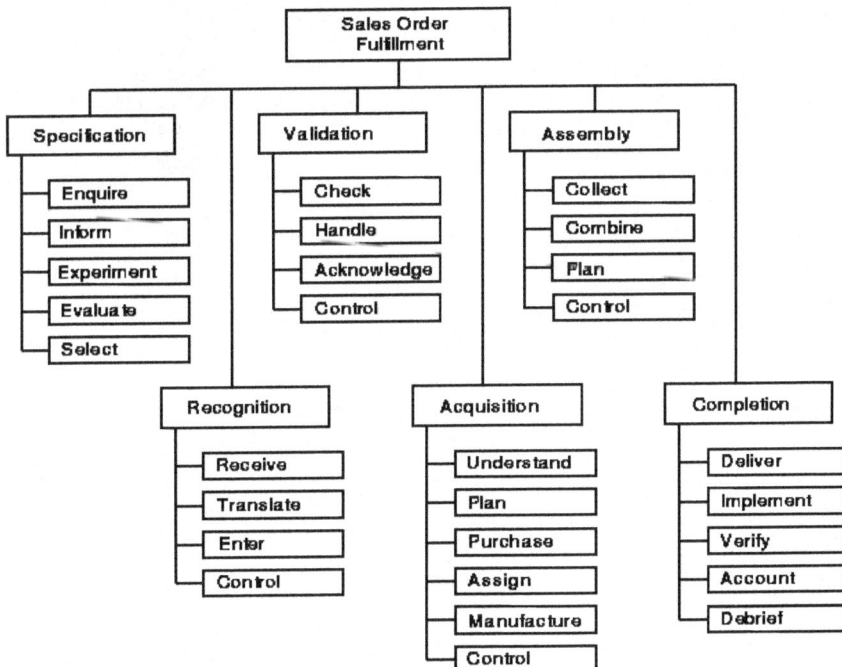

Systems Architecture Principles

We recommend that any of the components of an information architecture, including a systems architecture, be accompanied by a statement of principles to direct the activity and provide some rationale.

Table 4.1 lists some systems architecture principles. Any enterprise building a systems architecture should produce such a list, showing the appropriate linkages to other parts of an overall information architecture. Table 4.1 also shows some candidate alternatives.

Table 4.1 Systems Architecture Principles and Alternatives

Principle	*Alternatives*
A systems architecture identifies the information systems, manual and automated, needed to support the information needs of the enterprise.	The scope may exclude non-computerized systems; it may only be possible to prepare a systems architecture for separate enterprise departments.
A systems architecture should provide demonstrable financial benefits to the enterprise.	On a separate departmental basis it may only prove possible to provide efficiency and limited effectiveness.
The information systems are designed to provide the appropriate information to the people who need it, when they need it.	An initial portfolio may be restricted to operational and some management reporting activities.
The systems architecture must be affordable.	Identification of systems may be based more on intuition and preference than demonstrable cost-benefit.
A systems architecture must form part of a consistent, larger picture that includes other information architecture elements such as business, technical, and product architectures.	There may not be sufficient commitment in place for all elements of an information architecture, but useful system architecture work can still be performed.
The benefits of a systems architecture should be clear to its natural audiences.	Management education or awareness may be needed to accompany systems architecture work.
It is better to have a partial architecture than none at all.	Adequate resources may be available to complete a systems architecture quickly.
A systems architecture must be a living thing, subject to continuous evolution.	It may only be possible to start with a prototype systems architecture.

Systems Architecture Objectives

Once the principles for an enterprise's systems architecture have been established, more specific objectives can be defined. Figure 4.4 shows a candidate set of systems architecture objectives, which Table 4.2 treats in more detail.

Figure 4.4 Sample Systems Architecture Objectives

- Ensure investments in systems; support current and future business requirements.
- Ensure that information systems continue to meet enterprise goals.
- Provide a process to obtain explicit agreement on the implementation of information systems within specified time frames.
- Define clearly the automated system to be produced and its interfaces to other systems.
- Position the automated systems within a wider context.
- Make effective use of resources for implementing systems.
- Provide an internal and external communication tool by documenting the systems architecture.
- Provide a framework for working toward common objectives.
- Provide a forum for impact of organizational changes on systems.
- Provide guidelines to ensure that systems strategies and plans are congruent with higher-level strategies and plans.
- Help management focus on which systems to develop and deploy.
- Promote compatibility, interconnectivity, and integration.
- Help to protect investments.

Linkages with Systems Architectures

A systems architecture will never be used unless it is incorporated into the enterprise's planning, budgeting, and review processes and systems projects are linked back to the architecture. For example, there can be no data definitions and models without the involvement of the existing data management department, or without determining how the work will be managed.

Figure 4.5 shows schematically numerous possible linkages to a systems architecture. This view is systems-architecture-centered and does not attempt to map every flow of information.

We suggest that every enterprise producing a systems architecture obtains the necessary consulting help to produce its own systems architecture view of its activities and organization.

Table 4.2 Systems Architecture Objectives Explained

Objective	Explanation
Meet prioritized business requirements	Ensure that investment requirements and decisions regarding systems support current and future business requirements (as described within the business architecture, if it exists).
Information system performance and enterprise goals	Provide business management with sufficient supporting information to monitor and control information system performance in terms of contribution to enterprise goals.
Support priority identification	Provide a process to obtain explicit agreement within the enterprise about which information systems, automated and manual, are to be implemented within specified time frames.
Identify information systems required	Provide system development project teams with a clear definition of the automated systems to be produced and their interfaces to other systems.
Architectural need for each system	Provide a positioning of the automated systems within a wider context.
Optimize development resources	Make the most effective use of available resources for implementing information systems (for example, by designing common components, minimizing redundancy).
Document systems architectures	Provide an internal and external communication tool by documenting the systems architecture.
Common framework	Provide a framework for disparate groups to work toward common objectives.
Impact assessment	Provide a forum for the impact of changes in the enterprise's organizational structure and behavior on its information systems (and vice versa) to be assessed.
Information systems and business needs in sync	Provide guidelines to ensure that systems strategies and plans are congruent with higher-level strategies and plans.
Support management of information system deployment	Function as a management tool to direct the development and deployment of information systems within the enterprise.
Integration	Promote compatibility, interconnectivity, and integration by delimiting the required interfaces and common data requirements explicitly.
Investment protection	Help protect investments—the stability provided and the linkage of systems work to business objectives extend the useful life of automated systems.

Figure 4.5 Linkages to Systems Architecture

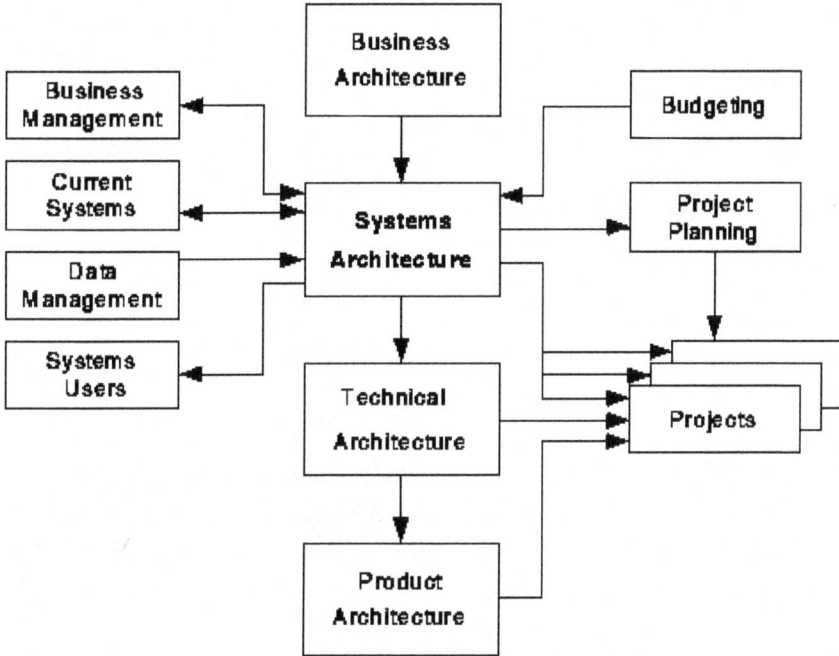

Systems Architecture Components

A systems architecture effort is based upon the following:

- Inputs or prerequisites
- Principles
- Tasks and processes
- Outputs
- Teams

There can be several possible inputs or prerequisites. A business architecture "feeds" into a systems architecture, and there is associated feedback. However, in many cases there is no business architecture, so systems architecture work will proceed without all the desirable initial information.

Whether or not a formal business architecture exists, several kinds of business inputs are needed for the systems architecture to work. These include:

- Overall enterprise information needs
- Business principles—statements of value and belief used by the enterprise to support decision making

- Business context—what industry is the enterprise in, and what are its performance characteristics
- Business objectives and well-designed metrics to measure them
- The results of an enterprise strategizing study
- An agreed business architecture model
- Current organizational structure
- Available and desired technology and identification of IT opportunities
- Identification of available resources
- Enterprise priorities
- Inventory of current systems

Of course, this list is not exhaustive. It will vary from enterprise to enterprise.

The results of a systems architecture will usually be embodied in various documents and databases, which describe systems, relationships between systems, and contributions to enterprise objectives. There are many ways in which such information can be represented. Figure 4.6 shows typical deliverables, for which Table 4.3 provides further detail.

Figure 4.6 Systems Architecture Deliverables

- Systems architecture definition
- Management overview
- Overall systems maps
- Automated systems maps
- Manual systems maps
- Implementation priorities and plans
- Systems architecture extract
- Communications relating to progress and problems

The construction of teams to drive a systems architecture effort is likely to be very important. Presumably, the effort is not merely academic, but intended to implement something.

Documentation and systems representations will depend on the objectives of the exercise. For example, many available techniques for producing charts and diagrams of system requirements are probably more suitable for helping a closed team reach consensus than for communicating a set of requirements to an independent group. This means that decisions should be documented and communicated carefully.

Table 4.3 Explanation of Systems Architecture Deliverables

Deliverable	Explanation
Systems architecture definition	Identify the scope and objectives of the work being undertaken.
Management overview	Inform management of the objectives, expected benefits and costs, and concepts of the systems architecture
Overall systems maps	Indicate the automated and manual systems to be developed or modified; this should indicate proposals or decisions which should be provided by infrastructure and which components will need to be provided by applications (some of these decisions may need to be deferred until further design work has been completed).
Automated systems maps	Identify automated systems and how they relate to other systems (manual and automated).
Manual systems maps	Identify manual systems and how they relate to other systems (manual and automated).
Implementation priorities and plans	Show the prioritized list of systems to be deployed, in decreasing enterprise added value.
Systems architecture extract	For each project initiated as a result of the whole process.
Communications	Keep appropriate people informed of activities, progress, and problems

A cross-functional systems architecture effort requires teams quite different from those engaged in an effort kept mainly within one department. In all cases senior management involvement and commitment must be sufficient to obtain the necessary resources and drive the required change programs throughout the enterprise.

We recommend that the effort be sponsored jointly by a business executive and a senior information executive and not simply by an IT or IS senior manager. The problem to be overcome is to prevent the systems architecture work being seen as essentially a technical effort; from the start it is very much a business effort, with much of the technical work being done only at later stages.

A realistic systems architecture is likely to involve the redesign of business processes, which will have heavy cross-departmental impact. The inherent relationships among the components of the enterprise's information architecture—business, systems, technical, and product—need to be represented, so systems architecture teams must provide:

- Vertical integration within each affected department between

senior management, project management, and design specialists
- Vertical integration between the different architectural efforts (business, systems, technical, and product)
- Horizontal integration across departments at senior management, project management, and technical specialization levels
- Horizontal integration across any architectural work performed in the different departments

Systems Architecture Processes

There are at least three categories of key systems architecture processes: creation, usage, and maintenance. By systems architecture creation we mean the steps to produce a complete systems architecture, from scope and objectives through identification of systems to be put in place.

Figure 4.7 illustrates such a set of steps. It shows inputs and signing milestones in the project and the major products of the creation process.

A systems architecture will be used in several essential ways:

- Extraction of information for project commencement, providing each project team with sufficient information for the required automated and manual information systems.
- Ensuring that project designs are compatible with the architecture. This check should be made for every system development project initiated. A design specification standard should be required to demonstrate architectural need and consistency for every project.
- Enterprise data model linkage. Where there is a separate data management activity, the initiated projects need to be consistent with the identified information needs of the enterprise.
- Consultancy to project teams. It is unreasonable to expect project teams to be familiar with all the existing and projected architectural work, so consulting must be provided as needed.
- Interaction with other systems architecture work. Every enterprise is likely to have several system architecture efforts under way, and these need to be coordinated.
- Infrastructure construction. Infrastructure will meet many of the systems needs. Here we mean a computerized and non-computerized information infrastructure.

For each kind of architecture in an enterprise, we distinguish its *definition* from its *occurrence*. For example, an enterprise will establish in general terms what its systems architectures will be used for and how the various efforts will be coordinated. This is a definition that (along with related processes) will be applied to specific enterprise situations to create an architecture occurrence. Maintenance for systems architecture work is at both the definition and the occurrence level.

Figure 4.7 Systems Architecture Creation

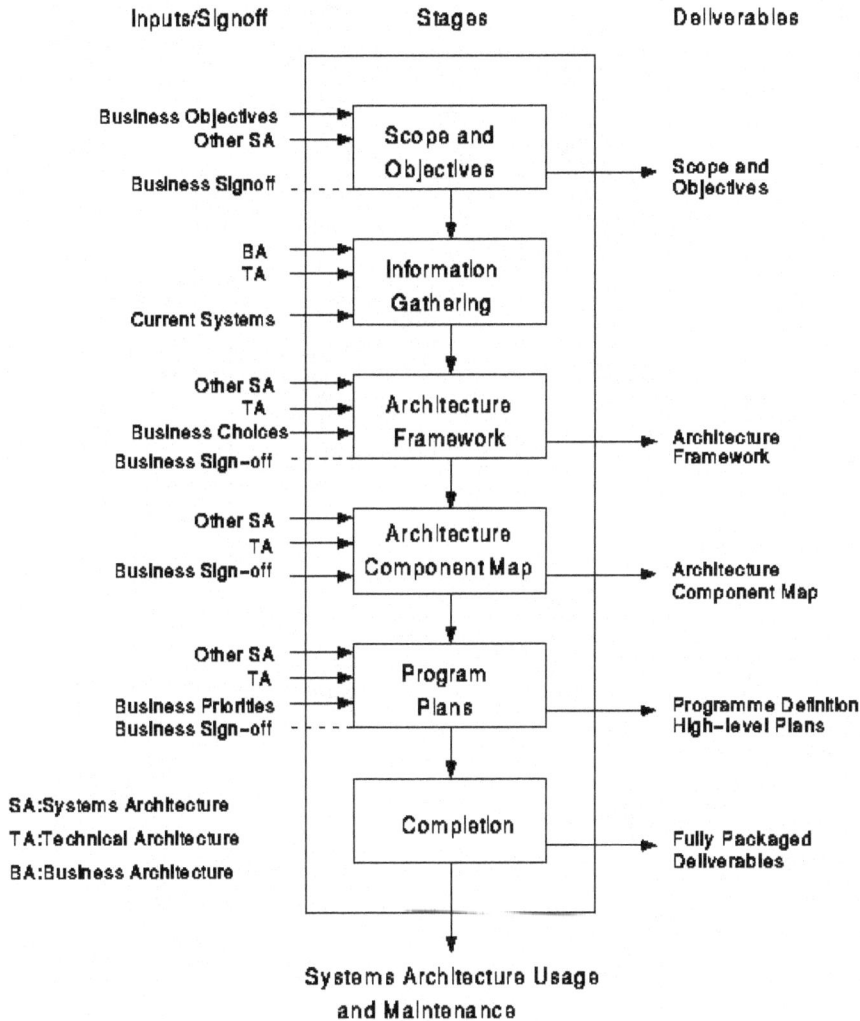

situations to create an architecture occurrence. Maintenance for systems architecture work is at both the definition and the occurrence level.

Figure 4.8 illustrates maintenance, showing that once an enterprise systems architecture definition is available, it will be applied to more than one business area[3]. This means that an enterprise usually has

---

3 In fact, this is one of the issues to be resolved when the scope of systems architecture work is defined. Some enterprises hold that there should only be one integrated systems architecture for the enterprise, as may be the case with a business architecture. Unless there is a sponsor, such as a computer technology independent information executive, in practice it will be very difficult to achieve complete cross-functional commitment and cooperation at the business level. For this reason the scope of most systems architecture efforts is only part of an enterprise. As soon as there is more than one architecture, coordination and cooperation become issues.

several systems architectures in differing states of activity, each of which will be used to some extent. Usage efforts provide opportunities for review, which will assist the review of the occurrences and the underlying systems architecture model used for the enterprise.

Figure 4.8 Systems Architecture Definition Maintenance

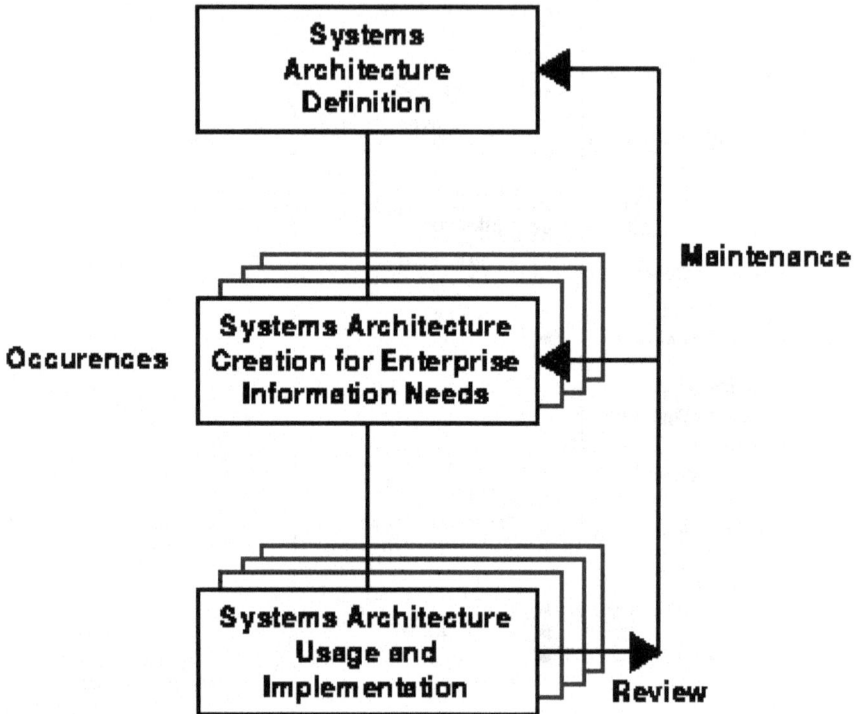

The information needs of an enterprise change continually, so systems architectures will require revision. In this sense, systems architecture work is never completed. The maintenance example shown in Figure 4.8 is modified in Figure 4.9 to indicate sources of change and review leading to continuous occurrence evolution. Obviously, definition itself can also be a source of change.

81

Figure 4.9 Systems Architecture Occurrence Maintenance

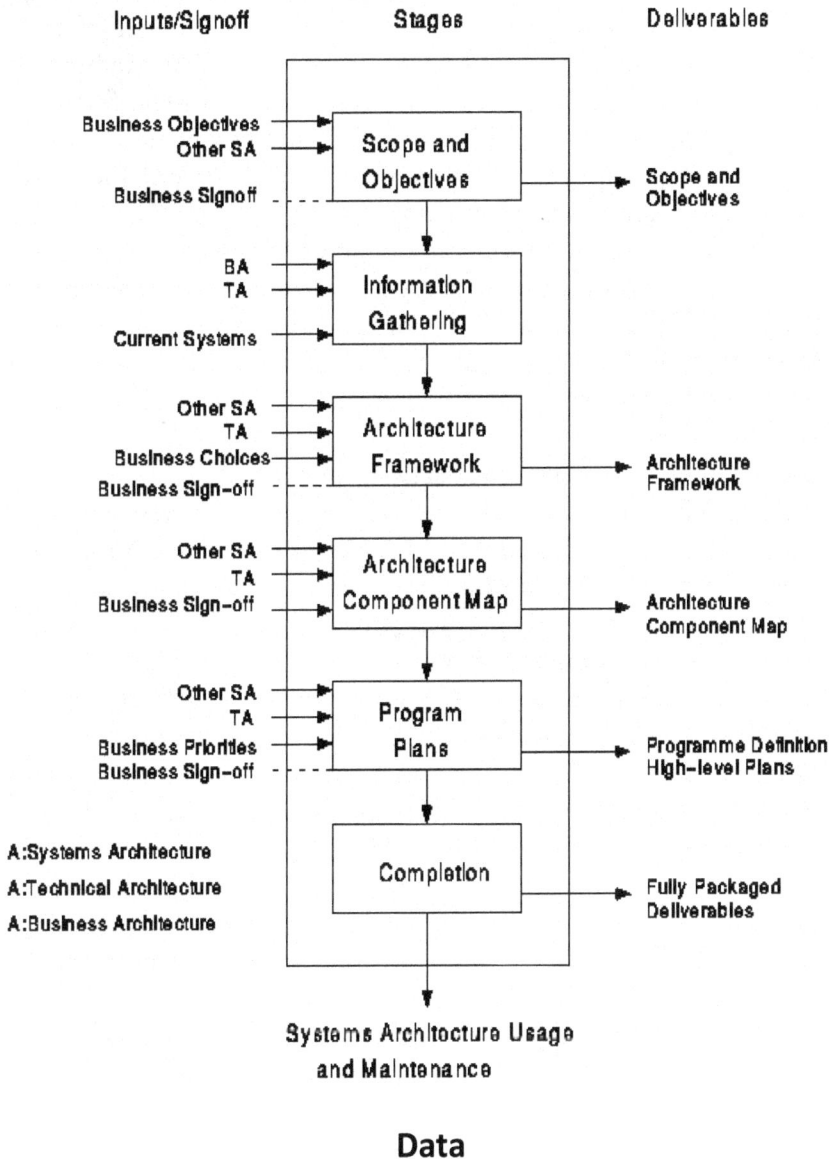

Inputs/Signoff	Stages	Deliverables
Business Objectives / Other SA / Business Signoff	Scope and Objectives	Scope and Objectives
BA / TA / Current Systems	Information Gathering	
Other SA / TA / Business Choices / Business Sign-off	Architecture Framework	Architecture Framework
Other SA / TA / Business Sign-off	Architecture Component Map	Architecture Component Map
Other SA / TA / Business Priorities / Business Sign-off	Program Plans	Programme Definition High-level Plans
A:Systems Architecture / A:Technical Architecture / A:Business Architecture	Completion	Fully Packaged Deliverables

Systems Architecture Usage and Maintenance

Data

A *data architecture* is related to an information architecture in the ways we discussed in Chapter 3. It contains the principles, standards, policies, models, practices, and activities necessary to the management of an enterprise's data. Whether a separate treatment of data is necessary will depend on factors such as the scope of systems architecture and the predominant application development paradigms.

We believe that enterprises should move from data management to information management to knowledge management. However, despite our belief, we are faced with the reality that much of the literature stresses the need for data management, and undoubtedly that is what executives in many enterprises still feel most comfortable with. At least it provides the illusion of understanding the information needs of the enterprise, even if it does not actually record the data usage within the computerized systems.

The historical roots of data management activity can be traced to literature about the role of the database administrator, which emerged to accompany developments in database management systems. To implement an enterprise-wide database or data model the enterprise must first identify and define all the data used within its computerized applications.

Very often, data management activity is restricted to a specific computing subculture[4] found in MIS-type operations. Data requirements within process control, or actually embedded in products and services, are frequently omitted from corporate data models.

Other ways in which data management activities may restrict themselves to certain computing subcultures are shown by the majority of the literature about data modeling, in which the most frequent presumption is that only structured data in some kind of formal record format is relevant for data management processes. We consider this an unreasonable presumption. There are many examples of unstructured data such as text, graphics, images, and voice that are inextricably linked to the essential information needs of an enterprise, and these are likely to be ignored completely by data management activity simply because they do not fit the mold of neat, structured, record-oriented technology.

We make what ought to be considered a superfluous recommendation, that data management processes should not ignore any essential information needs. The enterprise should not permit present-day technological limitations to drive the data management standards. Information needs should drive the standards, and, as technology evolves, one hopes a greater proportion of those needs can be IT-assisted in some way.

Figure 4.10 shows a sample set of principles for a data architecture.

Many different people interact with data for different purposes. Their roles can be classified as we show in Table 4.4.

---

4 An interesting approach to enterprise-wide data modeling that encompasses different computing subcultures can be found in Scheer (1989).

The custodians of data are responsible for maintaining what may be described as reference information and warehouses that contain data such as retired transactional records.

Figure 4.10 Sample Data Architecture Principles

- Data and information definitions are derived from the enterprise's information needs.
- Data and information definition should have representations that are independent of any technological implementations.
- Definitions and models must be consistent between different architectures and have appropriate representation for each architecture.
- Data are organized within a data managed environment that provides an infrastructure for people to obtain the data and information they need to do their work.
- Information is provided from data such that the value of the information exceeds its cost.
- Information is only provided where it has the possibility of affecting a decision.
- Data are collected once, are of the highest "quality" achievable, are made available to those who need it and at reasonable cost.

Table 4.4 Data Roles

Role	Explanation
Data producers	Those responsible for the origination of data
Data definers	Those responsible for defining data structures, standards, and representations (i.e., meta-data) and for identifying the basic operations performed on, or that "encapsulate" the data
Data custodians	Those responsible for "owning" data and keeping it up to date and relevant
Data consumers	Those who need access to data to support their work, e.g., operational systems needing reference information such as customer and price-product; or managers needing summaries of operational data

Applications

An application portfolio developed in accordance with the architectures and other Enterprise Information Management Model components should be:

- Flexible and supportive of change

- Highly consistent in its use of data
- Insulated as far as possible from business changes
- Insulated as far as possible from technology changes
- Highly stable in terms of basic enterprise data and principal operations on that data
- Well integrated, using a common infrastructure
- Appropriately supportive of skills to perform tasks for the enterprise

A broad strategy for applications development work would include the following rules:

- Maximize the use of available infrastructure components.
- Where application needs cannot be met from existing infrastructure and a decision is taken to build, the components that are commissioned should be designed to maximize their contribution to infrastructure evolution. Every case of functionality required by more than one application (present or future) is a candidate for adding to infrastructure.
- For every application requirement that cannot be met from infrastructure, ask the question, buy or build?
- Build every component to maximize reusability and distributability.
- As more infrastructure becomes available to support different application domains, consider developing very-high-level languages to increase productivity in the development of new applications.
- Establish design standards to encourage the development of reusable and distributable components using constructs such as clients and servers.

Roles and Responsibilities

A systems architecture effort is ongoing and thus needs the understanding and commitment of senior management to make it work. This can be considered a critical success factor for all of the architectural efforts we have described.

A major industry problem is that there are not enough "information architects" to support architecture work. The several architectural roles include:

- Information architecture definer, who is responsible for the overall definition of, maintenance of, and communication about an enterprise's architectural capabilities
- Information architectural consultants, who are able to advise on

the application of different architectures

- Methods engineers, who are responsible for formal behind-the-scenes modeling performed to underpin and verify various architectural efforts
- Architectural facilitators, who work with the enterprise departments in their architectural work

Portfolio managers (or those in a similar role) are needed to ensure consistency between applications and the relevance of applications to real enterprise needs. They are an essential part of systems architecture teams.

The information executive must act as a sponsor for systems architecture work. If no one fills this role, or if the executive comes from a technological background, the senior business managers should appoint people to sponsor and drive systems architecture work.

Application developers must feel (and exercise) considerable professional responsibility for the design and development of applications that are consistent with architectures and that maximize reusability and distributability. In many cases, developers can contribute to infrastructure development in the absence of explicit management decisions to do so. In this way, designers can make their own contribution to reducing potential costs of implementing strategies and architectures.

As a systems architecture identifies discrete systems and priorities for those systems, it provides the capability to make rational decisions about the economic and technical usefulness of each component.

In this chapter, we have described the importance of identifying a set of information systems to support the enterprise. This set will include computerized and noncomputerized systems. Most current literature on information systems places emphasis on the computerized aspects, even though overall information needs are much more extensive than the needs met by IT. A systems architecture provides a framework inclusive of all an enterprise's system. In the next chapter, the role of systems architecture will be positioned with respect to the overall needs of the enterprise in general, and information needs in particular.

[page left blank intentionally]

Chapter 5

Business Architecture

A Business Architecture was the last *technical* part of our information architecture model work (we say *technical* to distinguish the technical from the organizational issues, which we discuss in Chapter 6). There are good historical reasons for it being (almost) last:

- Dramatic changes in available information technology have altered the boundary of feasibility. A few years ago it was difficult and expensive to integrate a few computer applications and provide extensive online capability; now it is expected to achieve a high degree of enterprise integration.
- Extensive communications infrastructures, combined with changes in technological feasibility, now make global integration a means of achieving greater economies of scale.
- The increasing pervasiveness of IT means that it is very unwise to attempt enterprise strategy without considering information strategies.
- IT support makes new organizational forms possible, and the redesign of key enterprise processes, taking full advantage of those new organizational forms, is becoming a major competitive factor.

Business and It

In the past the development of computer systems to provide point solutions for specific isolated problems did not require much enterprise adjustment. New skills and approaches were necessary in the business domain using the new computer systems, but interaction between that domain and other business domains was limited to specific interfaces and flows of information from one department to another or from outside the enterprise itself.

As computer systems became more pervasive, it was increasingly difficult to insulate them from organization and other systems (personnel, manufacturing, logistics, legal, and so on). Now it is essential to consider both organizational and information system design and produce an appropriate combination of the needs of both. A systems architecture integrates the information systems, but a higher-level, enterprise-wide integration of all systems is also necessary. This is provided by a business architecture.

As part of the strategizing process for any enterprise, there are at least two levels of input to IT. The environmental-level input recognizes that within an industry as a whole, a great deal is IT related, and that an increasing percentage of IT is embedded in any product or service. Therefore, when management does the overall strategizing of the charter, mission, and strategy of the enterprise, it must take into account what IT and information bring in terms of market opportunity and how the product and service can be integrated into IT. The environmental level is the first point of interaction between IT strategy and business strategy.

After charter, mission, and strategy, have been determined, objectives, goals, and critical success factors are found, and business processes are designed. This is the second level (or "opportunity" level) of IT influence. Here it is necessary to understand how IT can be used to improve critical success factors, what kind of IT to include in the enterprise objectives, and how IT can change the design of business processes. For example, at a business process level, one of IT's major advantages is its ability to alleviate space and time limitations. Thus, thinking through all the business processes rather than taking a traditional departmental line, makes it easier to think about the added value in information chains.

Figure 5.1 illustrates IT's environmental influence. It shows how use of IT outside the enterprise affects the enterprise's charter, mission, and strategy. IT provides many opportunities for the rationalization, organization, and inherent flexibility of the enterprise and key business processes; IT may be embedded in the products and services themselves.

Traditional wisdom has it that a non-IT enterprise would only look at IT farther down the planning chain. In other words, once the strategy had been decided, IT would be examined in terms of improving efficiency or effectiveness. In this age we talk about strategic systems, many of which became strategic because IT was an integral part of the service role of the product[1]. Our argument here is that in the future it

---

1 Perhaps the most famous is the SABRE system, to which there are many references, for example Keen (1988).

will be very difficult to find any product or service that does not have an IT component. Therefore, IT strategy and overall enterprise strategy need to be planned at the same time. Also, since infrastructure in one company is connected to infrastructure in other companies, creating community or industry networks, IT infrastructure components can no longer be ignored at the very high level of business architecture. Today it would be very difficult to think of an industry that does not need some kind of IT built into products and services.

Figure 5.1 Environmental Influences of IT

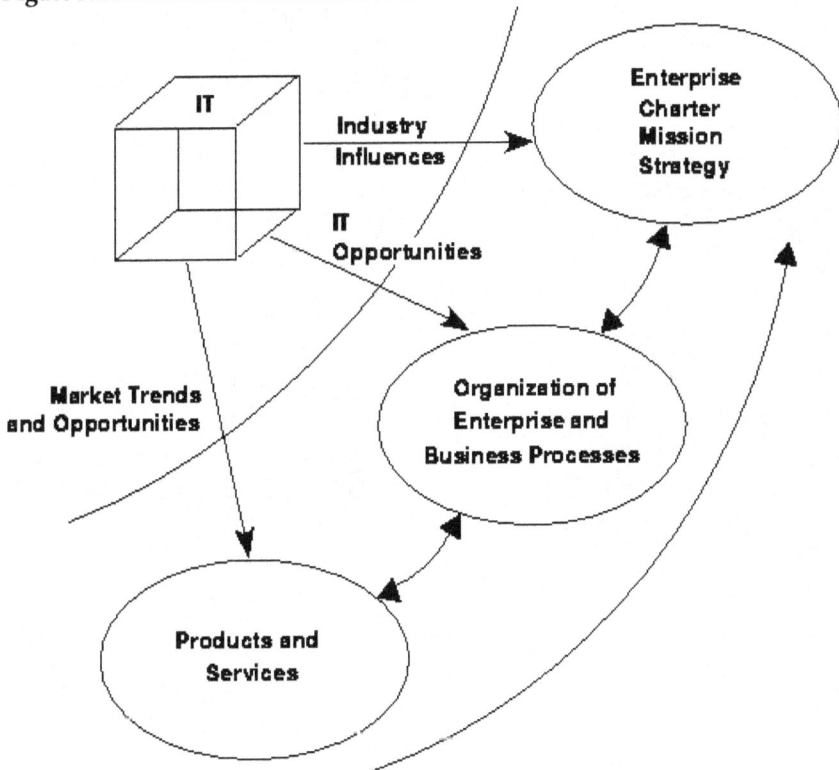

Take for example, the automotive industry, which uses a great deal of IT. There are more computers in a car these days than one imagines; IT is embedded in the product. When thinking about services provided by the automotive industry, it is very important to have direct links with the dealer and service networks. Therefore, IT is also embedded in the services the industry uses or provides—repair systems, diagnostic systems, fleet maintenance, scheduling, and so forth.

In general, the objectives of greater flexibility, reduced time to market, and mass customization are making IT in both product and service a necessity. IT makes products easier to customize because it allows for more soft-programmed, rather than hard-wired, components. Video recorders for an international market are a good example of this. They must overcome the local language problem in displaying information, which they do, not by embedding language in a chip or with hard-wired jumpers, but by controlling language with software. Similarly software can support multi-standard capabilities. In services IT enables the automation of links with the customer, the supplier, and distribution networks.

An even more advanced convergence of different technologies can be found in the most recent trend of cooperation between, and possible merging of, consumer electronics and entertainment companies. Such cooperation is essentially founded on information technology, where information and knowledge are fundamental to the purposes but independent of the technology. Multimedia training, for example, conveys knowledge and information, using information technology to enhance the process and improve learning—the same technological foundations can be used for very different subject matter. "Hardware" companies such as Sony have found it necessary to move into the "software" world of movie and music production. The next step will clearly be the integration of computer-based instruction and home entertainment through multimedia technology[2].

Technologies also converge when it comes to images. Camcorders and cameras are moving into the era of digital images, which can be edited by computer much the same way text is edited. CDROMs play an obvious part in this scenario, along with high-bandwidth communications that permit low-cost transmission of images, integration into multimedia environments, and enhanced cognitive models of information and knowledge. The information and knowledge bases become integral parts of the available information and IT infrastructures.

Traditionally, there has been a very wide gap between the enterprise's information systems and the IT embedded in its products and services. In many manufacturing companies, IS focuses on commercial applications, operational support systems, end-user computing, and so forth. R&D IS is usually totally separate from the rest of the company's IS and usually has a very different computing culture. Marketing systems, too, tend to be disconnected from some

---

2 Rothman, Grover, and Neff (1991) give an account of Sony's establishment of a software corporation responsible for products and services to complement their traditional "hardware" products. The extension to, or inclusion in, what we identify in Chapter 7 as individual information systems is obvious. Links such as this already exist for corporate, global, and individual information systems (CISs, GISs, and IISs) in such areas as training packages and trading systems.

of the other enterprise systems, and innovations in embedding IT in services such as marketing have been separate from the IS department.

These points are absolutely fundamental in the design of corporate information systems (CISs) and global information systems (GISs). Given the evolution of information and IT infrastructures and the increasing necessity to connect the external and internal worlds to community networks and infrastructures, it is no longer feasible for R&D to go off on its own embedding technology in products and services, isolated from the departments responsible for the logistics systems or from those managing the marketing databases.

Let us continue with the automotive industry example. After embedding microprocessors in a car, the next step is connecting the car to the diagnostic system at the repair station, then collecting the data and feeding it back to the manufacturing quality database to close the loop. It is very desirable to link the dealer systems, which are part of a marketing system, with the production planning system and the purchasing system. This kind of integration is illustrated in Figure 5.2. The final step is to integrate a consideration of actual car usage with patterns of work and information processing, and move as much work and leisure as possible to the individual rather than the other way around. As the value network expands to trading partners on the supply side and to customers on the demand side, information must be transferred all the way to where it is needed. This multiple linking makes it essential to think strategically of IT use-from IT-enhanced products and services through to IT efficiency.

Strategizing Elements

In developing our first business architecture, we took from the management literature many elements that we refer to generically as "strategizing elements."[3]. These allowed us to obtain a higher-level articulation of enterprise activity, and so we decided that our first business architecture version would identify some key features, including:
- Mission
- Strategy
- Objectives and goals
- Critical success and failure factors
- Business processes
- Strengths, weaknesses, opportunities, and threats

3 Chapter 9 discusses these in more detail.

Figure 5.2 IT as Strategy, Organization, and Product

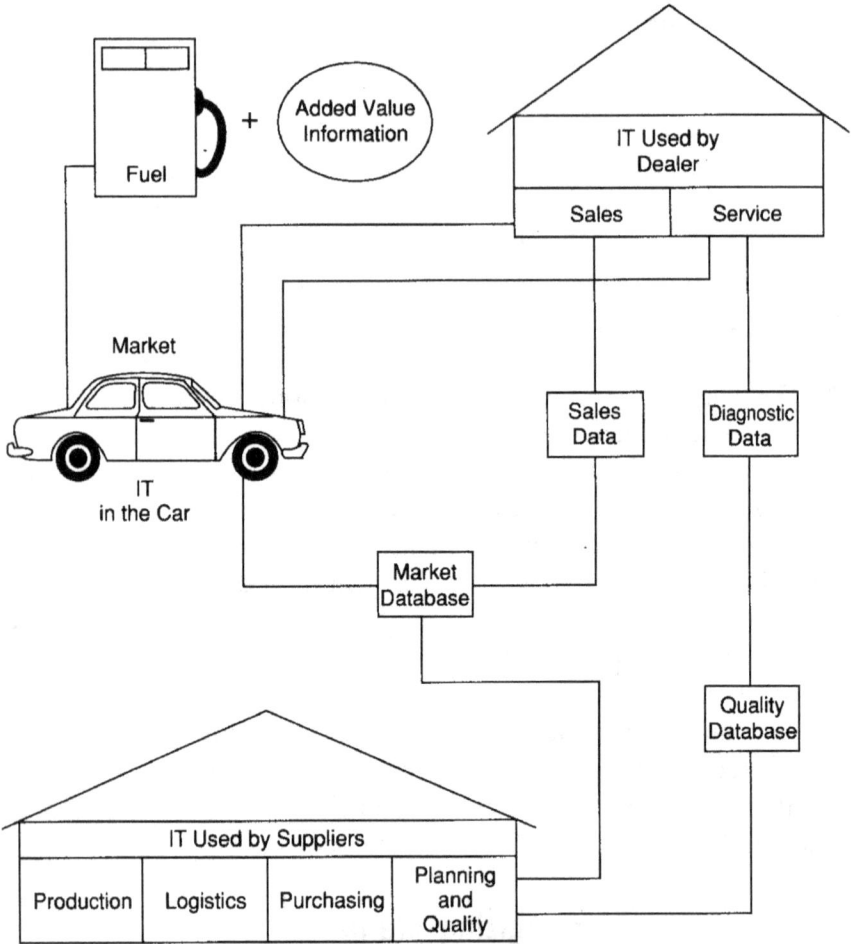

A business architecture can define these elements for the current state and the future state and then explore the dynamics of moving from one state to the other. Figure 5.3 illustrates this schematically. A desired future state is derived from a vision of the enterprise at some point in the future. Business processes are defined for all the necessary activities and based upon a set of business principles. Then various strategizing objects such as those listed above are related to the current and future state. A strategy helps to identify how the desired future state will be reached by a sequence of transitions from the present to the desired future.

The strategizing objects are inextricably related and can be explored through a variety of approaches and techniques, among them:

- Strategizing exercises
- Mission and objectives identification
- Critical success factors identification
- Identification of strengths, weaknesses, opportunities, and threats
- Program and project definitions to drive the mission and objectives into the enterprise

It is worth pointing out that these elements can apply either to a complete enterprise or to one of its major, identifiable parts (what some people call a strategic business unit).

Figure 5.3 Current to Desired Future State

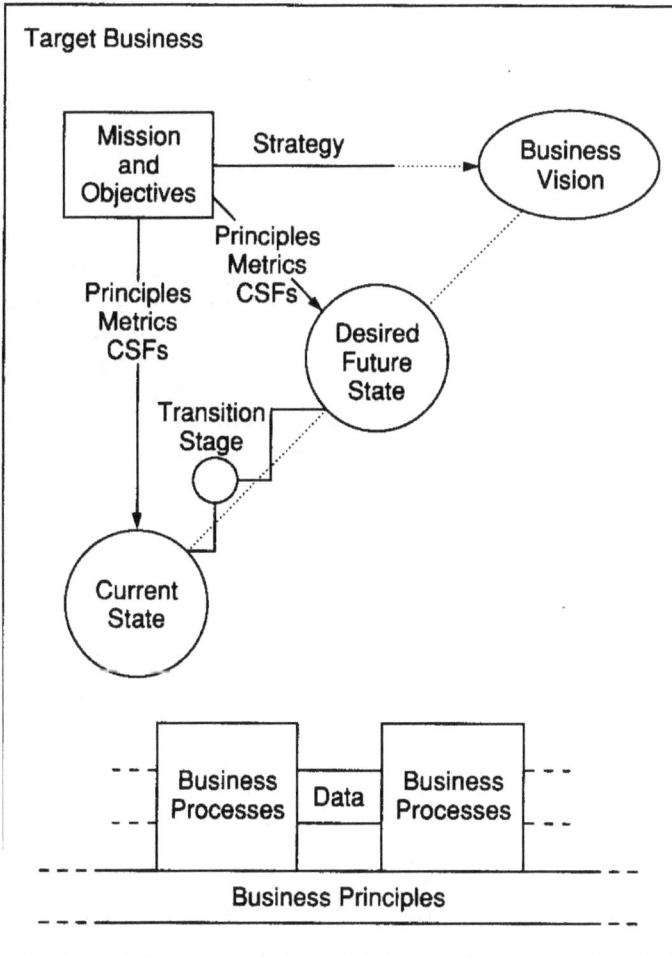

Enterprise Processes and Enterprise Departments

In many large companies much of the information systems planning is not only defined by the structure of the enterprise but also driven by people with a technological bias. As we have said, an enterprise's fundamental processes, not simply its organizational structure, must direct planning, and successful information systems depend on much wider sponsorship than from technology-based departments.

If the basic enterprise activities are not to be identified on the basis of the existing organizational structure, then on what basis? Common enterprise processes are often referred to as cross-functional activities. This is a somewhat misleading term that can be clarified as follows:

- A cross-functional activity is one that more than one department performs (for example, call handling, that is, the receiving and dispatching of calls of whatever kind). A rationalization process determines whether or not the activity is cross-functional on the basis of enterprise organization. (For example, if the decision is taken to have more entrepreneurial teams, then decisions will also be needed to decide where to locate marketing responsibility.)
- Ultimately, the different steps in all the enterprise processes will be performed by enterprise departments and teams, a fact organizational design needs to take into account, even though most enterprises do not assign clear responsibility for their overall information needs. The different departments will assume these responsibilities invarious ways.
- Some processes "should" exist but don't, and therefore will not be identified if only present departments are considered and their activities consolidated. (Total Quality Management is one example.)

So the fundamental reason for identifying enterprise processes is to identify opportunities for rationalizing them and thereby gain opportunities for greater advantage such as efficiency and flexibility.

The concept of redesigning business processes to take advantage of information technology has become popular over the last few years. Davenport and Short (1990), for example, propose the use of IT specifically for that purpose: "As we enter the 1990s, however, two newer tools are transforming organizations to the degree that Taylorism once did. These are *information technology*—the capabilities offered by computers, software applications, and telecommunications—and *business process redesign*—the analysis and design of work flows and processes within and between organizations". They present pointers to the volume of IT usage, suggest that "aggregate productivity figures for the United States have shown no increase since 1973," and point to a "growing dominance of service industries and office work in the western economies". They then prescribe five steps for business process redesign: develop business vision and process objectives; identify processes to be redesigned; understand and measure existing processes; identify IT levers; and design and build a prototype of the process. Keen (1991) also makes extensive suggestions for the role of IT in business design. He looks at trying to achieve competitive advantage as well as aspects of organizational design and personnel deployment.

Rather than an increasing dominance of service activities, we see more opportunity to obtain services (and components) from outside the enterprise when doing so makes economic sense, giving the impression of service industries replacing manufacturing industries. We also see more information and knowledge in products and services. The fundamental point, however, is that manufacturing continues to increase, not decline. Service industries and knowledge work *appear* to be replacing manufacturing because of changes in relative efficiencies and proportions of people employed, but the fact remains that manufacturing needs services, knowledge, and information, and knowledge and information become more important as they develop a foundation of solid manufacturing infrastructure and effective demand for manufacturing output. Two key questions start the identification of core enterprise processes:

- What does the enterprise actually do?
- What does the enterprise do it to?

Many texts propose core activities for enterprises [see, for example, Porter (1985), Davis and Olson (1984), and Martin and Leben (1989), and we see no need to offer alternatives. Each enterprise will create a unique set from this core and may also have others unique to itself.

We are strong advocates of simultaneous top-down and bottom-up approaches to problem solving, and this advocacy applies to the identification of business processes. One typical bottom-up approach is comparing what operations are performed on which data, and within which enterprise department, to identify common processing activities. It is based on a study of what the enterprise is doing at the moment.

The danger inherent in an exclusively bottom-up approach, however, is assuming that the enterprise is already doing what should be done but with unnecessary redundancy and inconsistency in different departments. It may be that the enterprise is in fact not doing all that should be done. As we observed before, data management within an IS department involves only the data used in computer-supported applications; perhaps nobody is studying the overall information needs of the enterprise (non-computer as well as computer-supported). A top-down approach is usually needed to remedy this kind of defect.

Here are some examples of enterprise-wide processes:

- Planning
- Administration
- Project management
- Cash resource management
- Logistics
- Human resources management
- Call handling
- Manufacturing
- Selling
- Service delivery
- Resource acquisition
- Information resource management
- Systems operation
- Research and advanced development
- Sales order fulfillment
- Purchase order fulfillment
- Performance monitoring of business departmental units
- Organization and task design

Clearly, many enterprises have chronic problems with the allocation of processes to their organizational units. We say that because of the frequency with which enterprises change their organization independently of any fundamental change in the external environment. This means that previous decisions did not produce desired results and there is a hope that the new ones will. Organizational changes can lead to a sense of achievement, whether or not they really improve the fundamentals of the enterprise! An inspection of the above list shows that some processes can be handled satisfactorily by one organizational unit (for example, enterprise treasury activity), whereas others can be divided into discrete parts, especially if it is relatively easy to make different units responsible for different stage transitions (for example, sales order fulfillment). In other cases it may be reasonable to replicate certain processes in several units (for example, call handling or task design).

Some words of caution are appropriate at this stage. It is common to show enterprise processes and departments in an overly simple form such as that in Figure 5.4. Oversimplification may work at a high level, but the danger is in delegating the de-composition of each process component to the department that performs the task. Doing so may mean each department still ends up defining its own customer database, for example. In other words, a chart of process and business departments may be created that takes the existing business departments for granted and assumes they will continue.

Figure 5.4 Enterprise Processes and Departments

Process \ Department	Sales	Manufacturing	Finance	
Order fulfilment	Enter order	Validate goods ordered Produce goods	Validate customer Produce invoice	
Call handling	Answer requests for information	Estimate delivery date	Produce duplicate invoice	

Figure 5.5 illustrates, in abstract form, some of Digital's experience. Its key point is the identification of business processes independently of existing business departments, although the departments are used as sources of the activities. The business processes are rationalized first, and the business departments are then based on organizational design to implement the processes and assign roles and responsibilities.

After each enterprise process has been de-composed and the different de-compositions compared (as shown in Figure 8.2) the many common building blocks, such as "get customer information", "check contract", and "validate product", should be identified and constructed independently of organizational structure. A de-composition of several high-level enterprise processes will probably lead to a complex network of elementary processes (not a simple hierarchy). Since each department will be able to take only a partial view of each process component, one major role for IS becomes the comparison and identification of true common, reusable building blocks. If IS does not take this responsibility and no one else does, duplication and inconsistency will be the inevitable consequences.

Figure 5.5 Digital Processes and Departments

Data Management									
SUPPLIERS	EDI	Manufacturing/ Engineering	Administration	Sales and Marketing	Customer Services	Finance	Human Resources	EDI	CUSTOMERS
		CAD/CAM							
		New Product Information							
		Material Management							
		Order Fulfillment							
		Selling							
		Solving							
		Servicing							
		Human Resources Management							
		Financial Processes							
		Management Reporting							

What is a Business Architecture?

A business architecture establishes a clear understanding of the nature of the enterprise and its main objectives and activities. It provides a top-level framework within which information systems, organizational units, and other kinds of systems can be placed in context, with interrelationships clearly understood.

We do not mean to imply that the business architecture must be defined for the whole enterprise. A model could be developed for a mission-critical business unit or process, a division, or a subsidiary. The key is that it must exist for a business and organizational entity with clear boundaries and a stated mission. Having a business architecture only for a function or a department is not adequate, although after the need for a business architecture has been established, we often see separate departments going off to do their own "business architecture". The only benefit to this is that it can be a valuable learning experience that can support subsequent cross-functional activities.

Interaction between IT and enterprise strategy takes place as feedback loops and feed-forward loops between the two. What this means is that IT or IS planning isolated from total company planning is becoming obsolete. The success of the enterprise could be accidental, but we suspect that as the interaction between enterprise and IT becomes more complex, success will become more dependent on enterprise planning. Our experience has been that an IS manager often tries to push a particular planning process for IS (using whatever "methodology" is in fashion) that clashes with the enterprise's culture. To combat this, many authors have suggested that a competitive framework for IS planning is needed, or that IS planning can only be done after corporate planning. We make a much stronger statement: *An IS plan should no longer be separate from the enterprise plan and vice versa.*

> *A business architecture establishes a clear understanding of the nature of the enterprise and its main objectives and activities. It provides a top-level framework within which information systems, organizational units, and other kinds of systems can be placed in context, with interrelationships clearly understood.*

A business architecture and the related planning processes are necessary but not sufficient for a successful IT Strategy, and the reverse is also true: IT Strategy must be able to influence the business architecture.

This book is about corporate and global information systems. The enterprise, information, IS, and IT strategies are linked in complex ways and are essentially inseparable. We are particularly concerned with the *information relevance* of business architecture and the interactions between its information-relevant pieces and other aspects of the enterprise (such as organization).

The business architecture work acts as input to systems architecture and organizational design work, so all activities related to these efforts should be kept in sync. Therefore, they cannot be sequential (that is, business architecture before systems architecture) but must be done in parallel with appropriate mutual feedback and feed-forward. These models must evolve together.

Many recommendations for IS and IT planning follow the simple model shown in Figure 5.6, in which enterprise strategy formulation is followed by IS/IT strategy formulation or perhaps IS planning. There are some fundamental problems with this model-for example:

- What happens to, and who is responsible for, the information needs of the enterprise that cannot at the moment (or perhaps ever) be met by the application of IT?
- The IS and IT strategies are considered subservient or merely subsequent to the enterprise strategy, so there is inadequate feedback.

Figure 5.6 Traditional Strategizing and ISP Model

```
┌─────────────┐                    ┌─────────────────┐
│  Enterprise │                    │ IS/IT Strategy —│
│  Strategy   │───────────────────▶│  IS Planning    │
└─────────────┘                    └─────────────────┘
```

Given these problems, we are dubious about the semantics of models like this. It is no longer reasonable to put the formulation of an enterprise strategy before that of an IT strategy. In fact, new IT, or new ways of organizing IS, often act as a trigger to enterprise strategy. We believe that up to the present many enterprises, including some very large ones, have not had a true enterprise strategy; instead, the strategizing work has been triggered by a recognition of the possibilities for integrating the enterprise, automating cross-functional activities, eliminating inconsistencies, and so forth. This is shown diagrammatically in Figure 5.7.

Figure 5.7 IT Strategy before Enterprise Strategy?

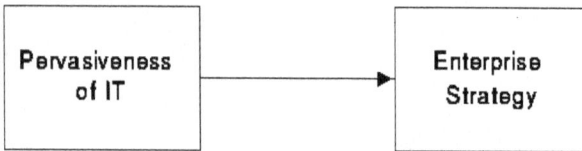

```
┌─────────────┐                    ┌─────────────┐
│ Pervasiveness│                   │  Enterprise │
│   of IT     │───────────────────▶│  Strategy   │
└─────────────┘                    └─────────────┘
```

Although very few enterprises have fully implemented strategies, many more are only now in the process of strategy formulation or have simply formulated statements about strategy. As a result, strategy studies consulting has become a growth business. Given this state of affairs, we are unable to assert that an enterprise strategy is either sufficient or necessary for success. If few implemented strategies exist, we are also unable to assert that the existence of a business strategy is an essential prerequisite for an information strategy, IT strategy, or IS planning.

The reality is that most successful enterprises precede an enterprise strategy. Since we do not know how many unsuccessful enterprises had strategies, we cannot judge any relation between the existence of strategies and relative success. So we are left with the intriguing possibility that the existence of IT applications and opportunities is a significant driver of the need for an enterprise strategy, and not vice versa. Moreover, since it is our experience that many enterprises do not implement the findings of their strategy studies, we suspect that adequate CISs and GISs do not exist, and so enterprise managers are subjected to information pollution—they are not only aware that they do not know all that is going on, they are also aware that there are real inconsistencies in what they do know. If this is the case, then conducting an enterprise strategy study without implementing its findings may at least be part of the enterprise managers' coping strategy. Many interesting empirical questions remain.

Traditional strategy studies focus on the range of strategizing elements we listed earlier. They must also deal with the fact that not all information needs can be met by IT applications, and the possibility, stated above, that IT applications or opportunities may be the drivers of an enterprise strategy.

For these reasons, a business architecture (which is itself a component of an information architecture) focuses on the information relevance of the components of the enterprise strategy, the overall information needs, IT opportunities, and interactions among all of these. This is shown in Figure 5.8.

We have found that high-level discussions about the information needs of the enterprise generally involve:

- Objects such as objectives, critical success factors, strengths, and weaknesses, which come from strategy studies
- The overall information needs of the enterprise, expressed in terms of support to such objects
- An initial consideration of ways in which information technology could be used to provide the enterprise with some significant benefits or competitive advantages

A business architecture, in the sense we describe here[4] consists of a set of:

- Principles—those that determine the rationale for the business architecture
- Components—typically a set of strategizing elements such as

4 In practice the business architecture for any particular enterprise will be unique to that enterprise. The example given here is for illustration only and is a subset of what would be expected from an actual full architecture.

those we have described earlier
- Needs—the specific information needs derived to support the enterprise
- Opportunities—the IT opportunities available to the enterprise
- We discuss what we term traditional strategizing elements in more detail in Chapter 9. Here we will discuss principles, needs, and IT opportunities

Figure 5.8 Major Components of a Business Architecture

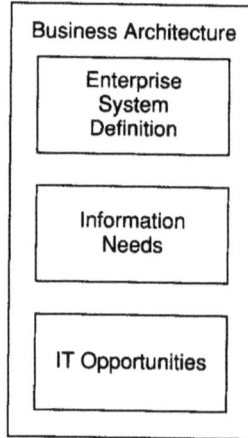

Principles

The creation of a business architecture is based on what the enterprise has decided to be an appropriate set of key principles. Figure 5.9 lists a candidate set of such principles that we believe is applicable to many different kinds of enterprise.

Information Needs

A business architecture must consider overall information needs explicitly. This is to avoid the model represented in Figure 5.6, in which business strategizing exercises come before information systems planning, thus emphasizing almost exclusively IT-based systems. There is very little information theory in this classical management consulting model, and the resulting implementation is quickly delegated to the organizational structure of the enterprise. The minimum required to change the classical model, therefore, is the addition of an information needs stage, as shown in Figure 5.10.

Figure 5.9 Business Architecture Principles

- A CIS or GIS should deliver appropriate information to the right people at the right time.
- A business architecture identifies the information needed:
  — For the enterprise to achieve its objectives.
  — By the enterprise and its organizational units to exercise effective control.
  — To know that the enterprise remains a viable system.
- A business architecture defines appropriate metrics and the necessary knowledge base to monitor the defined strategizing components.
- Information is provided at a cost that is less than its maximum value to the enterprise.
- Information is provided only if:
  — It has surprise value.
  — There is a statutory need to provide it.
  — The information is capable of affecting necessary decisions.
- The business architecture identifies all information needs independently of whether they can be met with IT.
- A business architecture considers interdependencies between the enterprise, IT, and organization.
- Information needs will be founded not only on theoretical desirability but also on organizational, technical, and economic feasibility.

We said earlier that enterprise strategy, information needs, and IT and IS strategy need to be considered simultaneously, and we have characterized this in Figure 5.11. The significance of the circle shown there is that the evolution of strategies and information needs is likely to be a cyclical, iterative process that will probably never stop. Even if a decision is taken to implement certain strategies, they will need to be kept under review and continually adapted to new situations.

104

Figure 5.10 Enterprise Strategy, Information Needs, and IT Strategy

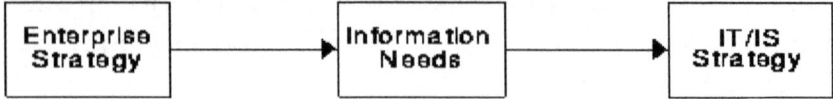

The enterprise must decide what to do about information needs that are not yet capable of IT support. In Chapter 8 we suggest the creation of an information management and technology executive position that would own not only IT, in terms of infrastructure and applications development, but also information management, whether or not it implies IT. Moreover in Figure 5.12 we have made another change to the classical model. This figure shows that the definition of information needs supports the evolution of an IT strategy, an IS strategy, *and a strategy to handle non-IT-based enterprise information needs.*

Figure 5.11 The Enterprise Information, and IS/IT Strategy Circle

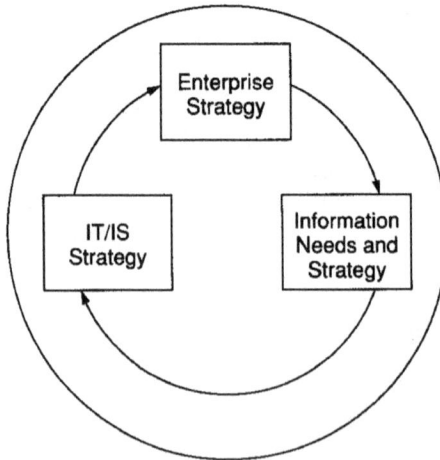

It may be worthwhile to take a brief look at how some enterprise information needs can be derived more formally from an understanding of enterprise strategy and IT opportunities[5]. This look is neither complete nor rigorous, but it will illustrate the point that information theory and principles must be applied systematically to the needs identified in the enterprise's various strategizing activities. Table 5.1 shows some possible information principles and examples of how they may be applied.

---

5 The interested reader who would like to explore such ideas in more detail is referred to more technical general systems theory and cybernetics books such as Beer (1979) and von Bertalanffy (1968).

We believe that in order to identify overall information needs, the enterprise should explore the formal cybernetic or information theory components given in Table 5.1 in the construction of a CIS or GIS. They should be an essential part of any business architecture effort.

Figure 5.12 Information Needs Factored Into Strategies

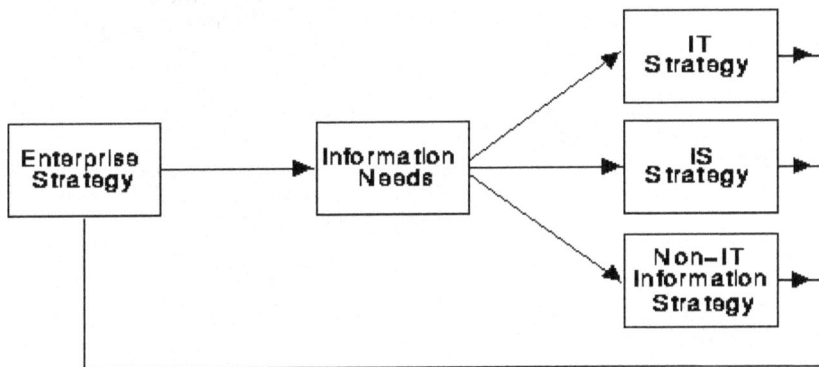

Table 5.1 Identifying Information Needs

Principle	Explanation	Examples
Attenuation	Information aggregated for appropriate audience	Management reports from one level to the next; business ratios to measure enterprise performance
Amplification	Enterprise objectives and decisions	Planning and forecasting systems with input from different levels; information communicated to team
Homeostasis	Self-regulating control mechanisms	Automated adjustment mechanisms, e.g., escalation of unclosed calls, generation of documents to collect cash, recalculation of projects after deadline slippages
Control	Decisions made and implemented for the allocation of resources or enterprise direction	Transmission of targets and budgets; allocations of resource
Coordination	Coordination of subsystem activities	Program management; "groupware," i.e., computer conferencing, electronic mail, etc

Principle	Explanation	Examples
Value of Information	Estimated maximum value of information to provide baseline for measures of economic feasibility	Simulation of possible outcomes after different investment strategies
Structure	Information structured to provide optimum information attenuation and amplification in organizational structure	Model flow of information within and between different possible organizational units
Transducers	Translation of information from one form to another	EDI feeders with suppliers and customers; construction of information warehouses based on historical data from different sources

IT Opportunities

Many books treat the possibilities IT offers, among them Porter (1985), Anderla and Dunning (1987), Schutte (1988), Cash (1988), OECD (1989), Cutaia (1990), and PA Consulting Group (1990).

Table 5.2 explores in detail a few of the ways IT can provide specific opportunities to support an enterprise's information needs.

Table 5.2 IT Opportunities

Opportunity	Explanation	Examples
Contribution to value chain	With particular reference to Porter's value chain (Porter (1985)), a systematic exploration of opportunities for IT could add value at different points in the chain or add value in coordination.	Providing the information infrastructure to implement the efficient flow of information from one value chain activity to the next; automated quality monitoring
Factor replacement	IT can replace factors such as people and soft capital; also information is significantly replacing cash, as more and more enterprises never see cash but only information about cash.	Simulation of alternative models of production for products and services; traffic control

Opportunity	Explanation	Examples
Factor substitutability	IT may improve the substitutability of factors of production.	Support for virtual teams, affecting factor substitutability between land and labor—e.g., making use of people located in different parts of the world; automated logistics systems
Cost reduction	IT adds greater efficiency	Flexible manufacturing systems; electronic conferencing; electronic mail
Revenue generation	IT improves revenue by supporting greater enterprise effectiveness.	Credit control; inventory control
Cost replacement	IT does not reduce costs, but some expenditure is transferred from another factor of production to IT.	Some accounting and administration; automatic aircraft landing
Integration	IT can make possible the integration of enterprises and "islands of automation".	Office automation environments; redesigned business processes; production control
Flexibility	IT can improve overall enterprise flexibility and responsiveness.	Just-in-time manufacturing; mass customization
Distributability	IT can support any organizational structure, and hence, given enough design for distributability, re-configuration options are wider.	Moving profit and loss responsibility from traditional enterprise departments to new entrepreneurial teams; remote control of oil pipelines
Knowledge of enterprise	More information can be assimilated and simulated more quickly, making possible better understanding of the enterprise.	Decision support systems; executive information systems; enterprise-wide videotex systems
Knowledge of environment	More information can be transferred between the enterprise and other enterprises; there can be more sensing of the environment.	Electronic data interchange; weather-sensing systems

Roles and Responsibilities

Looked at from a management point of view, a business architecture contains at least two classes of objects:

- Strategically oriented, such as mission, CSFs, and objectives
- Tactically oriented, such as business processes

Strategically oriented objects typically have been the responsibility of the top management of the enterprise or division, and they are often defined in isolation from IT strategy. Over the past few years, however, through various strategic planning exercises, IT has been included in overall strategy as a set of high-level statements about these objects.

Tactical activity is often carried out at two or three levels lower than top management in the enterprise and within a particular division or department, leading to the problem of defining the business processes not necessarily as they should be defined but according to organizational structure. This-is in spite of the fact, proven many times, that most of IT's benefits come after the enterprise has been restructured and business processes have been automated across multiple departments. A proper definition requires an overall map of the business processes of the enterprise, along with a clear understanding of their ownership.

To the question of who should lead the work of defining an overall map of business processes and stimulate the necessary organizational changes, we answer the IM&T executive or any other senior member of the board. An IM&T Executive who takes this role must be sure that the job is seen as a management task given to an individual, and not as part of general IT management.

Actually, there is a high risk in an IT Executive leading the business architecture work. Other members of the board may well perceive the job as technically oriented and miss the point of the exercise. For this reason we recommend that if an IT Executive is to lead the business architecture effort, a co-sponsor be sought from the board, ideally from the department that will be most affected, so that there is clear business ownership of the resulting architecture.

Rhetoric, Rigor, and Consultants

Consultants to the business architecture work must use both formal and informal methods, and *they must make sure to direct each to the right audiences.* The production of satisfactory conceptualizations of an enterprise, its strategy, and its information needs is very difficult, and it is probably true that no satisfactory and generally agreed method of doing so yet exists. There are as many approaches as there are consultants.

The language of enterprise strategy is new and only just beginning to penetrate the corporate world. The language of information needs, in terms of formal cybernetic (or similar) models, is only in its infancy and there are indeed few examples of formally constructed CISs and GISs (although many do exist as integrations of multiple applications).

At one level an enterprise information model with all its control mechanisms is a highly complex multidimensional representation, involving many technical terms and requirements. In this it is no different from, say, a full financial system, which also involves some very technical definitions and constructs. In the personnel world, models of motivation, personality development, and group dynamics are highly technical, with several important theories and a whole body of empirical work against which to make judgments.

We should not expect the general enterprise manager to be any more conversant with information theory than with accounting practices or psychological theory. Obviously, individuals will have different degrees and types of expertise and may take keen personal interest in particular technical areas.

As part of professional development, we suggest that the IM&T executive acquire either a solid background in subjects such as information theory and cybernetics or at least have immediate access to consulting resources with such background. This will help put the professional grounding of the information executive on a level similar to that of a chief financial officer or human resources manager. Other managers should be reasonably literate in information theory and cybernetics, just as they should be reasonably literate in accounts or personnel.

We can distinguish, at the extremes, two levels of knowledge and expression: a general literacy and ability to relate to the various management issues, and a much deeper technical knowledge of the relevant subject matter. The former we may label the level of rhetoric, the second the level of rigor.

Technical people with a level of rigor in one subject are likely to encounter problems communicating with someone with a level of rhetoric in another subject. A discussion between a highly skilled accountant and a personnel director about accounting will thus generally be within a narrow range of possibility and understanding. A technical person with a deep understanding of cybernetics may have a sense of frustration when talking to a general IS manager.

The formation of something like an enterprise strategy or a business architecture is generally by people who have a level of rhetoric in several enterprise management subjects and perhaps a level of rigor in one or more. The discussion can thus only be at a rhetorical level. Methods for dealing with a situation such as this are not common. One that participants in strategizing studies frequently use to communicate is some kind of "rich picture."[6]. Another one that Digital uses, known as TOP Mapping, is used for both internal and external system identification.

An example of TOP Mapping is shown in Figure 5.13, which illustrates total information flow from order receipt to delivery. From an initial map the information system(s) can be defined (initially, whether or not the system is computerized). TOP Mapping has proved to be a very powerful method for reaching consensus about part of an enterprise, and it does not require those involved to learn any difficult formal techniques. Although entirely at a rhetorical level, TOP Mapping is nevertheless based on a great deal of experience and insight about the enterprise, and after a TOP Mapping exercise can come a serious exploration of alternative ways of supporting the enterprise's information needs.

These kinds of pictures prove to be very useful exercises, and assist the participants to reach a consensus view of what they are dealing with.

Each subject area represented in a strategy study can be supported in depth with the necessary technical expertise. A rich picture or TOP Map requires elaboration and checking against more technically rigorous models, and these require the support of appropriate technical and methods consultants who generally will not communicate directly with the entire strategizing team but only with the consultants supporting the strategizing exercise. Figure 5.14 shows a typical scenario. The user world is supported by business consultants who facilitate the strategizing process. These consultants communicate rich pictures and other conceptualizations to the analyst world, where the models are expanded and checked for completeness and consistency. The analysts can then apply a level of rigor and convey back to the business consultants any sense of incompleteness or inconsistency that should be dealt with in the user world. Because the business consultants and analysis and methods consultants tend to use very different languages, "transducers," or mechanisms to facilitate communications between the business world and the analysis and modeling world are necessary.

The real strength in a more rigorous approach is that it makes possible maintaining control over a very complex multidimensional representation of the enterprise strategizing work. Powerful completeness and consistency checks can be carried out at any stage. For example, if the model includes strategies designed to overcome threats and weaknesses, it is possible to go into the database and identify those threats and weaknesses for which a corresponding strategy does not yet exist. In practice, we have extended this formal approach to what

---

6 The term "rich picture" is from Checkland (1981). Further discussions can be found in Wood-Harper (1985), Avison and Wood-Harper (1990), and Checkland (1990).

Figure 5.13 TOP Mapping

(Adapted from an illustration in Digital Equipment Corporation's
"TOP Consultancy" brochure, ® 1987 by Digital Equipment Corporation.)

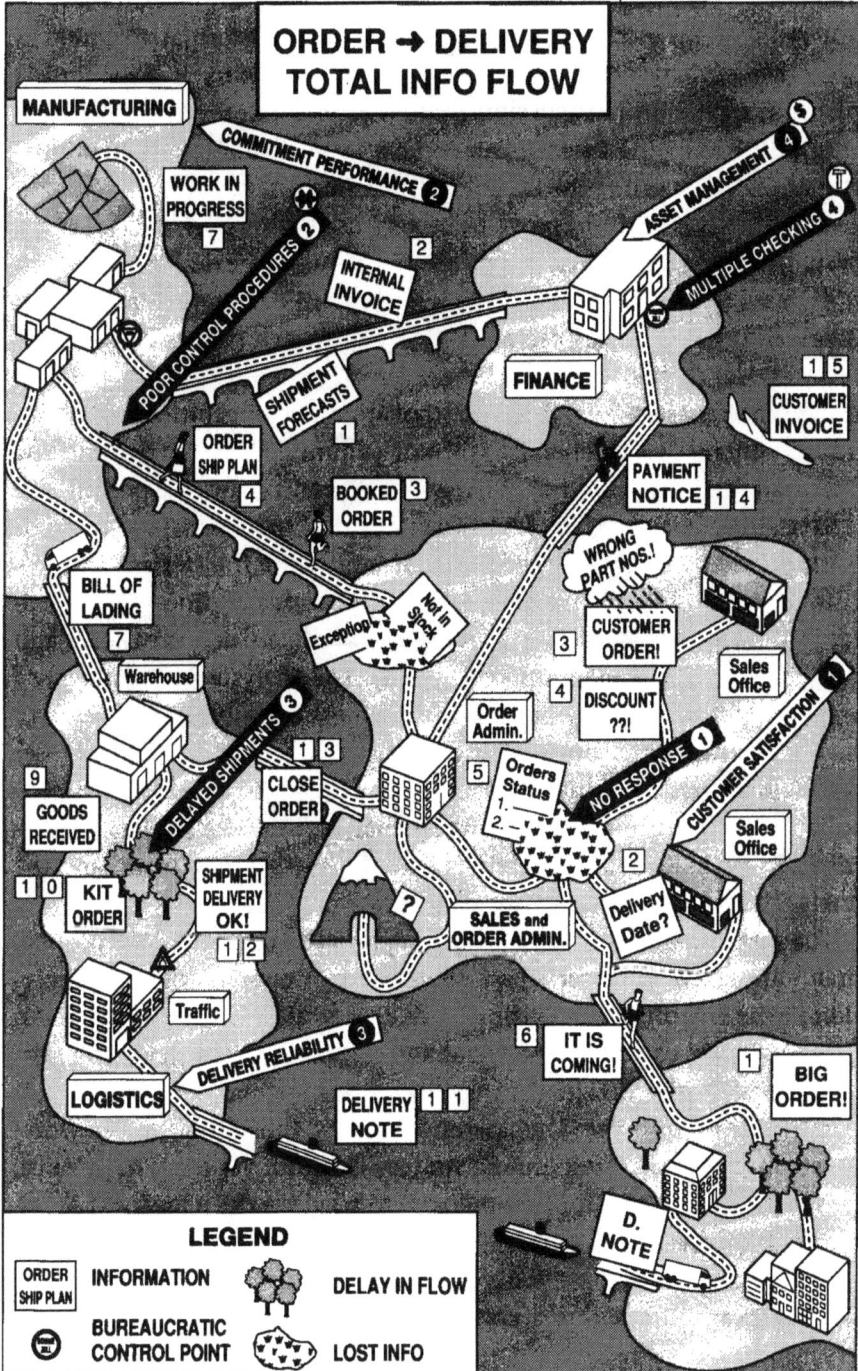

112

we call a Business Architecture Language.

In this chapter we have looked at some of the overall business issues that affect an information architecture. These range from ensuring that all aspects of an enterprise's IT and information usage are included, to establishing clear strategy, mission, and objectives for the enterprise and making sure that everyone thoroughly understands the information needs.

It is clear from this discussion that issues relating to an enterprise's organization, politics, and economics are crucial to the architecture. The next chapter discusses in more detail some of the organizational experiences arising from our information architecture work.

Figure 5.14 The Business User and Analyst Worlds

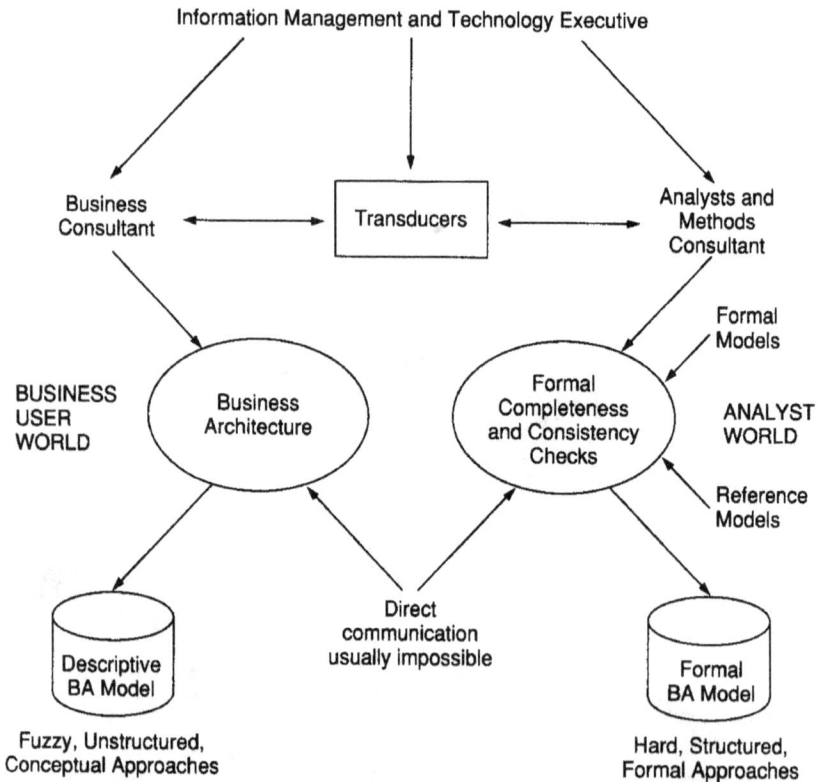

Organizational Impact

The Enterprise Information Management Model that we present in Chapter 3 started life with a technological focus. The perspectives of product and technical architectures make this clear. Organizational impacts were noticeable from the beginning. The provision of infrastructure capabilities, with easy global interconnection and communication, changed the ways people behave. The organizational dimensions were not so explicit or apparent from the documentation relating to the early product and technical architectures, but major behavioral and organizational changes were taking place, and some of these were critical success factors for effective infrastructure implementation. Traditional departments were giving up long cherished activities and responsibilities;   new departments were emerging; people were thinking in terms of impact across the enterprise; self-organizing teams were forming; and information was becoming much more readily available, with people making good use of it. Planned or not, organizational changes were happening in many enterprises in the 1980s. Along with them came the emergence of a new generation of management literature on the organizational impact of IT and alternative organizational forms.

As we moved into the systems and business architectures, organizational issues became more explicit. In fact, it became clear early on that if we wanted to make good use of our information assets, we needed to make enterprise strategy and organizational design work together with information planning. We are going through a revolution that is both organizational and technological, with information at its very core.

From both IS and IT points of view, it is important to understand organization as a collection of people who perform certain tasks, have certain skills, and organize their activities in particular ways. For applying IT to the working of the enterprise, and for embedding it in products and services, it is also important to understand how IT interacts with those tasks, skills, organization, products, and services. At a simple level the application of IT can be viewed as mere "automation" of those tasks for which automation becomes feasible. However, such a view does not make optimal use of the available IT, the people it affects, or the information and knowledge available.

Management change can be viewed from an IT perspective as an important consequence of interaction between technology and organization. The extensive use of IT leads to substantial changes in the way people work and organize. The application of IT leads to completely new services and products. With all of these changes the interaction is two way. Thus, people need additional skills to use the available IT, which creates changes in skills people have already. This is much more than mere "automation" of certain tasks.

Given such interaction between organization, tasks, and skills with respect to IT, it is clearly necessary for a closer involvement between human resources strategy and IT Strategy—with better "handshaking"—and that poses another set of challenges, but for different reasons. Human resources departments by and large ignored the input of technology to the enterprise, being one of the poorest users of IT (except for payroll). They are just starting to use IT now, with the consequence that integrating human resources and IT strategies will require many substantial adjustments to achieve mutual understanding as well as to plan and implement change.

It is, of course, wholly appropriate for human resources departments to act as a balance to prevailing "techno-centrist" viewpoints. Although the use of IT in support of enterprise processes may be seen simplistically as the identification of tasks that can be automated, in reality the "soft" aspects are likely to be more important than the "hard" ones. Ultimately, effective job design taking full advantage of IT opportunities is a highly complex problem.

The Claims for IT and the Organization

Many claims are made for IT's benefits to organizational structure, design, and behavior, and vice versa[1]. Nevertheless, it is not easy to sort out which changes have come about through organizational change, which have come about through IT changes, and which are really a result of an interaction between enterprise, organization, and IT. As a start, let us look at some of the effects on organization attributed to IT. A 1989 MIT report presents five levels of business reconfiguration

1 Rockart (1989) presents a useful survey of several studies on the organizational impact of information technology.

that are possible along two dimensions-"the degree of business transformation and the range of potential benefits from IT". These are shown in Table 6.1.

Table 6.1 MIT Levels of Business Reconfiguration

Level	Description	Characteristics
1	Localized exploitation	Efficiency in the performance of a particular task
2	Internal intergration	Effectiveness for the enterprise in improved performance with respect to some objective
3	Business Process Redesign	Revolutionary changes in the design of organizational processes, necessary to exploit the emerging technological capabilities; creation of differential market capabilities
4	Business Network Redesign	Exploiting sources of efficiency and effectiveness through integration of activities in a larger network, e.g., inclusion of trading partners
5	Business Scope Redefinition	Altering business scope proactively and reactively

The same report lists key attributes for a networked firm:

- Shared goals
- Shared experience
- Shared work
- Shared decision making
- Shared timing and issue priorities
- Shared responsibility, accountability, and trust
- Shared recognition and reward

According to Butler Cox and Partners (1987) "Information Technology has produced changes in formal organization charts . . . it has changed managerial roles, responsibilities, and influence; and it has changed the size and the composition of the workforce". They explain that in varying circumstances IT has made it possible to eliminate a complete layer of middle management, to distribute central departments to lower levels in the organization, and to concentrate some elementary activities, thus freeing up people for more productive activities; increased the power and influence of central managers; increased responsibility for high-value-added systems; reduced staffing levels; and shifted occupational mixes.

Child (1984) summarizes the benefits claimed from the introduction of new technology as:

- Reduced operating costs
- Increased flexibility
- Improved quality of the product or service
- Increased control and integration

There are many ways to use IT for integration between different organizational units, making appropriate use of skills and tasks. Rockart (1988) sees " . . . several specific ways to use IT to support interdependence:

- Integration across the value chain
- Integration across departments
- Inter-organizational integration
- Team support
- Planning and control"[2].

Johnson and Chappell (1990) present a very firm view that:

> "The computer integrated company (CIC) provides the platform for developing applications which are portable, reusable, and accessible across the organization by whoever needs them. It supports the transfer of information between computer systems without the need for human intervention, whether for translation, coding or simple physical transport. It provides for mutual communication between all the organization's staff, and also with suppliers, customers and business partners as required . . . the primary benefits of the CIC are a greatly enhanced ability to compete in time, and to add value to the organization's products and services by making them more 'information intensive'. Achieving these benefits will be essential to organizational success and even survival in the 1990s environment of global competition."

A global communication and information infrastructure, according to Johnson, has clear effects on the organization. These effects include:

- Flattening organizations
- Moving the work to the people
- Virtual teams
- Better horizontal flow of information

Our views here, as well as those of the commentators we have quoted, are all inherently optimistic, but there is a downside. As we observe in Chapters 1 and 7, IT provides threats as well as opportunities, and one of the symptoms of threats is that IT can actually reduce such enterprise characteristics as flexibility. Not all enterprises obtain

2 See Rockart and Short (1988) for a more detailed discussion on using IT to support interdependence.

satisfactory results from their investments in IT.
Vincent (1990), for example, points out:

> "Recent studies show dwindling or, in some cases, negative returns on IT investments made in the late 1970s and early 1980s. A recent working paper from MIT's Management in the 1990's Program reports that corporations would have earned a better return by investing the same money in non-IT capital such as production equipment. A Morgan Stanley economist claims that in the service industry, many large investments in IT have resulted in decreased productivity."[3]

Vincent explains that other corporations have achieved significant performance gains, which he attributes to their " . . . adroitly balancing the mix of strategy, management skill, and information technology".

In evaluating optimistic prognostications about the consequences of IT, it is important to bear in mind the phenomenon Friedman and Cornford (1989) call the "problem of tenses" and describe this way:

> "The tendency for the literature to anticipate events in the field refers primarily to positive technical events; to the existence and diffusion of new techniques, and to the potency of new techniques to overcome problems and increase efficiency or effectiveness. Negative effects of technical events are more likely to be delayed, to be reported after an accumulation of bad experiences. Those generating new techniques have a vested interest in reporting in anticipation of events. It can be useful for marketing those techniques. Those experiencing positive effects of new techniques have a vested interest in reporting them quickly . . . however, those experiencing negative effects of new techniques or other problems are likely to be reluctant to rush to report their experiences, at least until they are able to assure themselves that the problems they face have not been generated by their own incompetence."

IT as an Organizational Enabler

IT can support many different kinds of organization. Indeed, very few valid assertions can be made that only certain kinds of technology will work within certain kinds of organization and vice versa[4]. Many times technology has been applied incorrectly, or enterprises have been unprepared for the effective implementation of particular technologies.

What IT can deliver is much greater flexibility in organizational

---

3 The references Vincent uses are Loveman (1988) and Roach (1988).
4 There is much ongoing debate on this subject, which is beyond our scope here. For example, one of the most widely referenced approaches is the stage hypothesis approach of Nolan (1973 and 1979), which has received much positive comment in the management literature and is part of many management courses. There is an excellent discussion in Friedman and Cornford (1989), (which also summarizes and compares alternative approaches) about Nolan's approach and some of the subsequent empirical work carried out to test his ideas.

implementation. IT can support a whole range of organizational decisions, whether for centralization, distribution, or some hybrid. In this sense IT amplifies decisions about organization, but, of course, "appropriate" organization is necessary to leverage the benefits that are available from IT.

For example, if the decision is to divide the enterprise into distinct departments that commission their own information systems, in the absence of standards or cross-functional integration, then IT will amplify that decision, and there will be multiple and inconsistent definitions of the underlying data objects (customer, supplier, contract, call, and so forth). If the decision is to provide client/server mechanisms to manage the enterprise's information assets, then IT will amplify that decision, by providing both constraints and services to support implementation.

IT is also an enabler of training. With the increasing speed of change in most industries, training and retraining have become increasingly important. IT can play a key role in support of the human resource development and training strategy, because, more and more, it functions as on-the-job training and support. In this way the training, human development, and IT strategies can converge, supported by computer-assisted education and computer-based instruction. (We are not saying that computer-based training is appropriate for all kinds of training, but it is for many.) In Digital, for example, we have a plan to bring training to the workplace of the employees, instead of bringing students to the classroom.

Much training can be delivered in forms such as self-paced instruction. A CDROM can contain the equivalent of more than the text of two Encyclopedia Britannicas, so an enormous amount of material and training can be available to people as they work, perhaps as computer-based training programs combining interactive video (such as IVIS-Interactive Video Instructional System), with checking, feedback, and access to a large knowledge base. With CASE (computer assisted systems engineering), for example, training tools can be embedded in the computer, making access very simple for the programmer sitting at the computer all day.

As computer systems become more diffused there is no reason why they cannot be programmed to enforce laws or trading practices. A laptop, say, might contain auditing practices and laws so that auditors can provide appropriate consulting. This is not only on-the-job skilling and training; it is re-skilling to a higher level, and it can support significant job enrichment.

In most cases the appropriate use of IT must be decided with reference to other enterprise standards or policies. Figure 6.1 illustrates this, indicating that for particular policies or objectives, organizational and IT implementation together reinforce and amplify what is required.

Figure 6.1 Policy, Organization, and IT

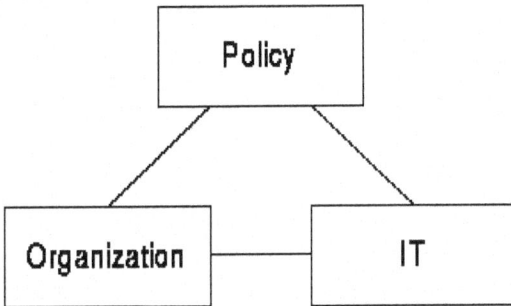

On what basis do we assert that IT and organization amplify each other's effects? Not enough empirical work has been done in this area, but our experience leads us to several conjectures, first about questions arising from the fact that on a superficial level, both organization and IT are either centralized or distributed.

What do these concepts mean with respect to organization? The survival of an enterprise can be an end in itself, but let us assume for the moment that the enterprise is formed not for that trivial purpose but to achieve its objectives. Quite independent of IT are important questions about the organization of work.

One characteristic of the Industrial Revolution was the emergence of an approach to organization in which production was reduced to a sequence of separate tasks performed by individuals. At the turn of the century, making cars was essentially an artisan-like entrepreneurial activity, very much in the tradition of modern coach building. Then came Henry Ford with the Model T and the production line. Around the same time (1911) Taylor was writing about scientific management and creating what eventually became known to organizational theorists and practitioners as Taylorism. Now we see a turnaround taking place. The production line is being replaced by teams, with examples provided early on in Volvo cars and recently in Apache helicopters, (Schlender 1991).

There is a major side effect on the way work processes are organized and coordinated between these two radically different styles of working.

The choice of team or production line creates planning problems above the level of work flow coordination. The focus of planners and strategists is likely to be fundamentally different once they receive feedback about the anticipated style of working. (If you are not too sure about this just imagine being involved in a strategy study: will the specification of requirements for a CIS or GIS and the strategic organizational requirements be the same or different, depending on whether the production processes will be production line or team-oriented?).

In these radically different styles of organizing work, different things are distributed or centralized, such as overall enterprise goal setting, individual performance setting and measurement, work organization, decision making, and the various information flows. As far as IT is concerned, the kinds of services that can be centralized or distributed include processing power, end user interfaces, data, and various peripherals such as printers, scanners, and magnetic media devices. An airline reservation system could operate with one centralized database and distributed access to the computer; the databases could be replicated in different locations; different subsets of a logical database could be located in different places as well.

There are no easy answers to questions about centralization versus distribution of organization or IT. The choice between options remains somewhat arbitrary, hence the importance of policy, indicated in Figure 6.1 (for example, policy about the scope of employee and managerial autonomy).

In order to establish clear dependencies between organization and IT, it is necessary to demonstrate how the emergent properties of an enterprise arise because some organizational forms come to depend upon properties of IT that cannot be obtained by some other substitute.

What does IT give that is not obtainable from alternatives? There are several properties that can be identified, that may act separately or in combination. They are time, space, interdependence between events, complexity, and knowledge. (See Table 1.6, page 16 for an explanation.)

Thus we conclude: *Any organizational form that comes to depend upon any of these properties of IT will support an enterprise with emergent properties derived from the interactions between IT and organization.*

What capabilities does organization provide that are difficult or impossible to obtain from alternatives? There are various characteristics obtainable from organization that otherwise would be difficult or impossible to achieve. They are cohesiveness, specialization, interdependence, mechanization, rationalism, implemented determinism, and power. (See Table 1.7 for an explanation.)

The conclusion we presented in Chapter 1 bears repeating: *Any IT that comes to depend upon any of these properties provided by organization will support an enterprise with emergent properties derived from the interactions between IT and organization.*

With this statement we come full circle to an earlier point, that the key issues of interaction between IT and organization are the "soft" ones, and not primarily the "hard" ones.

To explain the diverse ways in which IT can amplify different organizational and enterprise policies, Table 6.2 shows several examples in the range of contrasted possibilities.

Table 6.2 IT as an Organizational Enabler

Policy Options	First Scenario	Second Scenario
Degree of centralization	Greater centralization can be obtained through faster and more comprehensive aggregation of the enterprise's data.	Greater decentralization can be obtained by delegating more activity and decision making to business units, while overall and individual performance can be monitored.
Skills	There is a steady de-skilling of the workforce as computers take over more activity and decision making.	By removing a great deal of repetitive work, jobs become more varied, and there is an overall re-skilling with greater variety.
Control over work process	Work processes are all predefined, and people only provide services not yet automated	Greater control over work processes is achieved by providing people with more and higher quality of information to support their work.
Complexity	Activities become less complex as they are de-composed into constituent parts that are easier to automate.	It is possible to achieve much higher degrees of complex integration of many different activities.
Work location	Activities can be monitored in much more detail to evaluate performance when people work together in one location.	A communications infrastructure enables people to reduce commuting and work near or at home.
Documentation requirements	The fastest way to increase paper consumption is to make a computer available.	It is possible to move very quickly to a paperless office.

Policy Options	First Scenario	Second Scenario
Employment	Enterprises become sufficiently flexible to adapt very quickly to environmental change, thus protecting employment.	Greater rationalization of processes leads to lower formal employment and greater use of contract labor.
Status	Networked organizations and alternative working styles such as home working eliminate levels of management and produce a more egalitarian enterprise.	New status differences emerge between those at the center of planning and monitoring and those increasingly on the fringe.
Equal opportunity	Networked organizations and home working provide more equal opportunity less dependent on home situation.	Information workers become the next generation of badly paid home workers.
Power	Power structures are more resilient as they obtain more information more quickly.	Greater access by more people to more information leads to a greater democratization of enterprises.

There are elements of reality in all of these scenarios, and in essence, organizational strategy, information strategy, IT strategy, and enterprise strategy are all related. Enterprises should determine what they expect from their organizations and IT and then work systematically toward their objectives.

Organization, IT, and System

Perhaps one of the most fundamental problems an enterprise faces is the potentially limitless amount of information it must somehow manage from both its internal and external worlds. The Law of Requisite Variety we look at in Chapter 9 demonstrates how an enterprise must possess at least as much variety as it has to deal with, a requirement Beer (1979) sums up in the expression "variety absorbs variety".

Organization saves the enterprise from having to deal with limitless variety. Management must be able to exercise effective control, which means an appropriate combination of information amplifiers and attenuators, and this is the point at which IT really comes into its own. *We know of no technology other than IT that at a high level is capable of amplifying the enterprise's internal variety sufficiently to allow the enterprise to absorb the variety it encounters.*

Another serious problem facing the enterprise is handling the information once it crosses the boundary between the enterprise and its environment. The recipients must understand the information, which implies translation of some kind if necessary—that is, in a technical sense, transducers. The transducers themselves must also possess sufficient variety to handle the variety in those translation processes. (For example, if information is needed in English, French, and Italian, appropriate interpreters are necessary; if general statistical information from the environment is to be meaningful to the enterprise, appropriate tools must be available to support the analysis and interpretation of the statistics.)

As an enterprise becomes more complex, organization encounters exponentially increasing variety—exponentially, because as the enterprise deals with more "things" in its internal and external environment, it must also deal with more possible interactions between those "things". The enterprise must therefore be able to provide exponentially increasing variety with which to manage. Without the support of IT, managers reach a point beyond which they are really doing their job by accident and ignorance. IT is needed to amplify variety, thus enabling more complex enterprises to be managed.

In this sense, as we have said many times, enterprise strategy, organization strategy, information strategy, and IT strategy need to be considered together. To consider enterprise strategy first can mean that decided policies can inhibit organization and IT from providing the necessary variety.

We predict that fixed, large, centralized enterprises are less viable systems than smaller ones because they are less likely to possess sufficient variety to handle the variety they encounter. This is due in part to the skills available and in part to organizational capability. The normal strategy to deal with such centralization is to use bureaucratic organization and some IT to attenuate the variety encountered. (Of course, it is possible that in some cases such a strategy works.)

We would argue, on purely statistical grounds, that the larger an enterprise becomes, the greater the variety with which it must deal, and that the most effective way of handling the variety is the creation of flexible, purpose-driven teams with relevant skills and appropriately coordinated. The fact that many enterprises have discovered this for themselves is borne out by the continuing trend toward distributed processing and management.

Hence, the real interdependence between organization and IT lies in how IT can help the enterprise handle variety in ways that are not possible with other approaches. That is a bold high-level statement, and it is important to examine how to achieve the goals it entails. To do so, we return to our Enterprise Information Management model.

Organization, Tasks, and Skills

In supporting an information architecture, management must achieve a careful balance between:

- Information needs
- Organization structure and design
- Overall enterprise vision
- Enterprise strategies and policies
- Top-down planning
- Bottom-up implementation
- Appropriate management "styles"
- Tasks to be performed for the enterprise with corresponding required skills

Most enterprises establish what may be termed a "traditional" departmental structure. They delegate most tasks to that structure and implement a series of organizational changes, sometimes rarely and sometimes frequently. Moreover, within that structure important decisions must be made about such matters as the limits of decision making—that is, how far various managers are able to manage.

The Enterprise Information Management Model we have developed focuses on three aspects of organization: knowledge, skills, and tasks, as shown in Figure 6.2. Skills involve the acquisition and application of knowledge, and tasks are the processes to be performed by the enterprise. The enterprise organization itself will have structure, function, and behavior. Since an enterprise can be organized in many arbitrary ways, decisions are needed about skills and roles within its centralized and distributed parts.

Organizational structuring involves dividing the enterprise into smaller groups, or organizational units, and then determining the behavioral properties of the whole enterprise through some combination of the organizational units' extensive and intensive properties.

Management of the individual organizational units can be by setting policy, setting performance metrics for the units, or by some combination of those two. The units themselves can be relatively durable business departments or they could be much more transient task-oriented groups. Some tasks will be performed more efficiently by centralized groups, some more efficiently by distributed, or ad hoc, groups. Effectiveness needs to be managed by the coordination of activity in addition to the contribution of the units themselves.

Figure 6.2 Organization in the Enterprise information Management Model

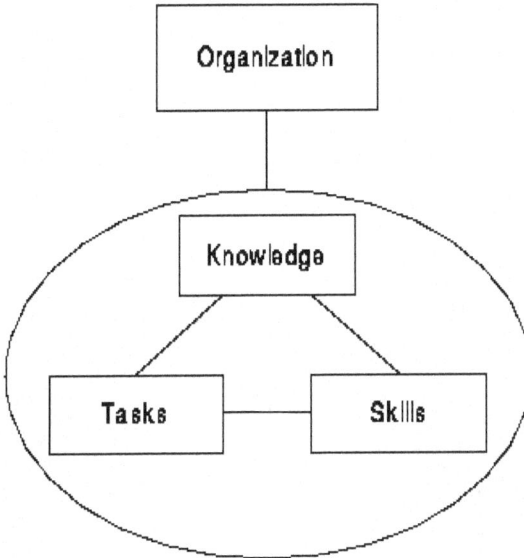

Whatever the division of the enterprise, it will be necessary to determine the tasks to be performed, the skills needed for the tasks, and the knowledge with which to work. There are additional inter-enterprise issues to be resolved and organizational decisions to be made on handling globalization and partnering matters.

Alternative organizational forms and appropriate IT support make it much more possible to run projects and project management with an excentralized model (that is, using resources owned or controlled by a centralized department but physically located in a different place).

Knowledge

Most of the information an enterprise needs is neither computerized nor structured. It must reside somewhere, and assuming that all aspects of the enterprise are handled within some organizational context, we have the knowledge component of organization.

Knowledge is applied by people with skills. IT brings together many people's knowledge, information, and expertise, making the knowledge available to an enterprise—not only the sum of the knowledge of its

126

people, but also the many ways in which individuals' knowledge can interact and solve problems at many levels. For example, a team of people from several disciplines will be more capable of handling a multidisciplinary problem-solving approach, and the individuals in the team will have the benefit of feedback from several disciplines, thus enriching approaches.

Part of the strategy for an enterprise should include making provision for identifying, capturing, and disseminating the knowledge it uses both as a whole and as constituent components.

Tasks

The tasks component of the Enterprise Information Management Model is the set of tasks to be performed in order for the enterprise to function. Identifying distinct tasks and providing specific IT to support them means that many different styles of management can be adopted. Examples of Task Principles are shown in Figure 6.3.

Figure 6.3 Task Principles

- Very high productivity gains for certain tasks are achievable through the appropriate use of IT.
- The quality of performing many tasks can be enhanced by the use of IT.
- There are many tasks the enterprise will need to perform independently of how those tasks are arranged in particular organizational structures.
- Information technology can provide significant support to tasks performed by teams and individuals.
- Job design should be as enriching as possible and strike a good balance between task efficiency and human satisfaction.

Skills

The skills component of the Enterprise Information Management Model identifies the various skills needed within the enterprise. Obviously, for the purpose of the model, this component is described with particular reference to implications for information and knowledge.

Skills are to some extent independent of tasks. For example, a new form of information technology may make it possible to perform a task differently, and doing so may involve different skills even though basically the task remains the same. A change in technology may also eliminate or create a need for particular tasks.

The creation of a skills component in an Enterprise Information Management Model is based on several principles. Some examples of these principles are shown in Figure 6.4.

Figure 6.4 Skills Principles

- The necessary skills will be acquired and propagated for the appropriate use of IT.
- The necessary skills will be acquired and propagated so that all tasks are performed effectively and efficiently.
- Appropriate skills will be identified for all tasks and technologies required by the enterprise.
- Skills will be matched to roles and combined so as to identify realistic job profiles that can also adapt as required tasks and skills change.
- Although the skills components of an Enterprise Information Management Model apply to computer-assisted information systems, the skills are likely to be a minor part of the total information and knowledge-related skills.

Flattening the Organization

An example of the close interdependence between organization and IT is the need for management hierarchies in enterprises. Several trends, listed here, enable very different management approaches to emerge:

- The extensive use of the network for decision making, routine reporting, information gathering and universal use, along with the use of virtual teams, enable managers, experts, and others to increase their span of influence.
- A change from relatively fixed management forms to much more flexible forms is accompanied by a change from management by direction to management by goal setting, with appropriate quantitative performance indicators and governed by objectives and ethics.
- The increasing capability for IT to replace soft capital and

become a major contributor to the formation of new soft capital.

- IT delivers extensive capability to amplify managerial and organizational variety.
- IT provides more information attenuation and amplification, which traditionally have been the responsibility of middle management.

As a result, the organization can be flattened, and the middle managers who mainly collect and distribute information can be transformed into individual contributors performing specific tasks. IT is not replacing labor here, but providing an opportunity to enhance labor and organizational effectiveness (not simply efficiency).

For example, in Digital a senior manager may have 15 to 20 managers and individual contributors as direct reports, but a great deal of attention is paid to people management issues, ensuring that all employees have clear objectives and that these objectives are regularly reviewed. Since so much information is available when needed in electronic form, the time normally spent in meetings to transfer information is used for real discussions on issues such as risk priorities, rather than for checking activities such as the progress of projects.

Over the past five to six years we have seen much squeezing of middle management through downsizing and elimination of layers[5]. Such squeezing is necessary because most middle management was put in place over the last 50 years not primarily as a span of control but mainly as a set of information processing nodes that would gather information, assimilate it, concentrate it, and pass it upward, then take direction from the top, interpreting and passing it downward. In this way many middle managers became information processors, performing the roles of information and variety attenuation and amplification.

However, with the availability of online information to every employee and the emergence of tools such as text retrieval databases, context-based query systems, mail filters, and other IT technologies that support information use, the need for middle management has decreased substantially.

Think, for example, of the impact of electronic communication. With the availability of electronic mail throughout the enterprise, it is now very easy to send one message to hundreds of people. In the past such communication would have had to go through the

---

5 In discussing future management, Drucker (1988) asserts that "The typical large business 20 years hence will have fewer than half the levels of management of its counterpart today, and no more than a third the managers." Some would argue that he is being very optimistic about such high future management staffing levels!

chain of command, but now there is much horizontal and vertical communication that skips many layers. As a result, that piece of value added provided by middle management's pure information gathering and distribution is no longer needed. To survive, middle managers must provide personal value added by being expert at something. More must become "coaches" who help to develop other people, not merely direct and coordinate them.

From a CIS and GIS point of view, the significance here is that the flattening of hierarchies is almost impossible without IT, because it is the tasks of information and variety amplification and attenuation that are being replaced. This means that the CISs and GISs must be designed, in part, with the specific objective of performing these tasks. An extreme example of organizational change within Digital Europe is the process called "inverting the pyramid," which is intended to give more authority to the field organization and specifically the account managers who deal with customers. To help them succeed, the account managers have been given a responsibility that cuts across traditional geographical lines to support national and international customers. In a reversal of the traditional hierarchical flow of information, IT is being used to implement an account-based management reporting system that provides account managers with the information they need. These changes in managerial roles have made it possible to remove layers of management, because a higher delegation enables a higher span of influence, effectiveness, and control. As an example, in Digital Europe, we have a goal to have only three layers of operational management for an operation of over 30,000 people. The "inverted pyramid" can be thought of as a parody of Anthony's pyramid, which is a traditional hierarchical view that has had great influence. For some people it is easier to develop a network model that departs from the traditional pyramid by going via an inverted pyramid rather than direct to the network. The essence of an inverted pyramid is shown in Figure 6.5.

Moving the Work to the People

Since the Industrial Revolution, the trend has been to concentrate people in industrial and then commercial centers—that is, to move people to the work. (Those have also been, of course, the social and cultural reasons for this demographic movement to urban centers.)

This trend has had a major demographic impact and has created social upheaval. Just one side effect has been increasing and massive

130

urban congestion in many parts of the developed world. Such a trend in congestion is not sustainable, and if repeated throughout the world, will probably be environmentally catastrophic.

For many service industries and activities, the growth of installed communications capacity makes it realistic to disperse many information—and knowledge-based tasks, because these tasks can be coordinated electronically.

Figure 6.5 Inverted Pyramid

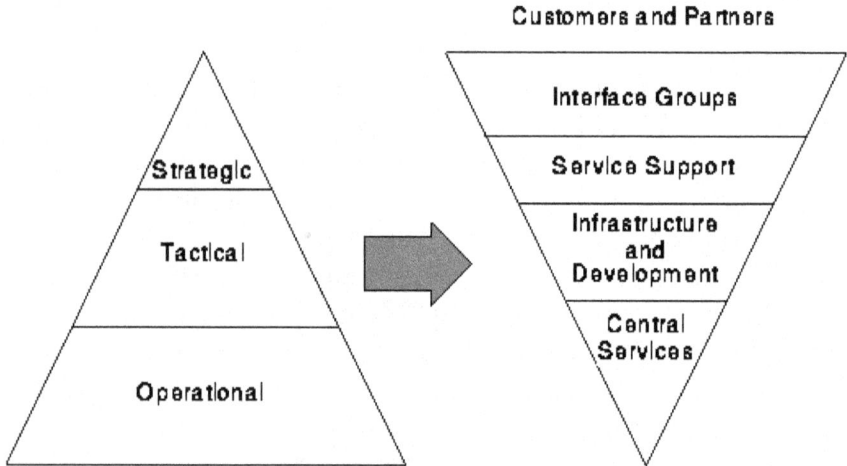

The competition for highly qualified IT people is fierce. Demand for some skills outpaces supply, both relatively in some areas and absolutely in others.

In macroeconomic terms, the highly variable production functions for different products and services use different technologies. Not many industries obtain optimum benefits from economies of scale resulting from large centralized production facilities. In many cases the efficiency of small specialized production and development units is higher. A great deal of innovation resides in small entrepreneurial companies, which can often react to environmental and market changes more rapidly than larger units.

By using a communications infrastructure effectively, it is possible to locate research, manufacturing, and service centers where it is possible to find good conditions and good people. For example, Digital has two centers for mass storage, one in Kaufbauren (Bavaria, Germany) and the other in Colorado Springs (Colorado, USA): they work on joint projects and are able to share component design and implement new processes in parallel. IT enables this distributed, concurrent engineering and manufacturing, because it compresses effective space and time, making coordination realistic. Other technologies could not achieve the same result.

Large companies can develop a number of small "entrepreneurial" units, which can coordinate their work according to an overall set of common objectives through intelligent use of the network.

Decreasing costs of processing power and increasing information storage capacity mean it is no longer necessary to move people to their work. One of the main reasons for a central workplace was personal interaction and information exchange; but now information is available electronically in a company or community network, and thus it can reach people wherever they are. Of course, social needs remain, and we are not advocating that people work in complete isolation. Even so, information gathering no longer needs to be done at the office, but can take place in the home, the car, or anywhere else.

At Digital we envisage taking information anywhere employees need it. It is conceivable that within the next few years, the sales engineer, software engineer, or service engineer will have a portable high-power workstation to access information from anywhere using wireless data networks, much like a salesperson today who uses a laptop to access information in a customer's office. Such use is becoming more and more common.

Moving the work to the people will make large buildings less necessary. It will also transform the time spent commuting into profitable time spent thinking, working, or seeing customers.

Project Teams and Virtual Teams

The next natural step in organizational change, after flattening the organization and bringing the work to the people, is establishing what we call virtual self-coordinated teams.

Using the network, companies can put together a project team made up of people located in various places in the world, who can do most of the work without meeting face to face. When they do meet they are more efficient, since all the preparation work has been done and documented and is available electronically. In this way, they can concentrate on the human and social dimensions of team work. One role of the information architecture and the Enterprise Information Management model in virtual project teams is to ensure consistency between members and projects.

Employees who perform similar activities and hold similar interests form virtual teams of peers that share information. This enables an enterprise to preserve unity and synergy in spite of its large size and geographical dispersion.

We are not advocating that all of a company's work can be carried out this way; there is still need for a mission, objectives, critical factors, and other "strategizing objects". Nevertheless it is very evident to us that an increasing number of company processes can be run in a project-like environment where people with different skills have been brought together. In other words, they need not be together physically, and it is easier to make them available for cross-functional projects. Construction and aerospace companies do this[6], and manufacturing and service companies will be doing it in the coming years, encouraged by critical success factors in customizing products and services.

Customization of products and services means bringing together off-the-shelf components, bringing together the skills of different people, and letting them work in a self-coordinated way under a set of principles of design. In the past it would have been necessary to bring those people together physically. In the future, with the exception of the initial team building and other essential social aspects, most of the work can be done remotely.

Such a phenomenon takes away even more power from line managers. No longer able to understand what is going on, they must trust professionals, project managers, account managers, and team leaders to do the work, which means changes to the traditional chain of command and traditional lines of authority. Authority no longer comes from the number of people controlled or from budget size, but more and more from the leadership provided, from personal value added, and from the ability as managers to set the direction for a team of professionals.

This is now happening at all levels and is particularly visible in service, professional, and project companies. The manufacturing world now has several examples of high performance teams, some going back more than ten years. A high-performance manufacturing team is self-coordinated within certain criteria. It is part of a larger detectable trend toward more customized manufacturing[7].

---

6 For example, the European Airbus Consortium.
7 Davis (1987) explains: "As the new economy matures, many new concepts, theories, models, and frameworks will develop that are appropriate to actual conditions, not holdovers from the industrial economy. One seems particularly ready to make its debut now: mass customization". Savage (1990) presents many ideas for achieving technological flexibility and market agility through ideas such as peer-to-peer networking, integrative processes, work as dialog, human time and timing, and virtual task-focusing teams. Belbin (1981) discusses research results on combinations of types of people that contribute to management team effectiveness. Boehm (1981) identifies team formation as a major cost driver in the software development world.

Grenier and Metes (1992) develop the idea of a capability-based environment in the context of enterprise networking. They define it as "a distributed stakeholder community working simultaneously toward both unique and shared goals. This environment is structured on strong yet flexible relationships, nourished by information moving through electronic networks, and facilitated by mutual trust and a commitment to distributed information".

Virtual teams, high-performance manufacturing teams, and capability-based environments require multidisciplinary abilities of the people who put the teams together and run the projects. These people must visualize the combination of skills and tasks needed for a team to be successful. Team building is a very important managerial skill.

Another example in Digital of IT being used to form virtual teams is for new telecommunications and networks products to achieve substantial reductions in the products' time to market. The problem was bringing together expertise in computer-aided product design, integrated circuit software and production, printed circuit board design and manufacturing, and final product testing. IT enabled creation of a virtual team with members and expertise located in Ireland, the United States, Japan, the United Kingdom, and Holland, without long lead times or expensive staff or facility relocation. Quantitatively, time to market decreased substantially, as did significant cycle time and lead times. Qualitatively, the best available expertise was brought to bear on the project goals, product design was very thorough to facilitate effective communication, and the distributed project management skills were excellent. To bring such a team together physically, complete with all necessary plant and buildings, would have proved to be prohibitively expensive and probably unrealistic.

Additional Impact on the Enterprise

The openness of various communications tools (such as electronic messages, videotex, and computer conferencing) enables information to flow freely within a company either horizontally or vertically and in any direction. This makes it increasingly difficult for a manager to withhold information in order to preserve "power," and forces all managers to be much more open and share with team members the information they need to do their jobs. It also requires all employees to mature over time so that they can make proper use of that information.

The role of line managers is changing in ways we discussed earlier. They are responsible for managing some of the enterprise's cash, people, information, and other assets. They must be skilled to a higher level and become multidisciplinary to be able to put together their own virtual teams as well as ensure that their people play a full part on other committed virtual teams.

Parts of an enterprise may develop core competencies, giving line managers the responsibility for them. However, if the core competencies serve the enterprise as a whole, they should be the responsibility of a series of cross-functional virtual teams.

Knowing what makes a high-performance team succeed will make it easier to know when to obtain resources and perhaps when to subcontract out parts of projects or call in outside people.

We see the continual evolution of multiple virtual teams, which are set up to deal with problems or take advantage of opportunities, as the establishment of a "global network of entrepreneurs" within a large enterprise. A good example is real estate planning, which is changing in many networked enterprises. Instead of planning by department (such as administration, sales, or marketing) it is becoming increasingly important to plan for cross-functional teams. Even more interesting, branch offices are planning for flexible space by choosing technologies such as portable cordless telephones and using desk-sharing facilities for a pool of people[8].

The Impact on Working and Management Styles

IT as a provider of enhanced information and variety amplification and attenuation, combined with different organizational forms, is leading to changes in work and management styles beyond those we have already identified. Here we present three concrete examples of using information and IT to empower managers and change the way people such as sales representatives perform their work.

Many traditional executive information systems are designed to provide a very few managers with such a great deal of information about the performance of their operational units that they know more than their people do. We believe, however, that managers should have access to information about their own performance, and that of their

---

8 This concept has been implemented in the Digital office in Finland. Sales and service people have no fixed desks. When they come into the office, they bring their own portable phone and a drawer on wheels, and look for a desk and terminal at which to work. Most of the office space has been converted to conversation and meeting areas, including pleasant relaxation points. This environment fosters teamwork and cross-functional fertilization, and it reduces stress.

peers, instead of just that of their subordinates. This way they can adjust their goals and strive to emulate the best in class performance.

One of the systems we have put in place at Digital (AMIS) is based on a client/server environment; it provides subsidiary operational managers with information about their own country's performance as well as that of all the other subsidiaries in Europe, thus enabling them to monitor not only their own performance, but also that of others. Information is no longer private to a few managers; clever managers can use it to their own advantage. Recently, we introduced an industry-based business dimension, in addition to the geographical dimension, and we are applying the same principle to share information between different business dimensions.

Using videotex technology we have established a pervasive set of information databases that transforms much paper information into electronic form and makes access to it instantaneous. We are working to empower Digital's sales representatives by providing them with more information more quickly. We have three specific databases available to the sales organization: (1) an online catalog containing all applications available on Digital hardware from partners and other software vendors; (2) a reference database that provides information on successful customer applications that can be used to support referrals for new sales; and (3) a competitive analysis database. Each is maintained in a distributed environment, with many people providing input. All three enable the sales organization to share information directly, and they reduce the workload of central marketing groups.

Originally, booked sales were consolidated at the end of the week and during the weekend consolidated reports were prepared for different management purposes. A logistics operation then ensured that the appropriate managers received their reports first thing Monday morning. This was an expensive way to provide the information needed to monitor business performance. IT was used to automate the collation of the data, making the necessary reports available in a distributed environment from which managers could pull the information they needed when they needed it. Using the technology to support a change from "pushing" reports to "pulling" them eliminated a great deal of analysis work and a whole logistics operation. It also freed many analysts to take on more complex tasks.

Savage (1990) discusses the evolution (or perhaps revolution?) of approaches to management and work in some detail. He explains that

136

> "... the transition [from second-generation steep hierarchies to fifth-generation human networking] cannot be bought from a systems integrator. True, there are companies that can install local and wide-area networks, interface one application with another, and help develop a unifying data architecture. But the real transition comes only when we look more deeply at the conceptual frameworks in which we operate. In order to break out of the confining quarters of second-generation management, we need to shift our attitudes and approaches."

Savage identifies the following conceptual principles associated with a human networking organization:

- Peer-to-peer networking
- Integrative processes
- Work as dialog
- Human time and timing
- Virtual task-focusing teams

He identifies some additional characteristics of this transition from steep hierarchies to human networking:

- The transition from the industrial era to the knowledge era
- The transition from *routine* to *complexity*
- The transition from *sequential* activities to *parallel* iterative activities
- The transition from industrial-era *conceptual principles* to those of the knowledge era
- The *management shifts* in structure, control, authority, and communication

Many of these changes and transitions we have achieved (or are working toward) in the examples presented so far.

According to Cash et al. (1988) in their discussion of IT and organization,

> "Organizational instability has been an enduring feature of the information technology (IT) environment ... Several key reasons lie behind this ... First, both for efficiency and for effectiveness, IT in the 1980s must include office automation, data and voice communications, and data processing, all managed in a co-ordinated and (in many situations) an integrated manner ... Second, ensuring the success of information technologies new to the organization requires approaches that are quite different from those used with technologies that the organization has had more experience with ... Third, where the firm's data and computer hardware resources should be located organizationally requires rethinking."

They speculate about four phases of IT assimilation and how those phases relate to the factors they state should be considered.

Some empirical studies of relationships between technology and organizational structure are presented in Byars (1984). He says that "Although much research has been concerned with whether size or technology is the most important variable, most studies have concluded that technology plays the key role in determining an organization's structure".

PA Consulting Group (1990) presents three nontechnical dimensions for a successful IT program: executive vision and leadership; culture and people (both senior management and staff); and environment, including the physical surroundings in which a business operates. The fundamental relationship between organization and IT is implied when they state that

> "The biggest single obstacle to organizations' progress in developing effective information systems is the belief that they are already in place. Much of the infrastructure of any company is there to prevent fresh innovation unsettling existing policies and procedures, purchasing restrictions and power bases ... This goes part of the way to explaining why few senior managers use computer terminals—yet there has been an explosion in the use of cellular radios by this same group of people because they pose no threat, offer no change to working habits and require no new skills."

Although we consider artifacts such as cellular telephones as part of an IT infrastructure and do not restrict the definition of IT to computers, nevertheless, PA Consulting Group's message about the need for organizational change is clear. We see the rapid adoption of machines such as faxes and cellular telephones as further evidence of the trend toward reducing the effects of time and space and increasing the speed with which events can be chained together.

Roles and Responsibilities

Some clear roles and responsibilities emerge out of the need to provide an appropriate match between organization and IT, for example:

- The IS department
    — At all levels there must be full awareness of the organizational impact of systems.
    — There must be much greater access to, and use of training in the "soft" and social sciences.
    — Organizational consultants must be part of major system

teams.
— IS at a top level must seek alliances with human resources to encourage company policies to exploit the benefits of IT fully.
— Most system development methods do not address the human aspects of system design, and they should because of the increasing evidence that non-technical factors are more important for productivity, quality, team performance, and so forth. They should interact more with human resources to address group and enterprise-wide issues of system development.

- Human resources
  — If the human resources department is not actively involved in IT issues, it will be confined to administrative roles and confronted by dissatisfaction arising from the conflict between traditional and new ways of working.
  — Human resource managers must seek alliances with IS managers to ensure that IT planning takes into consideration impact on human resources.
  — Human resources managers should have opportunities to use IT and understand its impact.
  — Human resources systems should move away from traditional payroll and other personnel administrative systems, and use IT for skills planning, team construction and support, and groupware systems.

Summary

This chapter has completed our walk through the history of the evolution of the Enterprise Information Management Model, looking at the business, systems, technical, and product components of the information architecture. This work identified significant organizational impact during a period of substantial change.

In the next chapter, we will move on to look in more depth at both information technology and information systems. We first present a more technical differentiation between information technology and IT, then describe several distinct kinds of information system.

PART I I I

Enterprise-wide
Information Infrastructures

Part III continues our journey through the worlds of information and IT infrastructure. Here we look at some of the background and theory that support our experience.

The following chapters will provide a deeper understanding of the topics we have described so far. We have used the terms "architecture" and "infrastructure" throughout, but what do they mean? Is architecture the right metaphor for what we are trying to say, or is there a better one? When we advocate a more extensive and formal application of information theory and principles for the future, what are we really saying?

Chapter 7 looks at information technology, exploring the importance of IT and then taking a high-level view of different kinds of information systems, including recent trends for global and individual information systems.

Chapter 8 continues with a look at information management challenges and then presents a generalized model for vertical integration between business departments, business processes, elementary computer processes, and computing platforms. We offer another simple model to show how planning for computer use or information technology often starts with some kind of deterministic model, which then, because of unpredictable behavioral and organizational changes, becomes a statistical model instead.

Substantial change is recommended for the management of enterprise information and knowledge assets independently of the technology.

Next, in Chapter 9, we consider more formally terms such as "information", "system", and "architecture", and offer formal definitions of "information architecture" and "information biology". We also discuss why we consider information to be a true enterprise asset.

Chapter 9 also treats general principles and concepts of information and IT infrastructures. Clients and servers are defined, and pointers are given on achieving greater application portability and interoperability. We summarize the key standards applying to IT infrastructures and based on identifiable open or industry standards. Finally, we offer a high-level view of information and IT infrastructure components.

Information Technology and Systems

What is Information Technology?

In order to explain how we use the term "information technology", we must consider both definitions and components.

Definitions

Here are a few definitions of information technology other commentators have proposed:

> "A term ... used to cover technologies used in the collection, processing and transmission of information. It includes micro-electronic and opto-electronic based technologies incorporated in many products and production processes and increasingly affecting the service sector. It covers, inter alia, computers, electronic office equipment, telecommunications, industrial robots and computer controlled machines, electronic components and software products." (OECD 1987)

> "A new techno-economic paradigm affecting the management and control of production and service systems throughout the economy, based on an inter-connected set of radical innovations in electronic computers, software engineering, control systems, integrated circuits and telecommunications, which have drastically reduced the cost of storing, processing, communicating and disseminating information. It comprises a set of firms and industries supplying new equipment and software, but its development and applications are not limited to this specialized IT sector." (OECD 1989b, at p. 136, quoting Freeman 1985)

> "IT consists of the following elements: 1. Hardware, 2. Software, 3. Networks, 4. Workstations, 5. Robotics, 6. Smart chips." (MIT 1989)

We bring together these meanings of the terms "information", "technology", and "information science"[1] for our definition of "information technology"; The systematic study of artifacts that can be used to give form or description to facts in order to provide meaning or support for decision making (that is, origination of information), and artifacts that can be used for the organization, processing, communication, and application of information.

The term "information technology" can be used in two different ways:

1. To mean the study or science of the artifacts involved with information and its use.
2. To refer to the artifacts themselves.

> *Information technology is the systematic study of artifacts that can be used to give form or description to facts in order to provide meaning or support for decision making (that is, origination of information), and artifacts that can be used for the organization, processing, communication, and application of information.*

Only the first sense is strictly correct, but most literature seems to use the term in its second sense. In order to be consistent with most extant literature, we use "IT", not as an abbreviation for Information Technology, but as a metaphor for the artifacts, and "information technology" to refer to the science or systematic study. This distinction

---

1   The term technology is derived from Greek, and a loose interpretation would be the science, systematic study, word, or speech of art and craft. It has come to mean primarily a systematic study of how to use artifacts to do things; it is commonly associated with tools and machines and in popular use frequently refers to the artifacts themselves.

   The meaning of the term information is somewhat more elusive. A popular distinction is made between data or facts and information, which is data rendered meaningful in some way. We examine more technical definitions of information later in the book, but a loose interpretation, from Latin, conveys the idea of giving form or describing. Cybernetics suggests that information is "formed" data, or a description of something, which is capable of affecting a decision. (For the purists, we will refine this interpretation later.)

   According to the Encyclopedia Britannica (15th ed.) information science was defined at a Georgia Institute of Technology conference in 1961 as "the science that investigates the properties and behavior of information, the forces governing the flow of information, and the means of processing information for optimum accessibility and usability. The processes include the origination, dissemination, collection, organization, storage, retrieval, interpretation, and use of information. The field is derived from, and related to, mathematics, logic, linguistics, psychology, computer technology, operations research, the graphic arts, communications, library science, management, and other fields".

is in keeping with our belief that many methods and processes for the use of IT are prescribed without sufficient consideration of information technology as a whole.

Figure 7.1 shows many of IT's components, as well as its functions and meanings.

Figure 7.1 What is IT?

Components	Functions Applied to Data Information
Microelectronics	Collecting
Optoelectronics	Processing
Computers	Communicating/Transmitting
Electronic office equipment	Storing
Telecommunications	Disseminating
Robots	Interpreting
Computer-controlled machines	
Computer-controlled services	
Software	
Computer input, output, and storage devices	
Control systems	

Meanings

Information technology as applied science
Information technology as machines and artifacts
IT concept
IT markets
IT industries

Components

Most people who come into contact with computers acquire an intuitive understanding of IT. However, IT has a much broader scope than its connection to computers implies. For example, "information infrastructure", one of our major themes, encompasses not only computers but also communications equipment as well as a few other kinds of technology. It is debatable whether some machines are valid information technology artifacts. Is a machine that counts out and dispenses currency notes an IT artifact? Some would say this depends on how such a machine is used.

There is fertile ground for confusion regarding "information technology" and "IT", as well as a risk that for some, the terms will have particularly narrow meanings. For these reasons, it can be helpful to identify the different categories of IT as it relates to information technology:

- "Pure" IT machines or services—the most appropriate examples being computers not used in conjunction with other machines
- IT-based machines or services—in which IT is an integral component. The IT and other mechanisms are tightly coupled; eliminating the IT would probably involve redesign.
- IT-assisted machines or services—in which IT provides assistance, but the machine or service could operate without it, albeit more slowly or less efficiently. In other words, the IT and other mechanisms are loosely coupled.
- Non-IT machines or services—in which there is no meaningful IT involvement

So, what kinds of uses does this list indicate? Figure 7.2 shows some different services IT provides within the various categories. Figure 7.3 shows some generic IT components. Computers are, of course, the most obvious, along with the various devices attached to them such as central processing units, memory, mass storage, and input/output devices. However, there are other devices for capturing or transmitting information, that is, communicating-for example, telephones, printing machines, and books-some of which are also used for transferring information between computers.

Figure 7.2 What is IT? (2)

IT use	Example Product	Example Service
"Pure" IT	Computer	Econometric modeling
IT–based	Automated teller machine Robot	Programmed share buying and selling
IT–assisted	Supermarket checkout	Traffic control

Figure 7.3 Generic Computer-Based IT Components

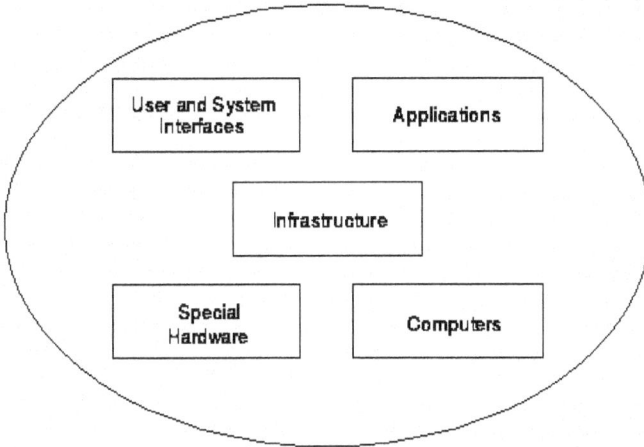

Electrical and physical connections and switching mechanisms have been used extensively for communications, and now, besides traditional wires connecting two locations with electrical signals, there are satellite communications and optical fibers providing light coupling. Mass storage, first paper and then magnetic tape, is now emerging as new devices including compact disks (CDs). All of this new technology is part of IT.

In its broadest sense, IT is *the artifacts for performing operations on information*. In its computer-based sense, depicted in Figure 7.3, it is computing platforms, infrastructure, applications, special hardware, and user and system interfaces. All forms of electronic information come under IT's umbrella. This includes data, voice, and images.

For any enterprise the introduction and use of IT is probably more evolution than revolution. Established working practices and systems are probably the major brake on its introduction. We believe that a pure top down approach to IT implementation will have little success. In fact, we know of few companies where strategic top-down decisions have had any major effects[2]. We advocate a combination of top-down and bottom-up approaches to the successful exploitation of information technology. Planning and deployment must be integral parts of any company's management system.

Given the fact that every company has built up its IT investment over the years, there is a need to rationalize that investment. Figure 7.4 shows in simple terms how the cost of implementing a corporate IT strategy decreases as the number of readily available and appropriate

---

2 Everyone has heard from many different sources about SABRE, American Hospital Supply, OTIS, and a few others. There are not many full-scale examples.

components of an IT infrastructure increases. This picture can be called an "investment gap", that is, the investment needed to deploy applications that cannot be constructed entirely from existing infrastructure components. Time to market is the time between the decision that a new application is wanted and the effective deployment of the application.

Figure 7.4 Investment Gap

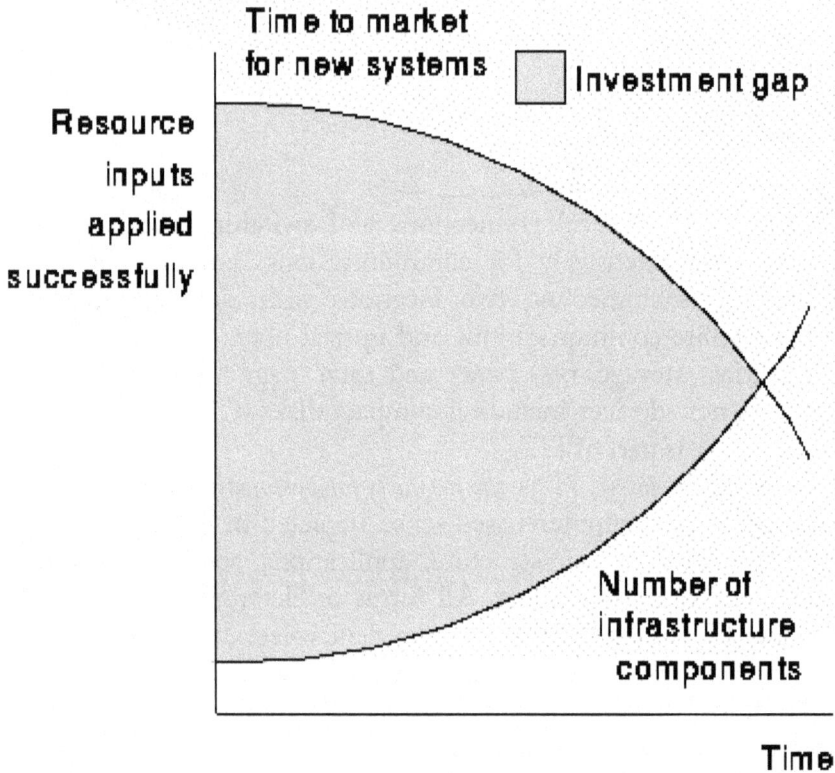

IT is the artifacts for performing operations on information. In its computer-based sense it is computing platforms, infrastructure, applications, special hardware, and user and system interfaces.

An infrastructure component is any part of IT that meets the needs of more than one application. Examples include shared processing units, shared devices such as printers, networks, shared software components, and shared databases. Non-IT information infrastructure components include policies, strategies, goals, knowledge, and clerical and managerial procedures. Perhaps the most common error is to equate infrastructure and network. In fact, however, a network is only part of infrastructure.

An IT application can be considered as an unique configuration of IT (as well as IT-based or IT-assisted) components used for a specific range of purposes. Some components may be shared, and some may be special to the application. Spreadsheet or document processing applications, for example, share the same processing units, mass storage, and printers; the only thing not shared is their actual contents. On the other hand, applications specially commissioned by separate business departments have much less to share with one another. An implemented corporate or global information system is likely to be a highly complex system of infrastructure components and applications.

The Importance of IT

Given current trends in technology and the dramatic decreases in per-unit costs of computing and communication, one could expect that companies will spend less on IT. However, trends in the past ten years or so show that spending on IT in successful companies is actually growing, or, at a minimum, staying flat[3]. What is happening is that increasingly available capacity is going into new applications such as multimedia, expert systems, group support systems, and massive simulation. Actually, we believe that in the coming years most of the incremental capacity will go into building more flexible organizations and providing more support to every individual.

Why is investment in information systems by some companies increasing by 10.5 percent per year? Several hypotheses are possible, among them:

- Companies find themselves in increasingly unpredictable environments and need to adapt more quickly. They believe information technology enables adaptability.
- There is a fundamental shift in social paradigms that views progress increasingly in terms of the application of technology.
- People increasingly enjoy using technology whether or not it leads to demonstrable and significant economies.
- The world is becoming so complex that the only way to manage increasing interaction is through the application of information technology.
- Available computing platforms were originally expensive and limited in capacity, so only a small proportion of an enterprise's activities could be computerized. Now there are many activities that can be computerized.

3 See, for example, Davis (1989), who asserts: "Despite a slowdown in the U.S. economy, the top companies in a dozen fields of industry and commerce are increasing their IS investment by 10.5%".

Whatever hypothesis one chooses, the result of increased IT spending is blurring the distinction between non-IT-based and IT-based processes and activities.

From our Western ethical and social point of view it is easy to assume that this is an unavoidable and only positive trend. We should not forget that many cultures have minimal levels of technology[4]; nor should we assume that a civilization predominantly based upon a technological paradigm is inherently superior. Regardless of one's point of view on such matters, IT is heavily implicated in both the present problems facing the world and their solutions.

There is an evolution to the results obtained from the successful application of IT. That evolution can be described as:

- Efficiency
- Effectiveness
- Enterprise integration
- Global interconnectivity

The outcome of the last stage should be greater flexibility, which we believe is one of the key advantages of IT applied properly.

Efficiency is characterized primarily by the displacement of labor for certain tasks that could be mechanized and, more generally, by rational combinations of resources needed for certain tasks. Computerization requires processes to be standardized and reduced to algorithms that can be executed by a definable and executable sequence of instructions. Efficiency usually influences an enterprise's cost structures.

Effectiveness is more than the automation of manual tasks; it involves applying the benefits of automation to improve the ability of the enterprise to achieve its objectives. It requires better use of information for decision making. Effectiveness affects factors such as revenue, market share, and meeting customer needs. Efforts to improve effectiveness have been accompanied by more individual computing (PCs) and networks. Many enterprises that have deployed IT successfully have achieved greater effectiveness, and we are tempted to assert that this is the position reached by the majority of such enterprises.

Enterprise integration has involved linking together various

---

4 Indeed, recent contacts from cultures with minimal technology, such as the Kayapo and Kogi, have been made with the specific purpose of explaining how technologically oriented cultures are responsible for a great deal of environmental damage. In such cases IT is neutral—it can be harnessed to compound environmental damage or to mitigate it. What may not be so neutral is the underlying ethical system that embraces a technological imperative in which the needs of technologically based cultures are considered sufficiently urgent and of high enough priority to justify damage to non-technologically based cultures.

"islands of automation". There has been an integration of personal and corporate computing. This has been achieved by the development of a computing infrastructure with components that support a wide range of requirements. There has been an emphasis on increasing flexibility of the deployed information systems. This is the position with which many enterprises are currently "struggling". We see a great deal of investment in many enterprises to achieve greater enterprise integration.

Global interconnectivity involves connecting together the information systems of different enterprises and individuals. This has been achieved in part by policies and developments that have made extensive communications infrastructure available. IT has lead to a tremendous growth in capacity. Emerging standards describing protocols for information systems to communicate with each other have reduced the need for negotiating individual protocols in the construction of a global information system. Not many enterprises are here yet.

The Importance of IT to the Global Economy

In a macroeconomic sense[5], information technology (including micro-electronics) can be considered the second largest sector of the global economy after transport and transport infrastructure. In the advanced economies the IT and IT-based sectors account for between 15 percent and 25 percent of total economic activity (OECD 1989b). IT is now a significant component in most other sectors of the advanced economies.

From the work of the OECD and other observers, it is possible to draw some general conclusions about the relationships between technology and other aspects of the economy:

- Labor productivity has increased in terms of output per unit of labor. (There are obvious problems with this statement, such as how one measures productivity for a totally automated factory.)
- Total output has increased.
- The level of capital productivity, in terms of the output per unit of capital input, has decreased.
- Capital-to-labor ratios have been increasing.
- The impact of information technology is essentially independent of whether it replaces labor or capital; it depends much more on the relationship between price and demand for the products or

5 For a more detailed and technical discussion of macroeconomic issues, see the publications of the OECD in their Information, Computer and Communication Policy series (OECD 1989a-c).

services of the industries introducing the technology.
- Separation of manufacturing and service activities has been increasing. Both have been growing in terms of total output, but there has been a shift from manufacturing to service employment.

The significance of systems of ethics, values, and beliefs is not apparent from much of the specialized literature on IT. We define these systems as "normative", and we believe, contrary to the literature, that they are interacting with technology on such a scale that global "macro" requirements and demands are changing beyond recognition. There is a saying that there are two roads to freedom: obtaining what one wants and not wanting in the first place. Technology-oriented cultures appear to be driven by very high levels of "wanting", and this, along with their beliefs and values, drives their behavior and lifestyles. The deployment of technology has a profound effect on future expectations.

Figure 7.5 shows a set of possible feedback and feed-forward loops between IT, applications, infrastructure, and normative systems. This is, of course, at a highly aggregated level, and no formal model has yet been constructed to test the ideas expressed. It illustrates the complex relationships between technology and other environmental factors. Various needs and wants prompt the development of certain IT and IT-based technologies, and these technologies drive the emergence of new needs and wants. Normative drivers are in the same macro loop: human needs and wants promote certain behaviors over others, including the use of technological solutions. Once the effects of these technological solutions become visible, they are evaluated against a wider range of norms, and this evaluation becomes another driver of subsequent generations of technology and its applications.

These subsequent generations of technology change the balance between applications and infrastructure. For example, as mechanisms and protocols for computer networking become more widely developed and used, pressure increases for more extensive communications infrastructure components for use by subsequent applications. Many enterprises are now investing heavily in the construction of intra-enterprise infrastructures.

Figure 7.5 IT and Normative Systems

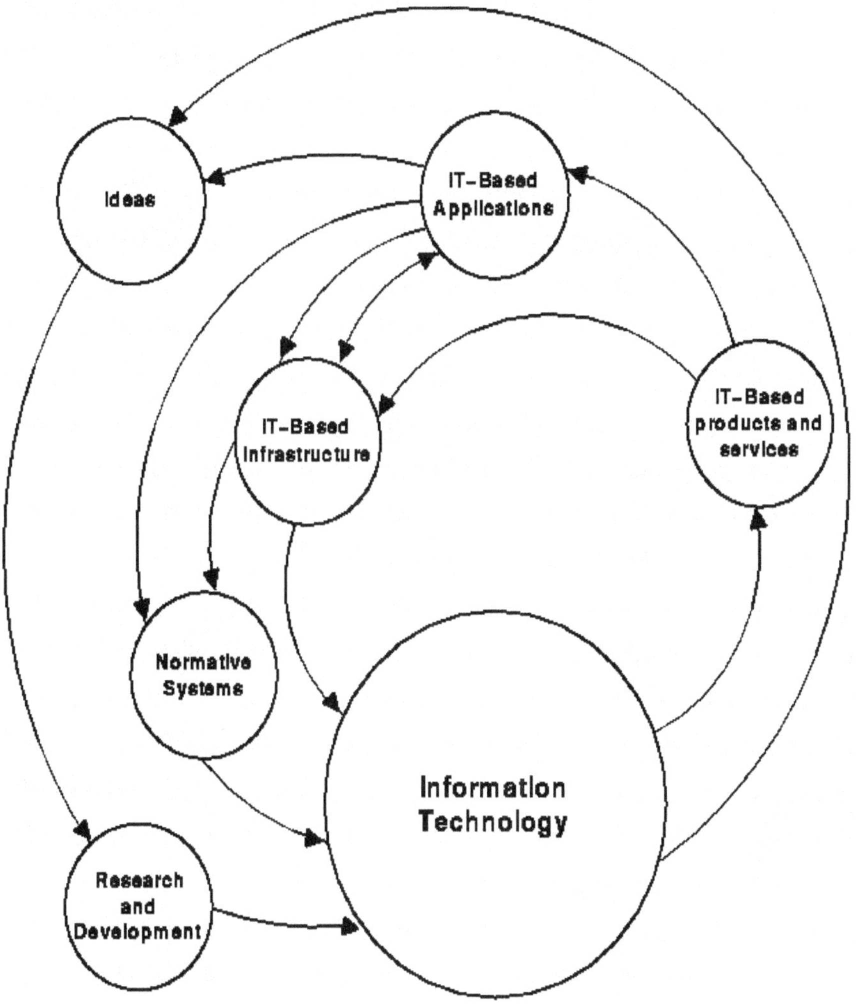

Ideas

IT–Based Applications

IT–Based products and services

IT–Based Infrastructure

Normative Systems

Information Technology

Research and Development

The Importance of IT to the Enterprise

There is much literature about using IT for competitive advantage, and hopefully in the coming years more data will emerge to provide a sounder basis for decision making on the deployment of IT to achieve particular goals[6].

For the individual enterprise, IT presents some important issues:

• In what ways can IT affect the overall cost structure?

---

6 To take a simple example, if a firm spends a great deal on R&D activity and is highly profitable, is it reasonable to infer that high R&D spending results in high profitability, or that high profitability results in high R&D spending?

- How can IT improve product and service quality?
- What are the possible relationships between the deployment of IT and available factor input combinations?
- Will the application of information technology result in the further growth or decline of an industry?
- Will employment rise or fall with the application of information technology?
- Can information technology improve capital productivity?
- How does IT increase the flexibility of an enterprise?
- Can IT be deployed to protect an enterprise against merger or takeover?

There is enormous variation in the amount enterprises spend on IT. The 1989 Datamation Industry by Industry Spending Survey Special Report (see Davis 1989), estimates IS spending overall at 2.3 percent of corporate revenue, with telecommunications, electronics, automotive, and industrial businesses among the most IS intensive, and retailers, food and beverage producers, and oil companies among the least. Companies in the banking and finance sector may spend up to 75 percent of profits as IS investments.

One way to judge perceptions of IT's competitive advantages is to look at the behavior of companies. The Datamation report identifies the main thrust of IT and IS spending as:

- Distributed computing
- Communications generally and electronic data interchange (EDI) specifically
- Computer-integrated manufacturing
- Database management software
- Computer-aided system engineering (CASE)
- Mass storage

Total IS spending on people is falling slightly, which the Datamation report attributes to top IS executives' reluctance to rely on their people: ". . . executives have already started paring back their ranks or moving them out to support business units". Datamation's implication that information technology leads not necessarily to the replacement of people but to their reassignment is echoed by the OECD. Companies that reduce their IS staff tend to move the displaced personnel to field business activities; moreover, reductions in overall headcount seem to be related more to overall business activity than to IT task automation.

Asset management is a major issue at the enterprise level— "information is an asset" is a recurring theme. Other assets are business goodwill, marketing, and R&D, all of which are much less tangible than buildings and machinery.

Accountants have well-established conventions for dealing with fixed and variable assets. In considering the impact of information technology, it is useful to make another distinction—between hard capital and soft capital assets. Soft capital assets include information, goodwill, information processing, marketing, research, and advanced development. Hard capital assets include machines that automate all or part of a process previously done manually. A machine can be "pure IT", IT-based, or non-IT. Depending on the kind of problem to be solved, IT can make a large or small contribution to a machine's construction.

A 1987 OECD report suggests that technological superiority is an important factor in determining the pattern of world trade in a majority of product groups. Competitive advantage at the enterprise level does not derive necessarily from IT superiority; rather, we think it derives from the superior utilization of information that is appropriately supported by IT.

The Importance of IT to the Individual

The standard and styles of living in developed (economically) countries are now heavily dependent on many applications of IT. The standard and styles of living in the developing world are impacted profoundly by developed countries. Therefore IT now has a profound impact, directly or indirectly, on most world cultures. (For the disbeliever, imagine life without any computer assistance!) The pervasiveness of direct computer assistance to individuals is increasing so quickly that in the future most households in industrial societies will see dozens of microcomputers embedded in various domestic services—for example:

- Knowledge, information, and image handling
- Computer-controlled domestic appliances
- Domestic communications (television, video, telephone, fax)
- Access to external information bases and services[7]
- Active and passive recreation
- Control of environment (electricity, air, water, heat)

---

7 For example, the Minitel in France enables people to reserve travel, theater, and restaurant bookings, and do personal banking, among other things.

Outside the home and office, IT influences daily life by reaching far into automobile and other means of transportation[8].

IT Opportunities and Threats

IT presents an enterprise with a wide range of opportunities and threats. It is important to remember that one enterprise's opportunity may be another enterprise's threat.

Table 1.1 on pages 7 and 8 explored IT's threats and opportunities. It illustrated the dilemma arising from the pursuit of a particular property of information systems because the property is considered "good" in its own right.

Opportunities

Some absolutely outstanding opportunities are available through information technology and IT. IT can provide many enterprises with significant competitive advantages and extremely efficient use of resources.

IT can replace various factors of production such as labor and capital. (Not all kinds of labor and capital can be replaced, so an enterprise needs to understand where IT will provide benefits and where it will not.) The skillful application of IT can also provide an enterprise with many more degrees of freedom in how it organizes its production of goods and services, meaning that it increases the flexibility of substituting one factor of production for another. For example, IT allows banks to be flexible in the way they do business by making it easy for customers to obtain cash or make payments electronically. It also provides for very rapid changes in the balance of payments by cash or electronically and thus makes knowledge about opportunities for investment more readily available. A bank can use IT to replace labor in some tasks and soft capital in others, add value to hard capital, or apply any combination of these.

The first kind of enterprise integration is usually the linking of different "islands of automation". The different systems are often highly inconsistent with reference to data structures and protocols. IT can support the translation of protocols so that data from one system can be fed into another; in this way it achieves an initial integration simply by providing feeders between systems along with the necessary

---

8 In the near future it will be possible to operate fax and other data devices from an automobile, which will then make it possible to have mobile offices connected to the corporate and global infrastructure.

translators.

In this sense IT is much better at integration support than are other kinds of technology. In the automobile industry, for example, the integration of different manufacturing stages has never been possible by purely mechanical means. However, significant integration has been achieved through IT support, IT-based machines, and robots. In such cases non-IT solutions have proven to be infeasible, too expensive, or too inflexible.

Integrating islands of computing becomes easier as standard facilities for interconnectivity become available. Tools such as electronic mail, EDI (electronic data interchange), and electronic conferencing provide opportunities for a general communications infrastructure available for many purposes.

An enterprise can be considered a system, and as such it has different needs for control and different ways in which it can be considered out of control. Enterprises that go bankrupt or are unable to survive after a disaster such as a fire are examples of enterprises out of control. In terms of information theory, information provides an essential part of the means by which control is exercised. Thus it can be said that IT provides an opportunity to construct a "brain" for the enterprise[9]. Continuing this biological analogy, we can say that a management information system is in some sense the brain, whereas a corporate information system is not just the brain, but also the nervous system, circulatory system, bone structure, sensor receptors, and so on.

There are some very concrete ways in which IT provides opportunities for organization, reorganization, and the way tasks are organized[10].

Deciding about organizational structure involves matters such as how much autonomous decision-making power managers have and what are the appropriate spans of control. Similarly, system design is in part concerned with putting points of control "in the right place". IT offers greater opportunities to distribute decision making, power, control mechanisms, and tasks where they will be most effective. With IT, business departments can be integrated more easily (both internally

9   This idea was expressed in its most detailed form in Beer (1972), The Brain of the Firm.
10 By way of example, consider the problem of inventory. First, models were proposed to reduce inventory; then just-in-time manufacturing was invented. Now the debate is about mass customization and manufacturing to order. IT has provided many opportunities in this area, and there are many examples of computers providing very high returns on investment from inventory savings alone. In reality, inventory problems are very difficult optimization problems. In some cases high inventories are completely justified (high inflation levels); in other cases low or zero inventories are preferable (low inflation and almost immediate delivery from suppliers). Manufacturing to order and mass customization work in certain cases (production within an acceptable period between order receipt and delivery), but in others (complex products with enormous resource inputs) the ability to accept an order may be heavily dependent on work in progress. IT not only supports different inventory paradigms, but also helps solve the underlying optimization problems. It can also switch between different solutions where appropriate.

and externally), and IT is an enabler for many changes to the way tasks are performed.

There are increasing problems caused by a paradigm of moving people to where the work is. Another significant opportunity resides in IT's support of moving the work to the people, as we discussed in Chapter 6. Such support could eventually provide a solution to the pervasive problems of commuting and traffic congestion.

Astonishing and exponential reductions in the price/performance ratios of most IT components can provide massive computing power at lower and lower cost. Moreover, much lower information processing, storage, and transmission costs mean that IT can make information available to everyone, in a real sense enabling much greater freedom of information.

Through its support for the rapid aggregation, filtering and dissemination of information, IT can replace and provide significant amounts of soft capital. For this reason alone, it is reasonable to assert that the application of IT makes information a true asset in its own right—precisely because information makes available some products and services that would be unavailable, or much more expensive, without it.

A recent study (Kearney 1990) identified the most important benefits deriving from IT applications. Here they are in decreasing order:

- Customer response
- Management information
- Productivity increase
- Cost control
- Improved quality
- Sales increase
- Market intelligence and market share
- New products
- New markets

Threats

Just like its opportunities, IT's threats arise from both its external availability and the way it is used. Symptoms of IT threats include:

- Competitors making much more effective use of factor input resources
- Increasing IT expenditure unaccompanied by an increase in productivity or profitability
- The installed base of computer applications significantly

inhibiting organizational change or the enterprise's ability to adapt to new environmental circumstances
- Too much time spent deciding what information is relevant and what is not
- Discussion about the need for a new information system, focusing rapidly on the computer aspects, to the neglect of noncomputer aspects
- An overwhelming emphasis on a single computing culture
- The installation of IT resulting in cost replacement rather than cost reduction, without any improvement in resource use or competitive advantage

There are perhaps three fundamental potential threats to an enterprise from IT:

1. Information pollution
2. Lack of information security
3. Serious difficulty changing work performance or business processes

Information pollution is the dysfunctional provision of information. It can arise in distinct ways:

- The amount of available information exceeds the capability to inspect and identify the relevant information.
- The cost of providing and managing information exceeds the possible maximum value to be obtained from it.
- The wrong information is provided, resulting in incorrect decisions and control that is not optimally effective.
- An extreme case of "GIGO" (garbage in, garbage out) occurs where computerized information systems are used to "sanitize" the garbage that becomes management information. (A notorious example is the macroeconomic simulations used by some governments that generate chronically incorrect forecasts that are then acted upon by governments and industries.)

Figure 7.6 illustrates the proposition that up to a certain point, more information leads to greater effectiveness of the enterprise, organization, group, or individual, but that after a while, diminishing marginal increases in effectiveness set in, ultimately leading to decreasing marginal effectiveness. This is another way of saying that information pollution is beginning to have its effect. The trick is for an enterprise to locate the optimum level of information, in terms of both quantity and quality.

158

Figure 7.6 Information and Marginal Effectiveness

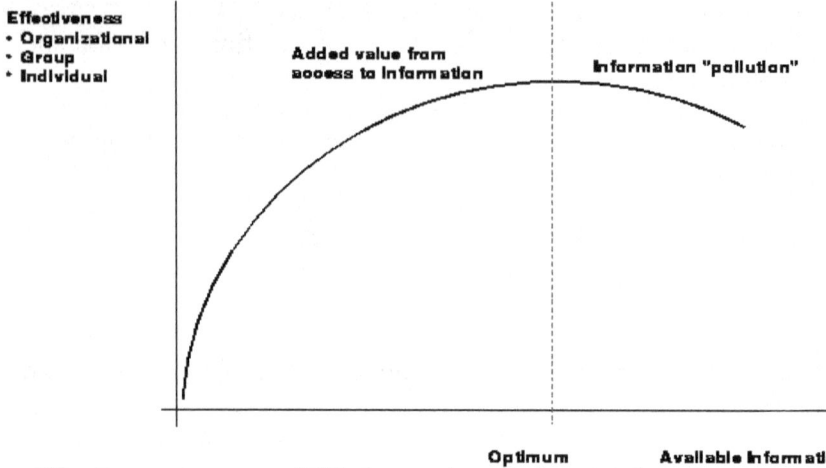

Effectiveness
- Organizational
- Group
- Individual

Added value from access to Information

Information "pollution"

Optimum   Available Information

The first symptom of IT threats listed above—that the amount of information available exceeds the enterprise's ability to deal with it—is epitomized by the traditional "manager's DIY (do-it-yourself) kit": a set of detailed reports the manager must examine in a short time and somehow detect all situations or deviations that require corrective or promotional decisions. Some professions have evolved strategies to deal with too much information. Accountants and investment analysts, for example, have a set of business ratios they apply to a set of accounts to support their comparisons and decision making.

> *Information pollution is the dysfunctional provision of information*

Information theory has the concept of the maximum value of information. This is linked to the maximum value that could be obtained from taking decisions under conditions of certainty; additional information cannot be worth more than the maximum return obtainable from an outcome that is certain, compared with an outcome that is probable. An interesting exercise is to compare increases in the rate of expenditure with increases in underlying profitability. If there is a greater increase in IT expenditure, it is necessary to determine if IT is contributing to cost replacement or cost reduction somewhere else. For example, if the rate of increase in electronic mail is twice the rate of increase in corporate profitability, is the electronic mail contributing to savings elsewhere? (The answer to this question can be found in Chapter 3.)

IT poses significant threats to the security of information. Just consider for a moment emerging compact disk (CD) technology. With writable CDs just around the corner, think about the security risk to all the company's data on a single disk. A CD can hold over 600 megabytes; this represents the complete telephone directory for the United Kingdom or more than one year's worth of The Times. The same security problems arise from PC and laptop use, which permits wide access to a company's information.

Many IT threats arise because a traditional approach has been simply to automate manual tasks without examining or reorganizing underlying business processes. Threats can also arise when an enterprise becomes locked into a monolithic computing culture. Examples of this abound: management may decide to standardize on UNIX regardless of how suitable a UNIX operating system may be for all the enterprise's needs; a standard user interface may be selected even though the underlying technology could inhibit integration or performance; or a single method may be chosen for the development of software to give the illusion of consistency, even though there may be problems the method does not help. (For example, many enterprises are heavily involved in implementing distributed systems, but most commercially available methods of development do not address problems of distributability.)

IT is usually a component in a socio-technical, not a purely technical, system. Unfortunately, many approaches to IT use focus primarily on the system's technical aspects, ignoring the social, psychological, and organizational. This overly technical emphasis can present a threat to IT's balanced use.

The increasing trend toward the commoditization of computing resources, both hardware and software, presents different threats to the enterprise, which can only be countered by the development of an appropriate infrastructure. To use a transport analogy, although more cars may appear to give more people greater flexibility and freedom of movement, the more cars there are on the road, the greater the need for a transport infrastructure.

Certain IT uses can lock an enterprise into specific organizational structures, business processes, or inappropriate technological dependencies. The almost unlimited availability of computing power means that more information is now available to everybody, creating a whole new set of behaviors. Enterprises risk their information becoming so unmanageable and unproductive that everybody in the company will have a great deal of information whether they need it or not.

Given that all applications talk to each other and that there are hundreds of these conversations in a sequence, it is very difficult to understand the consequences of a change. A decision in one department or one function to change a set of enterprise-wide organizational codes can affect many layers of the enterprise in unpredictable ways.

Finally, IT has the potential of supporting the construction of destabilizing systems. This is best exemplified by the 1987 stock market crash, during which programmed selling amplified the fall in many stock prices.

Information Systems

During the first few years of IT, computers were applied separately to automate different tasks and processes in different departments—accounting, administration, engineering, or production. Those *computer systems* typically were not connected; instead, there were manual interventions between the output of one computer system and the input to the next. As time went by, integration began in two parallel directions. Accounting and administration became what are usually referred to as *management information systems*. Engineering and production, less structured and less integrated until the emergence of computer-integrated manufacturing, became what are referred to as *operational information systems*.

In recent years there has been much integration of islands of automation across complete business processes. This has been a horizontal integration to link operational stages, combined with a vertical integration to provide management with more effective information about, and control of, those business processes. This level of integration has led to *corporate information systems*.

Now there is an increasing number of independent information vendors from which enterprises purchase information. At the same time the evolution of standards such as EDI has made it realistic to automate communications links between an enterprise and business partners such as suppliers and customers. In this way the *global information system is born*.

Finally, we come almost full circle. The trend toward outsourcing the supply of labor, consulting, and other value-added activities, combined with the growing availability of computing power at reasonable prices, is leading to more and more individuals who are able to act independently. Purely on personal initiative, many are building their own systems. This has lead to the emergence of *individual information systems* to serve individuals who interact with the world and provide services to their own customers.

Figure 7.7 shows the evolution from the small, or stand-alone information systems to the global and individual information systems.

Management Information Systems (MISs)

There are many texts about management information systems.

Anthony (1965) proposes a three-level hierarchy of management activity that includes:

- Strategic planning
- Management control and tactical planning
- Operational planning and control

Figure 7.7 Evolution of Information Systems

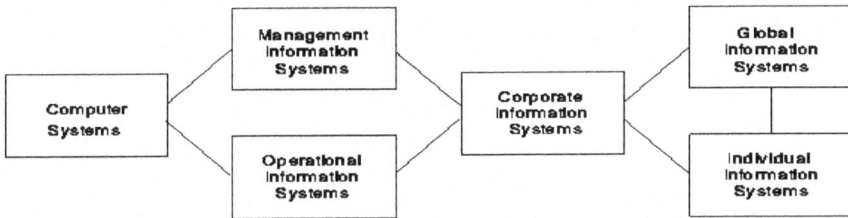

This hierarchy is usually presented as a pyramid. It is essentially a top-down hierarchical view, in contrast to the alternative "inverted pyramid" we show in Chapter 6. Both views are a simplification; they coexist in a modern organization, and better views are full networked and flexible organizations such as those discussed by Savage (1990) and Dumaine (1991), with multiple management centers.

The three levels in Anthony's hierarchy have different time horizons (long term, medium term, and short term) and different domains of concern. For example long-term planning deals with matters of overall business objectives; medium term, with the structuring of activities (and choice between alternative factor input mixes); and short term, with matters such as production and inventory levels. Activities such as pricing can occur in different levels, depending on the time frame within which price changes occur or the enterprise's pricing policy.

> *A management information system, in essence, is an effective integration of the subsystems responsible for strategic, tactical, and operational management and control*

Traditionally, responsibility in enterprises has been assigned to business departments, which have tended to develop their own management information systems. Many different MISs now exist for the different business departments and domains of concern, and their integration is often manual. In some cases figures from the different MISs can be consolidated by IT products such as spreadsheets. A management information system, in essence, is an effective integration of the subsystems responsible for strategic, tactical, and operational management and control. Borderlines are always difficult to define precisely. For example, word and document processing facilities may assist office functions. Other hardware and software combinations may support office activities. Word and document processing is not an MIS *per se*, but it may be integrated to provide management support. Similarly, a computer-controlled production machine is not an MIS *per se* but can be integrated with production planning and control MISs.

According to Davis and Olson (1984),

> "The conceptual structure of a management information system is defined as a federation of functional subsystems, each of which is divided into four major information processing components: transaction processing, operational control information system support, managerial control information system support, and strategic planning information system support. Each of the functional subsystems of the information system has some unique data files which are used only by that subsystem. There are also files which need to be accessed by more than one application and need to be available for general retrieval. These files are organized into a general database managed by a database management system."

This is a traditional view heavily conditioned by prior decisions about the departmental divisions of the enterprise. Software engineering principles suggest that enterprise-wide databases governed by a database management system may well violate several principles, such as coupling, cohesion, and information hiding. Nevertheless, Davis and Olson do give some useful hints about desirable levels of integration for an enterprise-wide MIS.

> *A logical management information system is an integration of all the information needs for the management of an enterprise, independent of either organizational or technological implementation.*

We have a stronger conceptual view of an MIS. All enterprises exist in an environment of potentially rapid change; most go through many organizational changes, which are accompanied by rapid changes in underlying IT platforms. An MIS exists at a logical level, however, which will continue to survive despite organizational and technological change; what will change are the ways MISs are implemented technologically and organizationally. On this basis we can distinguish between three types of MIS:

- Conceptual—concerned with the fundamental scope, rationale, and abstract concept of an MIS
- Logical—concerned with the functionality of an MIS independent of organization or technology
- Physical—actual implementation of a logical MIS into an organizational structure and on a technological platform

Therefore: A logical management information system is an integration of all the information needs for the management of an enterprise, independent of either organizational or technological implementation. A physical management information system is an organizational and technological implementation of an integrated set of requirements for the management of an enterprise.

> *A physical management information system is an organizational and technological implementation of an integrated set of requirements for the management of an enterprise.*

Clearly, defining a conceptual MIS is more difficult (especially so because those defining it are working in a "real world"). Nevertheless, we suggest that a conceptual management information system identifies the information needs of an enterprise with reference to the rationale and functions of management within the enterprise.

What does this rather abstract definition mean? Start with the question of how far the managers actually manage? That is, are they mainly responsible for collecting and consolidating information and passing it on to the next level of management; do they have autonomous responsibility for business performance, resource allocation, and the pursuit of enterprise objectives; or are they allowed a high degree of entrepreneurial autonomy, provided simply with resources, metrics against which to measure success, and policies to govern the limits of acceptable and ethical activity?

These are three very different views of the role of management, and they require a conceptual MIS at the beginning to take into account the

164

rationales behind management before any determination of the logical functionality MISs will provide in support of management activities. Unfortunately, there are usually very many hidden assumptions about the role of managers in an enterprise. They must be uncovered before an MIS can be defined.

> *A conceptual management information system identifies the information needs of an enterprise with reference to the rationale and functions of management within the enterprise.*

Figure 7.8 shows a simple cycle of MIS definition. First, a conceptual MIS is defined, along with a set of standards against which to define management roles. Then the required functionality is identified independently of organization and technology—that is, a logical MIS, which is implemented as a physical MIS by giving it organizational and technological form. Management performance is compared against appropriate standards and metrics.

Figure 7.8 MIS Cycle

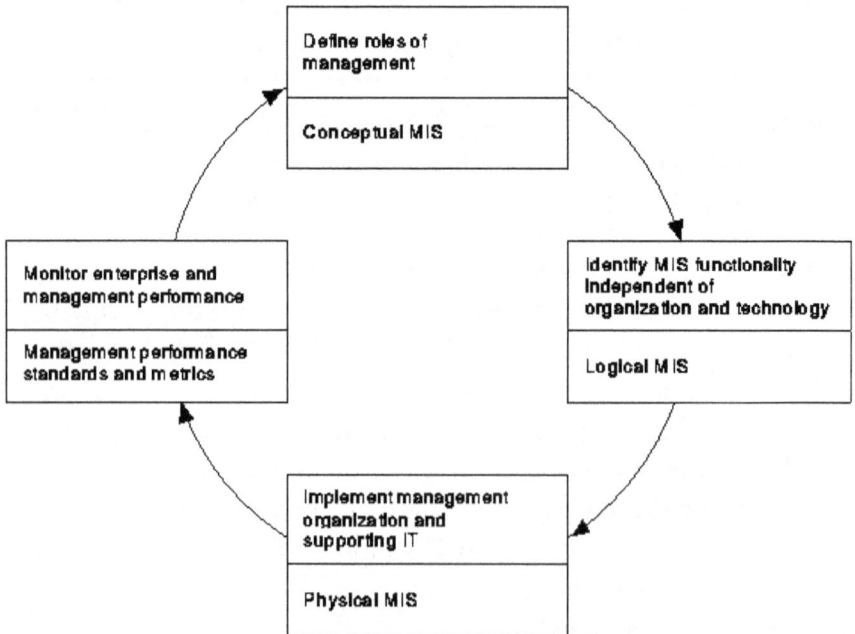

Operational Information Systems (OISs)

Operational information systems are the CIS components responsible for the transactional activities of the enterprise. Thus, they can be broken down as follows:

- Transaction processing systems to handle the commercial aspects of the enterprise's activities (sales orders, purchase orders, hiring, and so forth)
- Computer-aided manufacturing systems (including process control, computer-integrated manufacturing, and flexible manufacturing systems)
- Engineering production systems

The transaction processing systems implement the enterprise's definitions of the transactions. For example, some enterprises may consider a sale closed when the goods are available for collection, whereas others may consider it closed only when payment has been received. Essentially, transactions are "opened", or started, and proceed through a sequence of "state" transitions until they are considered closed. The information systems involved in such transactions are concerned with:

- Recording and opening the transactions
- Controlling valid sequences of state transitions
- Reporting on the status of transactions
- Closing transactions; archiving any required information

Process control systems usually control some specific mechanism such as a machine or sequence of machines. Their operation may be manual or automated. One key aspect of integrated manufacturing systems is a higher level of control that can sequence and trigger the appropriate control systems at the right stage in a process.

Computer-integrated manufacturing uses computers to integrate production processes. It comprises all the activities taking place within a manufacturing enterprise. Gerelle and Stark (1988) identify the following CIM subsystems:

- Marketing
- Decision support
- Engineering

- Production management
- Production

They define the CIM infrastructure as " . . . the technological foundation of the CIM system . . . built up from the most elementary objects and actions associated with information and materials", and they list its components as processing, storage and retrieval, user interface, and communications.

Corporate Information Systems (CISs)

The essential difference between a management information system and a corporate information system is that a CIS integrates all the information subsystems of an enterprise[11], whereas an MIS integrates only those responsible for strategic, tactical, and operational management.

A system is more than the sum of its parts. In other words, there is a level of information system for the whole enterprise that transcends the mere combining of each department's information needs. This is why historically in many enterprises, although individual business departments may have implemented information systems, there is not enough effective information for control at an overall enterprise level. These enterprises have trouble identifying the overall information needs because they cannot visualize themselves as independent of their organizational structure.

Beer's (1972, 1981) analogy of the "brain of the firm" is very useful for understanding overall enterprise control needs.

A corporate information system needs to provide information for defining strategy as well as for monitoring performance against objectives. In this, a conceptual MIS and a CIS are alike. An enterprise can be implemented and operated in many way. A CIS should provide information to aid the choice of implementation and monitor the implementation's effectiveness.

An enterprise must pursue its purposes (which evolve over time) and function satisfactorily within its external environment. It must also organize itself and function appropriately in its internal environment.

A corporate information system is not the whole enterprise, just one part. Personnel, transport, production, logistics, and value systems, among others, are not part of a CIS but are supported by and interact with it.

---

11 Some of the literature uses the terminology CIM to include all the information subsystems in a manufacturing enterprise; we use CIS as a broader term that encompasses CIM as an occurrence relative to manufacturing industry.

Hence a CIS includes the information needs of the enterprise with respect to:

- The overall enterprise and context within a wider environment—what distinguishes the enterprise from the rest of its environment?
- The organization of the enterprise itself
- Structure
- Communications
- Logistics
- Function, that is, what the enterprise does and why
- Production, that is, the actual conversion and combination of factor inputs into outputs
- Recognition by the enterprise of various stimuli and its responses
- Information attenuation and amplification, that is, making the relevant information available to the right people or mechanisms
- Knowledge
- Management

A particularly difficult aspect of establishing a CIS is providing it with a knowledge base. Doing so requires finding the relevant information, expressing it as knowledge, and then knowing what to do with it. A knowledge component of a CIS must consider:

- Facts about the enterprise
- Facts about the environment
- Rules for the classification and interpretation of facts, and responding to knowledge
- Alternatives available to the enterprise, including interactions with the wider environment and internal enterprise organization, structure, and control
- Decisions, both external and internal
- The impact of events and decisions, internal and external
- Simulation of actions and the consequences of actions
- A vision of possible future states

Also of great importance to a CIS is its static-dynamic dimension. Its information must represent not only static snapshots of a particular point in time but also the dynamics of changes in the enterprise and its environment.

Figure 7.9 summarizes the primary information asset domains a CIS must integrate. Information needs should be represented on internal-external and static-dynamic dimensions.

Figure 7.9 CIS Information Asset Domains

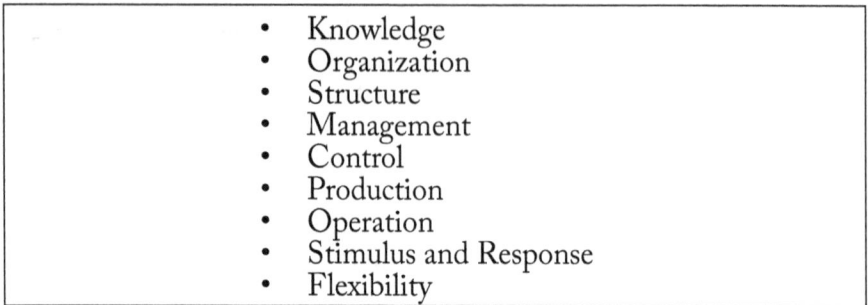

> - Knowledge
> - Organization
> - Structure
> - Management
> - Control
> - Production
> - Operation
> - Stimulus and Response
> - Flexibility

Global Information Systems (GISs)

Imagine that a particular activity requires information from independently owned sources and that this information is internally and externally available. Examples of such activity include:

- Evaluating a particular market in order to make product, production, and pricing decisions
- Automating the supply of goods or services where part of the value added is provided either by trading partners or independent con-tractors
- Several independent enterprises cooperating in the definition and subsequent implementation of agreed standards
- Joint research, development, or production ventures

Since in any of these situations IT offers a great deal of support, we can say that GISs are essentially IT-based systems.

Implementing a global information system involves establishing communication with other enterprises and sources of information. Figure 7.10 offers a stylized illustration of GIS implementation. Most of the diagram is self-explanatory, but a "policy engine" has been added to resolve certain specific problems:

- How are mutually binding commitments created between cooperating enterprises?
- How do the parties know that a mutually binding commitment has been created, and what is the appropriate level of evidence of the commitment?
- How are mutual commitments carried out or in some cases

enforced?

As for the uses for a GIS, it is clear that individual enterprises will have different ideas from those of individuals and administrative groups. On the basis of our own experience, we believe that GISs in the enterprise will aid the exchange of information in support of distributed processes (including those combining voice, video, and data) and knowledge and information handling and sharing (for example, electronic conferencing and services such as videotex or mediatex combining video with audio and perhaps other forms).

Between the enterprise and the outside world, we think GISs will support substantial growth in electronic information and knowledge interchange (that is, an initial expansion of electronic data interchange (EDI) followed very quickly by electronic knowledge interchange (EKI), which supports the transfer of knowledge and the different ways of interpreting and applying it). Soon many enterprises will be making trade agreements with major partners that stipulate EDI or EKI.

Figure 7.10 Enterprise Global Information System Implementation

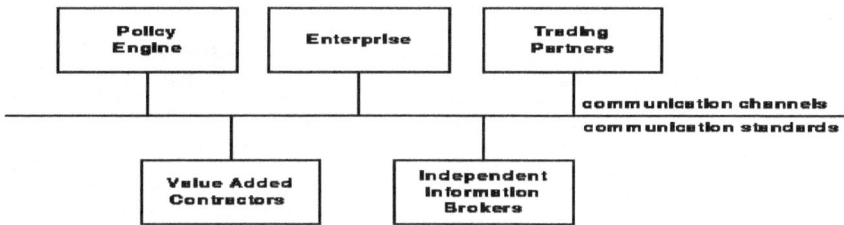

On a more global level, GISs (such as Facebook and Google?) will be used for knowledge transfer, news, entertainment, changes to systems of democracy, environmental monitoring, monitoring of governments and public organizations, and providing an infrastructure for individuals and enterprises.

Individual Information Systems (IISs)

Changing organizational structures, production paradigms, and the general availability of information are contributing to a growing pool of individuals who work independently as consultants or contractors for different enterprises. Individual information systems (depicted in Figure 7.11) can be considered similar to global information systems. There are needs to connect to information systems owned by other individuals and enterprises.

Access to many sources of information, including competing sources, is increasing. Nevertheless, having the information is not sufficient: There are often many ways to interpret information, so there must be not only access to multiple and competing sources of information but also access to alternative ways of interpreting it.

In addition to its opportunities for global interconnectivity, individuals are also likely to take advantage of IT to integrate household appliances and other equipment that is IT-based or can be IT-supported.

Figure 7.11 Individual Information System Implementation

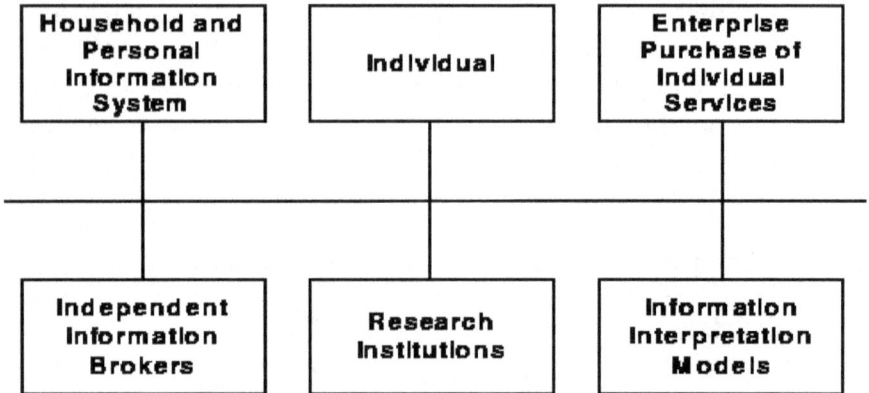

Household and Personal Information System	Individual	Enterprise Purchase of Individual Services
Independent Information Brokers	Research Institutions	Information Interpretation Models

Summary

In this chapter we have explored in some detail how information technology is broader than IT and described several types of information systems.

Information and information processing are of increasing importance at all levels of the economy from global to each individual and enterprise. We see no reason to believe that this trend will not continue for the foreseeable future.

In the next chapter we describe a range of challenges with which everyone will have to cope in order to manage and use this increased volume and importance of information.

Chapter 8

The Information Management Challenges

There are several major challenges in the evolution of corporate and global information systems, and it is important to recognize how extensive and pervasive they are.

- Information challenges—few enterprises recognize the totality of the information they need for their activities. Even if they do, the information is often so extensive and dispersed that managing it is probably an illusory concept.
- Knowledge challenges—what information is needed, why it is needed, and what can be done with it.
- Integration challenges—many enterprises are already running a large number of different information processing applications; for many reasons some or all of these must be integrated, not the least reason being problems of inconsistency between applications.
- Technical challenges—information management is achieved with the support of many technological approaches, often with very different technical computing platforms in different departments.
- Interpersonal communication challenges—information management is concerned with identifying the enterprise's information needs and then implementing the information systems to meet them. Different departments use different languages and special terms, and often they have great difficulty understanding each other.
- People management challenges—so many changes in organization, management roles, and empowerment are taking place that there are now substantial challenges in motivating and managing people.
- Cultural challenges—up to now, information and IT have been used in very different ways, involving the development of different information use and different computing cultures.
- Directional challenges—many enterprises are embarked on programs to integrate information needs and resources in

pursuit of some "vision"; how can information help them choose the vision and then keep them on course (or help them change course if circumstances change)?

Every enterprise must have its own way of meeting these challenges, particularly if it hopes to gain competitive advantage. Some solutions are more effective than others. Some involve many unrecognized assumptions, whereas others recognize and manage limitations on the basis of assumptions they have made explicit. The goal is to manage these challenges well rather than let solutions just "happen".

Information Challenges

The total information needs of the enterprise are more extensive than just those handled by information technology. In turn, information technology is more extensive than just computer-based systems. Enterprises must recognize their total information assets and understand what can be handled by IT generally, what can be handled by computer-based systems, and how to manage it all. Detailed discussion of this topic is in Chapter 1.

Knowledge Challenges

In order for a collection of information to be an asset or system, there should be some sense in which it can be said that the information is fulfilling some purpose. Moreover, the data on which it is based must have been made meaningful in order for the information to support decision making or gaining advantage.

Most enterprises use far more unstructured than structured information; the same is true for knowledge.

Taking a rather simplistic and pragmatic view (because this is not a philosophical text), knowledge is concerned with applying experience to information to make the most effective use of the information available. It involves cognition (perceiving and recognizing things and situations), experience about the significance of what is perceived or recognized, and judgment about the various outcomes of decisions.

Enterprises apply a huge mass of unstructured knowledge in the course of their activities, which often gives rise to long debate and discussion about its meaning and what to do with it. Different people can suggest completely opposite courses of action—and quite validly—because their knowledge is different.

The value of appropriate knowledge is that it improves the probability of a "correct" decision, or one that leads to the most desirable outcome out of a range of possible outcomes. An "expert" is someone who is more efficient than most people at making correct decisions, understanding the significance of certain information, and applying knowledge to it. Of course, in dealing with knowledge one must remember that a judgment about the most desirable outcome can be a matter of pure preference or prejudice.

Ideally, an expert can articulate the rules to be applied to information in order for it to support decision making. This is the essence of what computer-based expert systems do. However, real experts, unlike computers, are also stimulated by new thoughts, new data, and new and conflicting ideas. The difficulty in creating expert systems is usually finding experts in the first place. Sometimes it seems that the hope for artificial intelligence is that, in some magical way, we will be able to use a computer as a substitute for an expert without having to capture all of the expert's appropriate knowledge.

How can an enterprise use the available, unstructured mass of knowledge to its best advantage? Recognizing knowledge is the first step.

Figure 8.1 illustrates some of the steps to be carried out by the enterprise in dealing with some of the knowledge challenges. Below we explain the steps:

Figure 8.1 Managing Knowledge in the Enterprise

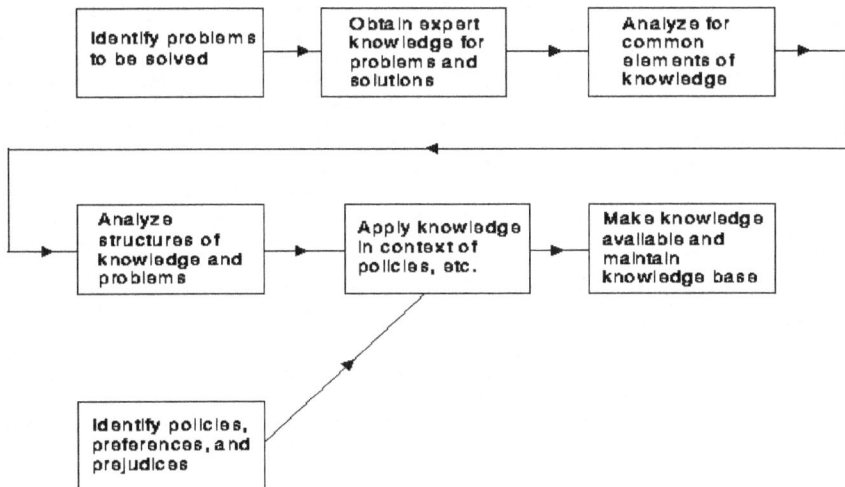

- Identify the problems to be solved—as a result of a strategizing or other kind of workshop, determine the problem domain for which knowledge and expert assistance are required.

- Obtain expert knowledge—it may be difficult to find experts who understand the identified problem domains and solutions required; recognize that different experts are likely to have different knowledge, and then identify the consensus among them.
- Look for common elements of knowledge—perhaps there will be certain levels of agreement among the different experts; even if there are few common elements, try to identify the disparate ones.
- Analyze structures of knowledge and problems—someone who specializes in epistemology should look for the abstract structures in the knowledge and problems that are independent of the problem domain, and determine how different knowledge structures apply to different problems, depending on actual objectives (that is, knowledge can be used for the same problem, but may produce different results depending on the objectives of the enterprise—for example, if the problem is deciding an appropriate product mix, how knowledge is applied depends on whether the objective is maximizing profit or maximizing market share.)
- Identify policies, preferences, and prejudices—there are many arbitrary objectives available to an enterprise; its choices influence the application of knowledge. (For example, a policy not to pay commissions to salespeople will impact the application of knowledge about motivation.
- Determine how to apply knowledge in context—relate knowledge and decisions about policies and preferences.
- Determine how to implement knowledge within the enterprise— how should knowledge be made available? Deciding how to maintain the knowledge base is an issue frequently ignored. Rules for the application of knowledge are often probabilistic, and thus the relevant probabilities may change as the environment and experience change.

A growing body of literature is devoted to the role of knowledge workers in enterprises. (See, for example, Zuboff 1988, Toffler 1990, and Nolan 1990.) Much of it addresses issues such as how information technology can supplement people's skills and lead to greater job enhancement rather than merely automating manual tasks. Along these lines, the OECD has published a detailed discussion of the way in which the balance between manufacturing and service industries is changing.

Integration Challenges

Many enterprises must deal with a large number of different information systems, some of which may have been created:

- At different times
- By different business departments
- To process information at very different levels of granularity
- To run on different computing platforms
- As a point solution to a point problem
- To automate manual procedures

A major cause for concern in many enterprises is the number of inconsistencies that has arisen between existing implemented systems. The systems may also have been modified in an unplanned way. Combined with poor or nonexistent system documentation, this results in an absence of effective knowledge about what many applications do or how they do it.

There are some scenarios that are typical of integration problems enterprises try to solve:

- Shared computing resources—more than one application can execute on the same computing platform, and they are integrated at the level of sharing the same basic hardware and software resources.
- Integration within one business department—for example, the accounting department may start with many different component applications and then integrate them.
- Cross-functional integration—data from one department's application are required by another department's application, so the departments agree to a greater degree of integration between the two. For example, a sales order processing cycle is likely to involve several departments in a complete value chain.
- Disparate computing platforms—there are two or more different computing platforms, and the data from an application on one computing platform is to be transferred to an application on another. For example, some specialized hardware, say a document scanner, may be running on a PC, and the resulting documents are to be transferred to another machine for further processing; another example which is quite common occurs where there is a relatively centralized mainframe-type platform providing something like basic accounting, but it is too expensive to allow end users ad hoc access to the databases to take extractions and manipulate the resulting data. Some mechanism is therefore

created to make extracts and transfer them to PCs for local processing.

- Integrated package environments—packages for particular applications that will become part of a complete environment are purchased from different vendors, and it is necessary to create "umbrella" environments for the various tools to operate and share information.
- Merger—two or more enterprises are merged, and their information systems are to be made consistent and compatible, with an appropriate level of information sharing.

These are relatively traditional scenarios for integration; however, an enterprise embarking on a complete enterprise-wide information systems strategy frequently has in mind a much higher degree of integration than we have described.

Figure 8.2 shows some of the issues in and rationale behind achieving a high degree of integration. Near the center of the diagram are the many logical objects[1] the enterprise will have to deal with independently of its organizational structure (that is, unless it makes a radical change in its business). It must manage information about customers, suppliers, products, contracts, calls, facilities, and people regardless of the business departments individually responsible for them.

Above the data objects are the elementary computer operations that must be performed on each—creating, using, changing, removing, and so forth. We call these processes elementary because it makes no sense to break them down into smaller processing units.

At one level up from the elementary computer processes are the elementary business processes, many of which are in fact the basic transactional activities of the enterprise, such as making a sale or hiring an employee. Each elementary business process usually represents a sequence of elementary computer processes.

At the next higher level, elementary business processes combine into the main business processes of the enterprise. Examples are selling, marketing, production, logistics, accounting, and hiring.

Finally, at the highest level, most enterprises organize into business departments such as sales, finance, and manufacturing. These departments are in place to achieve enterprise objectives and goals.

Note that the data objects and elementary processes are logical— that is, they exist independently of how the enterprise is organized and

---

1 See, for example, the discussions in Martin and Leben (1989) and Scheer (1989) about candidate data subjects and processes that may be performed on them.

of the computing platform used to provide computing support. They are then implemented on a particular computing platform, ideally in such a way that the technology will be appropriate to the information processing needs of the enterprise.

Figure 8.2 Enterprise Needs and Technology integration Technology

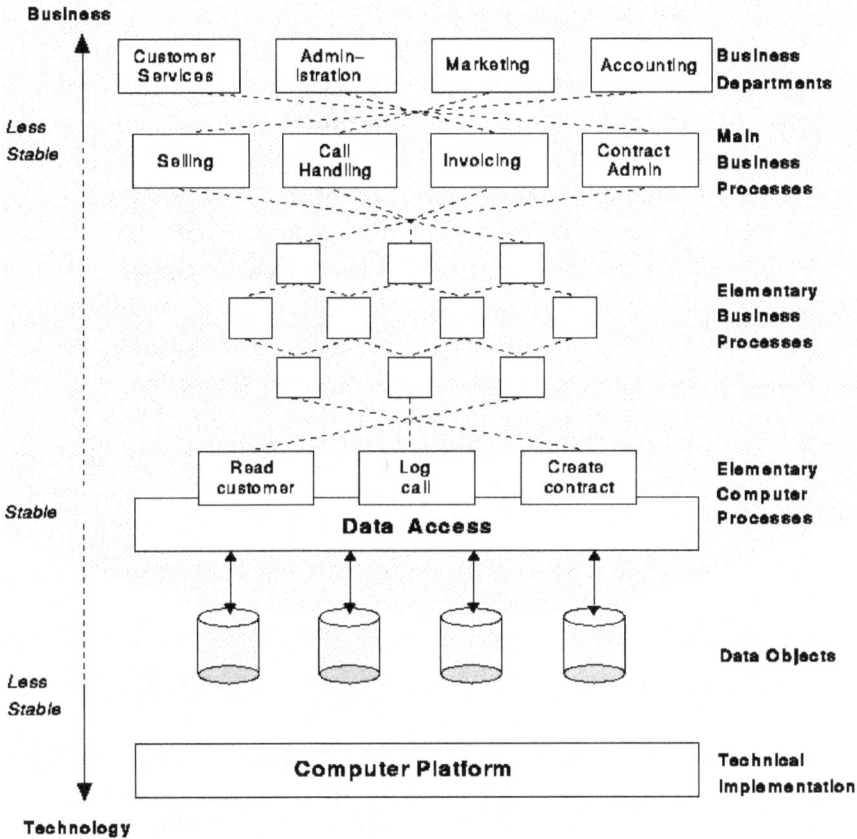

Two very important principles arise from such a highly integrated schematic as that represented in Figure 8.2.

First, the data objects and elementary computer processes are highly stable as *logical requirements* because they will not change much unless the enterprise changes significantly what it does. Instability increases toward the top and bottom of the diagram. That is, the elementary computer processes are more stable than the main elementary business processes, which are more stable than the main business processes, which are more stable than the business departments. The business departments are probably the least stable, since they are the most likely to change as management adjusts the organizational structure. This speaks against a traditional top-down de-composition technique for the development of information systems, because the starting point for analysis should not be the most unstable part of the enterprise. The increasing instability toward the bottom of the diagram results from the evolution of technology; customer information will be stored, whether in a person's memory, on paper, in a simple computer file, or in a complex database.

Second, the diagram shows a very high degree of *vertical and horizontal integration*—vertical integration because the objectives of the enterprise are implemented by maximum process sharing; horizontal integration because information flows from one elementary process to the next, independently of the organization of the enterprise.

From the perspective of information management, what is important in a high-level integration is that it allows changes in enterprise organization, or the addition of new functionality, at significantly lower cost than would be possible if the changes or additions were commissioned by separate, unintegrated business departments. It is surprising that even now, no elementary software building blocks have been created to enable an enterprise to put together a comprehensive set of applications without significant investment or integration effort. In reality, most applications stand alone, and so does their information, which is perhaps why so many enterprises do not see substantial benefits from IT; they have allowed themselves to be organized along strictly departmental lines, with no cross-functional responsibilities, *and the departments have been permitted to commission their own information systems* without being required to coordinate their work.

We advocate the implementation of an integrated model through a distributed client/server infrastructure. In this way there will be maximum support throughout the enterprise at all the necessary points of activity and control, the highest return on investment will be achieved, and creating new applications will be much simpler.

At a more technical level, there are several different ways to achieve integration:

- Multiple applications installed on the same computing platform achieve initial integration through the sharing of computing platform resources.
- Many computer applications in the past were linked manually— that is, feeders took the output from one system and entered it into another. Enterprises then followed the path of least resistance by automating manual tasks, so these feeders received

more automated support through innovations such as creating tapes from the output of one information system and using them as another system's input.

- Databases containing the data for several applications reduce the need for applications to feed results from one to another.
- Often, making multiple applications available from a common entry point, such as a set of menus, provides an elementary integration.
- Slowly and painfully, many enterprises have realized that often they perform the same logical operation in several ways; they integrate these operations by extracting some of the common ones, and implement them with some shareable resources.
- Client/server computing enables a much higher degree of reusability by making significant information processing capability generally available.

Of course, there is a deeper integration problem beyond the integration of IT systems. This involves the integration of many other forms of technology (such as robots, automated teller machines, and many other kinds of machines or control mechanisms).

Technical Challenges

The enterprise faces many technical challenges to its effective management of information, among them:

- Dealing with different technical platforms in the same or different departments
- Establishing costs and benefits
- Creating naming conventions
- Distributing or centralizing computing
- Establishing and enforcing standards
- Dealing with the proliferation of computers
- Messaging
- Predicting required capacity
- Minimizing the number of people needed to manage infrastructure
- Balancing applications and infrastructure

However, perhaps the greatest technical challenge is that at any point in time it is only possible to provide IT support for a subset of enterprise information needs. The life story of a computer application, from the time the idea for it is established to the time the final version is up and running, involves many levels of abstraction. For this reason it is very important to incorporate in an information management program a set of naming conventions that will identify not only the object described but also the level of abstraction at which it is described. Recall that in Chapter 1 we identified three levels of abstraction: conceptual, logical, and physical. An application for controlling customer orders, say, cannot be implemented fully until certain issues at each of these levels are resolved:

- What management style has been selected?
- How will the system be integrated with other systems?
- What basic functionality is needed?

Whether systems "should" be centralized or distributed is a somewhat sterile debate. It is not really a technical question, but it does have difficult technical implications. The physical implementation of an information system is often confused with the degree of control that can be exercised by business and information management. If an enterprise decides to maximize the flexibility of its supporting information systems, then building strictly centralized or distributed systems is unwise. The proper strategy is to build systems that *maximize distributability*—that is, they can be reconfigured for different environments without more "surgery" on the applications. Distribution results from configuration or reconfiguration rather than from being fixed in a design.

With a distributed system the technical challenge is to optimize the distribution of computing resources for maximum support of enterprise objectives at minimum cost. The use of overall system resources in the final implemented system will be at an optimal level if the points of control have been located in the "right" places. This means that when control in a system is exercised in the "wrong" place, the system will probably cost more to construct and operate.

Certain functions are more suited to centralized operation, whereas others are more suited to distributed operation. There is no general answer to the question of whether centralized or distributed is better. It depends upon the problem and the enterprise. A higher-level principle than the question of distributed or centralized computing is that anyone who has a task to perform should have available the information, resources, and control mechanisms necessary to carry it out. How this is provided is a cost-optimization problem that attempts to balance the following factors:

- The relative costs of making information available locally or remotely
- The need for information consistency
- Enterprise tolerance for interruption of business due to technological failure
- The need to monitor enterprise objectives

The question of standards is a difficult technical challenge. First, the enterprise must choose the ones it will adopt, from many sources, both internal and external.

External standards, existing or proposed, can come from:

- "Independent" standards bodies (sometimes subject to enormous commercial pressure during the definition and acceptance stages for new standards)
- Consortia of enterprises that work together to define standards
- A profit-making enterprise that owns or substantially controls proprietary "standards"
- Simple market penetration, which can create "de facto" standards

Internal standards, on the other hand, develop because:

- There is an absence of appropriate external standards.
- Available external standards are not suitable for various reasons.
- Available external standards need customization to be implemented.

Once a standard has been adopted, the enterprise must then decide how far to enforce it. This is of particular concern when a problem is encountered, and the adopted standards are either silent on the matter, or are demonstrably wrong. The adoption of an information system development method is notorious in this regard. Most commonly used methods are unable to handle the wide range of problems they are supposed to solve.

The technical challenges increase as the number of available computers (internal or external) increases. Several requirements contribute to this growing complexity:

- Software must be installed or made available to all computers. It is not sufficient to keep all systems "up to date" with their software installations; in some cases they must retain their older versions of software because of an installed base; in other cases they must run new or proposed releases of software, for evaluation and impact assessment. Different machines may require very different software installations.

- Maintenance of both hardware and software must be considered.
- Change control involves procedures that must be implemented before changes are made to particular machines (hardware or software); the need for prior testing as part of change control procedures will depend to some extent on the priority of the application and its potential impact on the enterprise.
- Where copies of data and subsets of data have been circulated to different machines, and decisions are being made on the basis of available information, it is necessary to understand and control requirements for consistency of the information available to the enterprise. In some cases a consistency constraint may be very high; in others there may be a high degree of tolerance for inconsistency; and in still others inconsistency may be necessary2.
- Backups, both on- and off-site, must be performed, coordinated, and archived appropriately.
- Information is used by an enterprise at different levels of aggregation and for different purposes; a piece of data may have several dimensions that are meaningful to different people. (For example, a sum of money in one currency may be converted at an actual rate of exchange on a given day so that that day's cash position is known, or it may be converted at a planned rate of exchange so that it can be balanced against forward-budgeted currency options.) There must be an appropriate match between who owns what data and how the data are implemented in the available systems.

Many of these problems are much more severe wherever PCs proliferate. Most end users with PCs have neither the knowledge nor willingness to perform essentially technical operations on their machines. Thus, the greater the number of PCs, the greater the related IS costs for software acquisition, maintenance, and installation. There may well be severe problems of responsibility for the integrity of data expressed by appropriate backup and recovery procedures, and data security, expressed by the controls for preventing the unauthorized transfer of privileged information.

The more extensive a network, the greater the need for communications and data passing. Because computer-readable information can be structured, unstructured, or in the form of knowledge, an enterprise faces the technical challenge of providing a messaging infrastructure that will ease communication among the constituent parts.

---

2 For example: 1) A consolidated set of accounts, by definition, should be consistent, and there is unlikely to be much need for concurrent update access to it; 2) It is desirable to have an up-to-date price list, but if prices are modified and it takes a little time to update all copies, the updating can usually be done after hours, minimizing the risk that an order will be accepted at an incorrect price (and even if it is, it may not matter very much); 3) the database for available seats on an aircraft may require inconsistency in that each seat should be sold more than once in order to permit a certain amount of overbooking.

There are very few deterministic models available that can predict the overall demand for IT. Demand is particularly difficult to predict after computing resources have been available to users for any length of time. Computer use creates some very strong feedback loops, so that after users have been working with computer-based applications for a certain period of time, they wish for more. In other words, their expectations increase. If people do not know what is possible, they do not have wants, but once they know, the wants develop, and over time they become expressed as "needs". More to the point, the use of IT and knowledge about IT can change the way people live and the way tasks are organized.

Figure 8.3 illustrates a basic feedback mechanism. It shows that various initial needs are fed into the actual use of computers in order to produce certain results. Current computer use increases expectations, and subsequent computer use is determined by these expectations as well as previous use.

Figure 8.3 Basic Feedback Mechanism for Computer Use

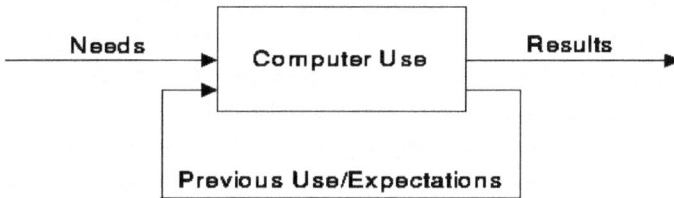

Figure 8.4 illustrates this feedback process in much more detail. It also illustrates how deterministic and statistical models help solve the technical issue of what computing resources to provide. Changing expectations and behavior are of particular importance because they are difficult to predict. The reality is, of course, that very rarely do we deal primarily with technical systems; rather, we deal with socio-technical systems, so "soft" methods (such as described in Checkland 1990 and Espejo and Harnden 1989) have a major role to play. At the project level prototyping techniques can address some of the socio-technical issues.

The diagram in Figure 8.4 has four quadrants that illustrate four general phases:

- Use of deterministic models
- Implementation of a designed system

- Behavioral change as a result of system use
- Use of statistical models to monitor and manage demand. This loop is followed by another loop, which starts with an attempt to revert to a deterministic model through an understanding of what is happening and a further attempt to understand the components, volume, and key drivers of demand.

Figure 8.4 Computer Use Feedback

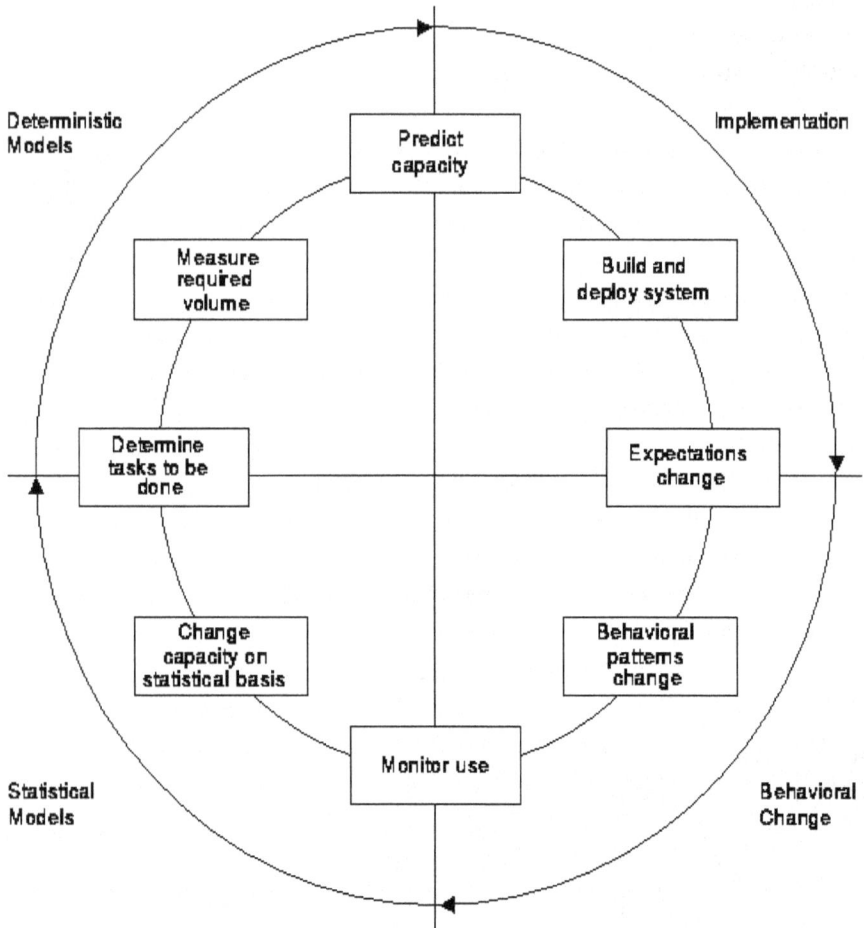

Within the four quadrants there are at least eight distinct subphases:

- Determining what tasks the information systems will perform
- Measuring the expected volume of activity to be performed
- Predicting the required capacity (and network topology, and so forth)
- Building and developing the system

- Monitoring changing expectations as users become used to the new computer-assisted tasks
- Monitoring evolving behavior and attitudes that result in unpredicted use of the available computing platforms
- Measuring the increase in unpredicted use and, if necessary, controlling demand
- Changing the available installed capacity on the basis of a statistical understanding of users' desires, tempered by what the enterprise can afford and perhaps demonstrable returns on investment

Here we must repeat our disclaimer at the beginning of the book: We are not attempting to assert "correctness" in diagrams such as Figure 8.4. Much systematic research remains to be done to extract, test, and correct appropriate hypotheses from such proposed explanations. This diagram and others like it give a stylized representation of our experiences and some of the factors we believe to explain those experiences. In reality, it will probably take far more sophisticated models to explain the mechanisms behind our observation that current use of computer applications affects demand for computer applications in the future.

We believe two other factors influence the effect of feedback from current computer use on subsequent demand. At the moment we do not have the data to support this belief, but we suspect these factors will provide useful research ideas:

- Users of computer-supported applications need some "critical mass" of computer experience before they start demanding more applications[3]. (Indeed, below a certain critical mass, individuals may well feel intimidated because they do not understand what is possible or they lack familiarity with an appropriate computing culture; in such a case there is no feedback.)
- The more flexible a computing environment, and the greater the ease of use, the more likely is it that users will invent new applications for the technology and contribute positive feedback in the loop.

Very few applications today can be considered "pure" in the sense that they do not need to share resources with other applications. A shared part of an application can be considered infrastructure.

---

3 By way of analogy, in epidemiological theory a certain threshold of susceptibles and a minimum level of infectiousness in individuals is required for an epidemic. (For a more technical description of this, see Bailey 1957.) An alternative approach to the idea of critical mass is presented in Rogers (1989), in which the author asserts, "Interactivity is one reason why a 'critical mass' of individuals usually must occur before the rate of adoption of an interactive technology takes off into rapid growth".

It is major technical challenge to identify and implement an appropriate infrastructure and keep it up to date. At the outset, for example, there is an economic requirement that the cost of building an infrastructure component must be less than the savings from not providing equivalent functionality in all the applications that would share the component.

Identifying candidate infrastructure components involves a degree of application component generalization. It is often the responsibility of some kind of methods and tools group, who find it easy to be enthusiastic about the technical merits of a proposed tool and to believe that many applications should want to use it. What may not be so easy is obtaining the necessary agreements and mutual commitments to support the tool.

What is certain is that most enterprises that have allowed individual departments to build their own infrastructures will find that the same logical component has in many cases been implemented in different ways, which is wasteful. A common infrastructure avoids waste and duplication and so building one creates the potential for substantial savings.

Many applications have several possible, and correct, ways to achieve similar results, but there may be no simple way to select among the available options. Put another way, ten programmers working on a well-defined algorithm are likely to produce ten correct solutions, all of which may be acceptable according to predetermined performance criteria. How does one choose among them?

The answer lies in management owning the problem so that only one solution is produced that will satisfy the needs of all applications requiring the same functionality. For example, most enterprises do not commission their own printing machines for output (of course, there are some very special exceptions), but rather adapt to standard machines available on the market. Once management chooses a solution, it still faces the technical challenge of deciding what functionality is common to several applications and what is particular to each.

An enterprise strategy may well be to meet as many application needs as possible from infrastructure components. Figure 8.5 shows an increase in applications requirements being met from infrastructure components and a decrease in those being met from application components.

Figure 8.5 Application and Infrastructure Balance

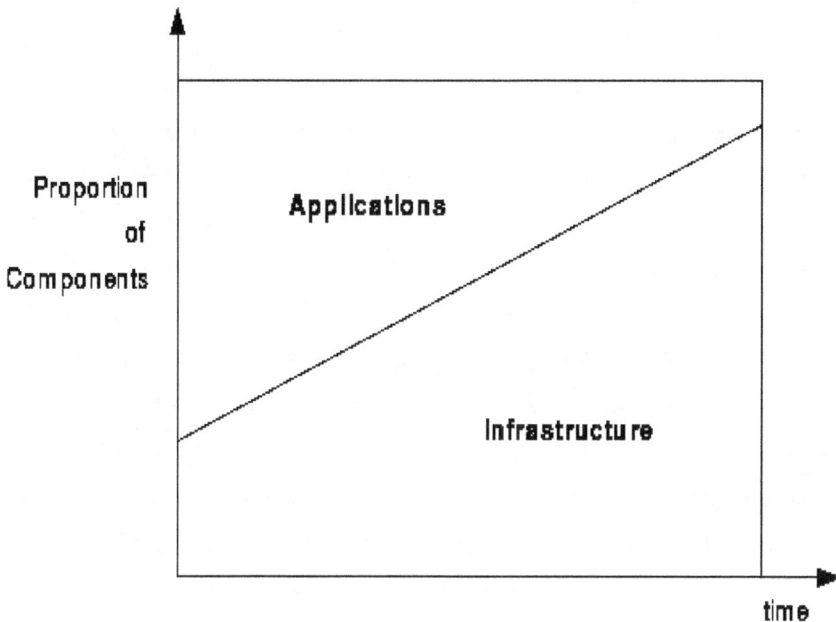

Interpersonal Communication Challenges

Different groups in an enterprise use different "languages", which lead to some difficult communication problems. These problems should not be underestimated.

Within the context of information technology are at least four likely subcultures, each using different terms and language in their work:

- Business managers in the enterprise, the people responsible for defining and controlling the overall direction of the enterprise
- Department managers, who are responsible for the performance of a particular business department
- IT-oriented people, who are responsible for the selection and implementation of a computing platform and the implementation of the many computer applications supporting the enterprise
- System development people, who build or implement the specific hardware and software solutions that make up the available computing platform

Business managers talk in terms of mission, objectives, strategies, business goals, financial targets, market opportunities, product mix, competitors, profitability, return on investment, government regulations, and so on. Department managers talk in terms of their area of responsibility and sometimes their expertise. The department managers' views and concerns are a subset of the business managers', but they are more deeply involved with departmental needs. The manager of finance sees the enterprise differently from the manager of engineering, who in turn sees the enterprise differently from the manager of sales. All of them use terms specific to their departments and subcultures.

On the technical side, IT people talk about information systems, computer platforms, development methods, operational systems, computing strategies, application portfolios, databases, human interfaces, project management, packages, and so on. System developers use concepts such as programming languages, database management systems, peripherals, structured or object-oriented techniques, CASE tools, transaction processing systems, expert systems, windowing, and backups.

The consequences of these different languages, and the cultural gaps they represent, are sometimes very serious. An enterprise must therefore have enough "interpreters" to translate. Consider this simple scenario.

Business and IT people meet with software developers to discuss a new information system. The developers say their method for developing software is a life cycle to ensure the quality of the final product. They have selected the phases of the method and the sign-off procedures after examining many methods available, and they feel they have chosen the best. The resulting software will represent what the business and IT people really want. In fact the IT and business managers approved the idea of a single method, so that all information systems will be developed in the same way and that problems of duplication and inconsistency will be substantially reduced, if not actually eliminated.

During the discussion the developers use various explanatory techniques, such as data flow diagrams and data modeling, because they say these techniques ensure that the business people really understand what the required system must do. The business people are not comfortable about some of the techniques, because they are not sure about the correspondence between what they want and the way the information is represented. Anyhow, the developers are the technical people, so they must know what they are talking about, and the business people go along with it.

Eventually, something is agreed upon and written into some kind of specification. If the business people have not already done it, they now choose someone to represent them who works with the developers while the system is being built. The system, for example order processing, goes through the phases outlined in the developers' life cycle, and the software is ready and available for installation and use.

After the system has been in use for some time, the auditors have a look at it. They ask, "How do you know that all the orders received have actually been processed and either accepted or rejected?". The answer comes back that the system performs a validation of the customer and a technical validation of the contents of the order. However, that is not what the auditors were asking. They want to know how the system records the number of orders that have been received and how the orders are dealt with.

In this way the business people discover that the system has no facility for basic controls over the total number of transactions received by the enterprise, and that it will only operate on orders entered into the system; there is no way the post room or the telephone operators can tell it how many orders have been received and should be accounted for.

What has gone wrong? The business people complain that the delivered system does not do what it should; the developers say they only built what they were asked to build and that, in any case, the requirements had been too vague for them to know what was actually wanted in the first place. The business people also complain that despite the new development method, the fundamental problems of duplicated effort and inconsistency still remain.

There are some valuable lessons to be learned from this kind of situation, which is not atypical of many enterprises:

- The business people and the developers operate with different languages and on very different levels of abstraction. By definition, until the software has been produced, several possible ways of producing it remain. It is unreasonable to expect business people to specify how a solution should be produced—they are the customer, after all, relying on professionals to help them.
- The developers receive a set of incomplete requirements, and they know they are incomplete because many questions remain to be answered before they can write all the software.

- The developers say they have defined the customer file several ways, because that was the specification; if the business people had wanted a completely uniform and cross-functional database of customers, then that is what the specification should have been for. The business people need to go back and make the necessary decisions and commitments to define, build, and use a consistent database.
- The method chosen by the developers followed a traditional life cycle, which did not allow for the specification to evolve as its incompleteness became clear. The developers need to go back and select a method that will allow a flexible approach to evolving and implementing a set of requirements.
- At the beginning of the project, the business people assumed that the developers would automatically include a set of appropriate data processing controls for the transactions, and the developers assumed that what was not in the specification was not needed. Neither talked to the auditors.

IT strategy can give rise to another source of language difficulty. Business people talk of IT providing them with a strategic competitive advantage. They want information in the form they need it, when they need it. They want flexible information systems so that when they decide to change the structure of the enterprise, they can adjust the information systems to provide support without waiting three years. They want accurate cost-benefit studies that will show their IT investment's contribution to the bottom line or its effects on their overall cost structures.

Technical people, on the other hand, talk of an IT strategy in terms of relational databases, UNIX, windowing, PCs connected to mainframes, peer-to-peer networks, and CASE or SQL. They are technologically enthusiastic, but often cannot bridge the gap and explain the relevance of strategic proposals in business terms.

The challenge of interpersonal communication is at the heart of all the other information management challenges.

Cultural Challenges

There are several dimensions to the challenge of dealing with the different cultures that use information and information technology. Table 8.1 summarizes several[4]. It is easy to underestimate the importance of these different cultures, but in fact their effects can be profound.

4 Darnton and Teichroew (1992) present a much more substantial discussion of these points.

Table 8.1 Cultural Challenge Dimensions

Dimension	Issues
Reasons for producing systems	For sale as a product, for use in part of another product, for sale in support of the sale of other products, for enterprise use, under contract to deliver working software, part of research, in furtherance of an occupation
Reasons for using systems	Management, operations, leisure, education, research
Application domain	MIS-type systems, expert systems, process control, office environments, government and administration, embedded systems, manufacturing
Computing cultures	Big "MIS" shop, UNIX world, single user, individual programmer, scientific and engineering programming, software and hardware product production, artificial intelligence, computer and software product engineering departments, system integration
Style of system acquisition	Traditional life cycle, prototyping, incremental development, subcontracting, outsourcing, resource box
Information users	Computer literate, no computer experience, libraries, external reports, computer terminals, workstations with windows
Level of aggregation	Information use at different levels: individual, team, department, enterprise

In some cases we see the effects of "culture collisions", which are now happening with greater frequency as enterprises attempt greater integration of disparate systems. For example, those involved with software development methods see the explicit culture collision represented by "real-time extension" to more traditional methods; those who dealt previously with mainly structured data are now having to learn to handle unstructured information and knowledge.

People Management Challenges

Hierarchies are flattening. The role of middle management is changing such that managers must now lead teams and add value to the tasks being performed. The role of senior management is also changing, such that high-level executives must lead the development of the vision of the enterprise, be able to coach others to pursue the enterprise mission and achieve its objectives, and make major adjustments to the enterprise as the environment changes whilst keeping a high degree of awareness and sensitivity to the implementation issues as they affect people. There is increasing utilization of knowledge. IT is replacing some jobs and enhancing the skill level of others. The role of the employee is changing such that individuals are taking on increased responsibility for the assets of the enterprise, including information.

It is essential to avoid the information pollution that is affecting more and more people in modern enterprises. A flattened hierarchy makes information much more available and thus promotes information pollution. However, in such an environment IT can provide information filters that support people and prevent them from having to deal with more information than they need to do their jobs. Conversely, IT can amplify policies and decisions; we have demonstrated how this can present both opportunities and threats. Greater education on the value of information will enable people to be more self-regulating about the information they seek and disseminate.

Devolving responsibility and decision making, by definition, are making people more responsible. IT can provide the infrastructure that will give them the confidence they need to take on more responsibility, precisely because more information is available that is relevant to the tasks they must perform.

People must be encouraged to share information rather than try to keep hold of it. There is a shift from obtaining power by controlling information, to obtaining power by providing it. Information should be provided in an organized way, in order to help avoid increasing potential problems of information pollution.

Job descriptions and rewards systems should be adjusted to meet the challenges of organizational management. Without such adjustments, effective management by objectives and tasks will be more difficult. Organizational structures will generally need to be redesigned to take advantage of IT.

Knowledge can be organized into the ultimate network: expensive to create, cheap and fast to use, accessible from any point at any time, valuable in geometric relation to the number of its parts . . . The greatest challenge for the manager of intellectual capital is to create an organization that can share the knowledge. (Stewart 1991)

Increasingly, managers must lead not primarily by authority but by their personal skills and value added. This necessity is blurring some of the distinctions between managers, consultants, and employees.

The trends we have described pose substantial challenges for people management regarding role definitions, patterns of authority, reward systems, information utilization, and enterprise organization. These challenges will lead to major changes in the role of human resources departments.

Directional Challenges

The critical directional challenge lies in the enterprise choosing a vision for the future—a desired future state—and then deciding how to achieve it. This challenge confronts the enterprise at the macro level as well as at the level of its constituent parts. Once the enterprise chooses its vision of where it wants to be at a certain time in the future, it must choose among its many present options in deciding how to get there.

The further away the enterprise is from its vision, the more choices it has. As it makes choices and obtains feedback about their consequences, it narrows its focus to those most likely to be successful. The process of reaching a desired state is often discontinuous, as shown in Figure 8.6, and punctuated by alternating periods of slow and rapid change. Rarely does it move continuously, at a constant rate.

Three ways information systems and IT can help an enterprise meet some of these directional challenges are particularly important:

1. Information is necessary to determine and qualify possible visions and desired states, and to choose between alternatives.
2. Strategies to achieve a vision need monitoring against the criteria established for recognizing the vision.
3. Once a vision or desired state is selected and strategies are in place to achieve it, continued monitoring of the validity of the choices is necessary; many changes could occur that invalidate the vision or the strategies, and information is needed to provide feedback and, if necessary, make corrections in the vision and movement toward it.

194

Figure 8.6 Steps from Current to Desired State

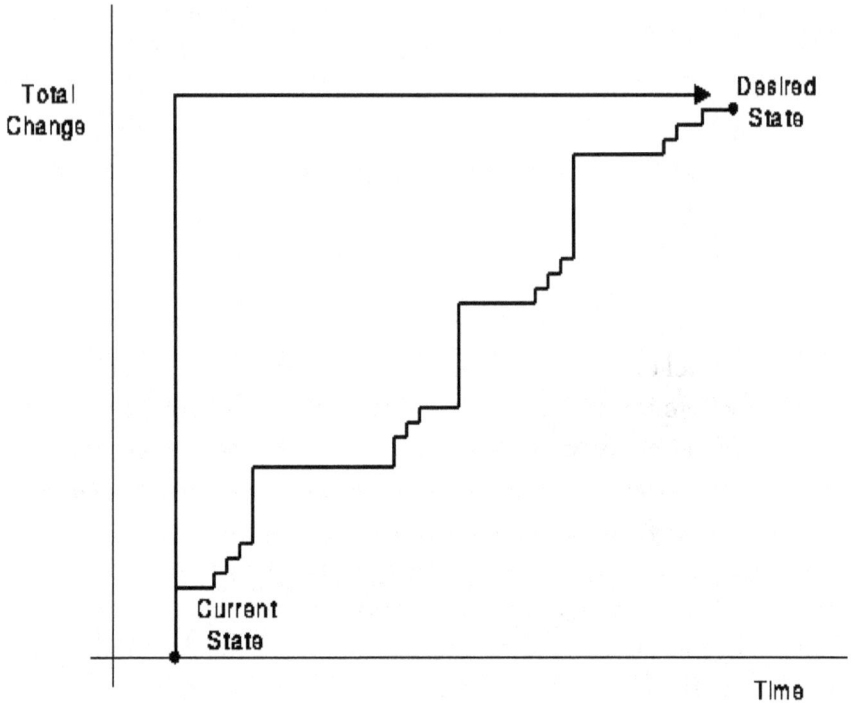

Evolving Roles of the IS Department

IT use can be organized in many ways, and the terms used to describe the organization can be confusing because they refer sometimes to the IT activity and other times to the *business department* responsible for it. These terms include "DP", "EDP", "ADP", "IS", and "systems".

When we talk about an information services (IS) department we mean that part of the enterprise that is chartered with particular responsibility for providing some enterprise-wide information or IT-based services. Since this is clearly not a book on IS organization, we will not attempt any comprehensive study of it; instead, we will draw a broad sketch of some of the problems confronting IS, particularly problems of information management. The IS department has evolved a great deal and will continue to do so.

Originally, price-performance ratios and the absolute cost of computers meant that they could be used only for limited, dedicated operations. There was no possibility of creating an "information integrated enterprise". IT was not advanced enough to handle the huge volumes of information actually used, and more traditional forms of organization were used to aggregate, interpret, and act on the limited information available. Aggregating information was essentially a manual task, highly skilled and hence expensive. In this scenario IT provided automated support to a narrow range of applications sharply divided between the commercial, technical, and scientific. Very different computing cultures developed for these application domains, and even today people talk about commercial and real-time systems as though there is still a meaningful distinction.

In the past computers supported many independent requirements, the most important to the enterprise as a whole being an accounting system (typically owned by the finance department) or an early version of a management information system. This is shown in Figure 8.7. More departments acquired IT-based solutions in response to point problems and budgets they could negotiate to fund the IT acquisitions. Today strong, independent departments in some enterprises may still acquire their own IT, including department-owned and -operated networks.

Figure 8.7 Traditional Responsibility for DP

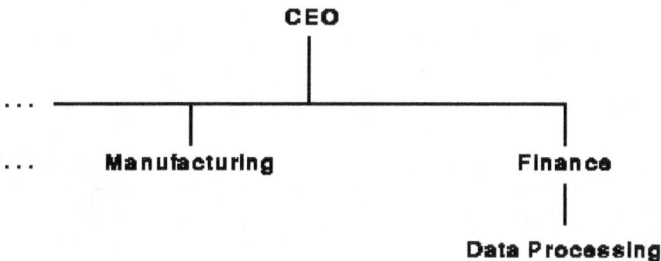

Once the finance department owns a centralized DP operation other departments usually follow, acquiring their own systems in an uncoordinated fashion. To repeat a point we made earlier, if the enterprise has 20 different business departments, all of which have some direct contact with customers, there should be no surprise that there will exist at least 20 different definitions of a customer!

As IT proliferates, top-level management eventually becomes aware of the pervasive uses. This realization usually comes about not through technical observation, but by observing the rapid growth in IT-driven budgets. It may also result from the volume of articles in the business literature about the potential benefits from IT, which makes members of the board ask what is being done about it. Thus the systems organization or information services (IS) is born. It then receives equal status at the top of an enterprise's organizational chart. This chart is shown in Figure 8.8.

Figure 8.8 IS Department

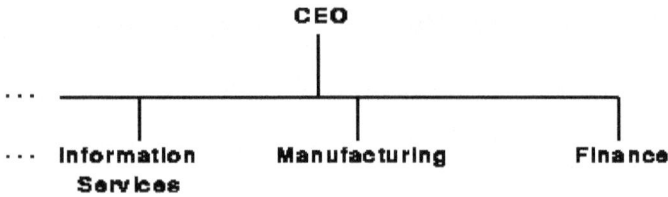

```
                              CEO
                               |
  ...   _____
  ...   |                      |                           |
     Information          Manufacturing                 Finance
      Services
```

The IS Department performs the functions depicted in Figure 8.9. It carries out system development projects on behalf of different business departments; builds and manages a common operational platform and infrastructure; and maintains and supports the common computing infrastructure and the departmental applications. Other groups using computers receive services from IS such as computer and software supply negotiation, maintenance contracts, updating, and perhaps some training. This is where many enterprises are today.

Figure 8.9 IS Department Responsibilities

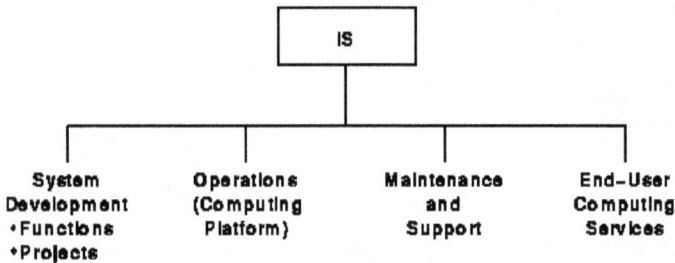

```
                        _____
                       |   IS   |
                       |_____|
                           |
   _____
   |               |                 |                    |
 System        Operations        Maintenance          End-User
Development    (Computing            and              Computing
•Functions      Platform)          Support             Services
•Projects
```

There are some inherent problems with this very common approach to managing IT. Perhaps the two greatest are these:

- The IS department essentially grew out of *technological* need; overall enterprise *information needs* are still not addressed properly.
- In order to provide a cross-company service, IS must have mechanisms for consultation with other departments— ownership of cross-functional integration is still defined according to the structure of the enterprise.

As IS departments begin to realize that there is no overall enterprise view of information needs independent of organizational structure, they start offering data management and some kind of enterprise modeling service, as shown in Figure 8.10.

Figure 8.10 Extended IS Departrment

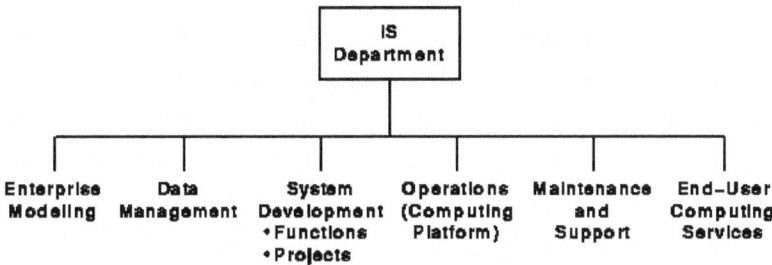

However, the combination of overall information management and management of traditional IS is made less effective by the persistent perception of IS managers as technically oriented. Some enterprises have tried to remedy this defect by appointing chief information officers (CIOs) with nontechnical backgrounds, but the success of this depends on the extent to which the CIO's responsibilities include non-IT information needs and the amount of co-sponsorship they receive from other departments and top enterprise management. Very few prospective managers can combine information management and traditional IS effectively, because as we have said before, *the information needs of an enterprise are far more extensive than just its IT-based activities.*

It may be better to combine information management with the quality assurance or human resources department, or perhaps organization and methods. After all, information management has nothing to do with computers apart from the support computers can provide for some aspects of the enterprise's information needs. To put this another way, we did not see business departments set up for filing cabincts or other information processing devices.

In our experience combining information and computer infrastructure management is counterproductive. The job of IS manager has one of the highest turnover rates. If there is a problem with profit and loss responsibilities, it is the business unit manager who is responsible, not the chief finance officer (CFO). If there is a people quality problem, it is first the line manager, not the human resources manager who has responsibility. Yet, if there is a problem with information, it is the IS manager who is fired, who is responsible first!

198

The second major problem was how to bridge the IS department and the users in the other departments. Traditionally, this has been resolved in the past by creating structures like account managers, portfolio managers, business IS groups[5]. This still does not ensure a truly cross-company view of the information flows in the enterprise, or true ownership of the solutions by the actual users. The bridging structures still refer back to the organization of the enterprise, which means a finance IS manager or portfolio manager or account manager, and the same for marketing, engineering, and so on. Systems and solutions remain locked into a stove-piped organizational and departmental structure.

It bears repeating that an enterprise must look at its information flows and business processes independently of its automated systems[6]—even though almost every process has some automated support. True cross-functional activities are an absolute necessity in meeting the challenges of information management, and developing them should be technology-independent. That is, the initial analysis should ignore the technology platform, and then further analysis should determine how technology fits into the overall plan.

IS managers have always tried to cast the problem of creating cross-functional activities in a technical light. For this they have often been accused of being empire builders, separated from the business and centralized. In fairness, if the system does not work, it is usually because the business processes have not been adjusted or information does not flow properly. In most enterprises there is no single person responsible for the overall information problem except the IS manager, who tries to do something—but from a technological perspective and with technological resources. Data management activities within an IS department also focus on computerized systems and often do not address overall enterprise information needs.

Historically, the computerized parts of the enterprise do not represent a systematic cross-functional computerization but more an arbitrary, piecemeal automation that depends on technological feasibility, negotiated budgets, and technological prejudices.

Figure 8.11 is a schematic diagram illustrating the many business processes, and information flows between them, at the enterprise level.

5 See, for example, McFarlan (1981) and Cash (1983) for a more detailed discussion of portfolio management related to overall risk management.
6 Savage (1990) has substantial ideas and advice on this.

Some processes (or a very partial departmental view of a process) have been automated, and if technologically and organizationally feasible, some of these "islands of automation" have been linked together, usually by feeders. Even so, integration of these islands of automation and their feeders to provide a complete enterprise-wide view of business processes still requires significant manual (or, rather, non-automated) effort.

Figure 8.11 Business and Automated Processes

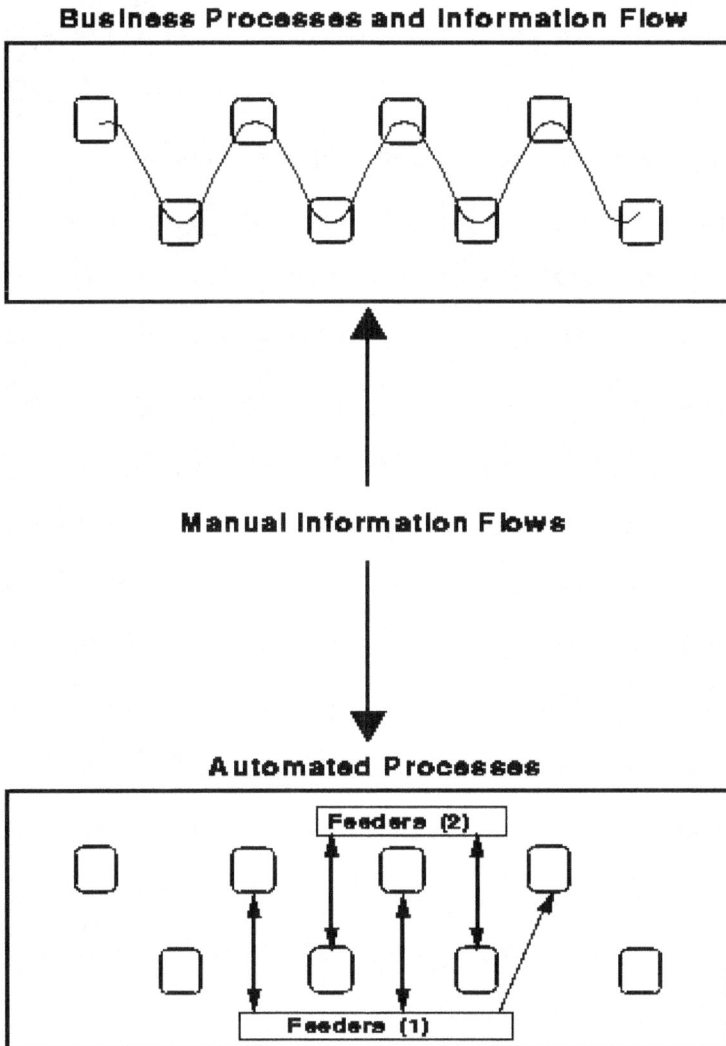

Information Management—Roles and Responsibilities

The previous discussion showed clear roles emerging for the IS department, and some of these have to do with maintaining, developing, and owning infrastructure. However, it must be decided if IS will be the actual provider of these services to the rest of the enterprise or if it will buy them from third parties. The fact that IS is responsible for the total infrastructure does not necessarily mean that it must carry out itself all the work that responsibility entails. Indeed, more and more enterprises now subcontract their network and operations to outside vendors[7].

Given that the infrastructure is company-wide and that IS owns the IT infrastructure, the question remains, who owns the non-IT related part of the information infrastructure? We believe that a counterpart to IT is needed—a unit of the enterprise that claims ownership of its non-IT infrastructure components. At one time O&M (organization and methods) held the responsibility, but this department seems to have almost disappeared over the past 30 years[8]. Then IS took over, but neglected to do some of the basic work the O&M people had done. This was partly because, being technology-oriented, IS tended to treat non-computer problems of analysis less thoroughly that it did computer problems, and partly because no one now truly owned the problems.

Information is emerging as a major asset for many enterprises[9]. What is not yet clear, though, is how it should be managed and what the roles and responsibilities of its managers will be. This is a major information management challenge.

Perhaps a couple of analogies are in order. The chief financial officer (CFO) is responsible for the accounting and financial policies of a company, but does not own all the profit and loss. Similarly, the human resources manager is responsible for personnel policies and procedures, but the line managers manage the people.

In many financial departments someone writes the financial and

---

7 Krass (1990) discusses some of the financial reasons for this kind of subcontracting.
8 Norton (1989) asks "Whatever Happened to the Systems Approach?" as his title and presents an interesting history of what he terms the systems approach. This is a useful high-level discussion, but we would add to it the history of systems thinking, lines of investigation represented by authors such as Ashby, Beer, von Bertalanffy, and Checkland.
9 Clemons (1991), in discussing American Airlines Sabre reservation system (one of the most widely cited examples of IT providing a competitive advantage), states: "Wall Street placed a value of $1.5 billion on Sabre—at a time when the market capitalization of AMR [American's parent] itself was only $2.9 billion. . . . and its [Sabre's] market value had become greater than that of the airline's core business".)

accounting rules—there is even a certified set of accounts—but every cost center manager or business manager is responsible for profit and loss (P&L). In personnel, there is a certain number of company policies, but it is the line manager who has responsibility for development and hiring.

The question then becomes, who writes the rules for the proper management of information? The IS manager has been trying to perform this role without a clear charter, and this has been the source of conflict for the last ten to twenty years.

Given the vast difference in tasks, skills, span of control, and issues between IT and non-IT information management, we believe the job is more than one person can handle. We see two very different roles—IT and non-IT—that should be performed separately by two people. From the enterprise point of view, this means a senior executive responsible for the information strategy and the business architecture and an IT manager responsible for the IT strategy and infrastructure. If these two people share the same goals, they have a much greater chance of driving their messages to other departments.

If the enterprise chooses to keep both roles in the hands of one person, it should establish an information management and technology (IM&T) executive position, which is much like that of CIO (Synott 1981, 1987)[10]. However, the CIO position has raised controversy in many enterprises and in most cases has been reduced to that of IT executive. The enterprise should be aware that the IM&T executive may well meet the same fate.

Let us return to the cash and people analogies. As shown in Figure 8.12, the CFO typically has central authority over accounting services, treasury and tax, and business unit finance.

Figure 8.12 CFO Responsibilities

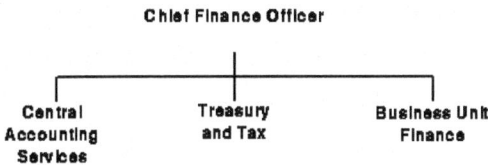

Chief Finance Officer

| Central Accounting Services | Treasury and Tax | Business Unit Finance |

As shown in Figure 8.13, the human resources executive typically controls central personnel services, compensation and benefits, and

---

10 Although Synott's (1981, 1987) exposition of the role is a useful consideration of general information issues, he places it firmly in the IT space by asserting "The final challenge for CIOs is to make a bid for the top slot by demonstrating the kind of leadership and ability that brings information technology into the mainstream of business. . . .

business unit support. The roles and responsibilities in both Figures 8.12 and 8.13 have been expressed as central services, policy determination and management, and services to business units. "Business units" does not necessarily mean traditional business departments, but can be units set up for specific tasks or to handle key business functions.

Figure 8.13 HRE Responsibilities

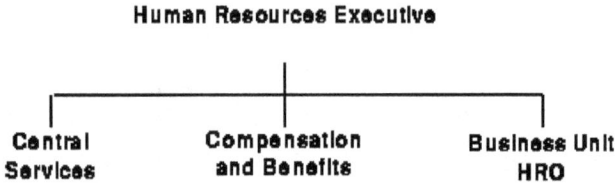

Human Resources Executive

Central Services	Compensation and Benefits	Business Unit HRO

By analogy with cash and people, if information is an enterprise asset, its central services include infrastructure services and systems development (both of which can be outsourced, of course); its policy determination and management might be an Enterprise Information Management model; and its services to business units are the information systems that support their activities. Together, these make up the structure shown in Figure 8.14.

Figure 8.14 IM&T Executive Responsibilities

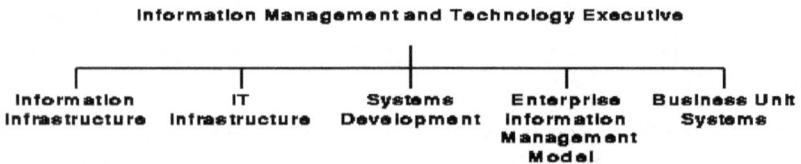

Information Management and Technology Executive

Information Infrastructure	IT Infrastructure	Systems Development	Enterprise Information Management Model	Business Unit Systems

Each business department should be both an information provider and an information consumer. This implies implementing the right procedures for managing information according to company policy, just as it is responsible for the correct use of other enterprise assets such as cash, people, and facilities. Sometimes this means changes may have to be made in how people work. For example, they must not give away valuable information free of charge but use it to add value within a value network.

Enterprise, Organization, and IT

After analyzing all the different management challenges and their implications for the enterprise, we conclude that every enterprise should take a holistic view and integrate its overall enterprise information needs with its organization, information, technology, and IT. The Enterprise Information Management Model we use works most satisfactorily when they are carefully balanced.

These components interact, producing mutually reinforcing critical success factors. This is shown in Figure 8.15, which makes certain assumptions about IT:

- In any enterprise, certain organizational structures and behaviors are likely to be more supportive of the enterprise than others in meeting its objectives.
- Certain forms of organization are not suitable for certain kinds of enterprise.
- Some enterprises are more likely to succeed with certain uses of IT than with others.
- Some IT is primarily for the support of particular kinds of enterprise.
- Certain forms of organization need the support of certain kinds of IT.
- Certain kinds of IT will only be used effectively with certain organizational forms.

Figure 8.15 Enterprise, Organization, and IT CSFs

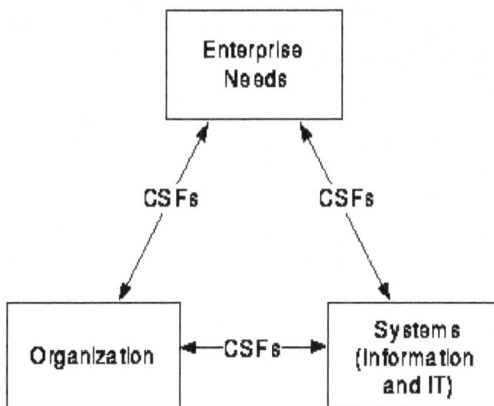

A successful enterprise is one that has achieved the right balance of all components, but if a serious imbalance develops somewhere, the enterprise's achievement of its fundamental goals may be threatened. (This is lightheartedly depicted in Figure 8.16.)

204

Figure 8.16 Enterprise Imbalance

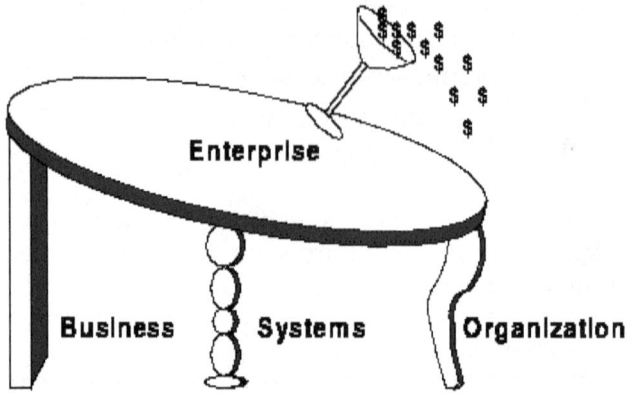

Summary

We have described a broad range of challenges facing people who manage and use information. These challenges range from ethics, objectives, and organization, right through to specific technical challenges related to the operations performed on information.

Various terms are used to designate these many and varied information management challenges; in particular, many people are concerned with information, systems, information systems, architecture, and various other possible combinations of these words. We look more deeply at their various meanings in the next chapter.

Chapter 9

Information, Systems, and Architecture

In this chapter we discuss words such as "information", "system", "architecture", and "infrastructure", exploring some of their deeper meanings—what people are talking about and hoping for when they use them. We also present some key points these words entail that we feel will become increasingly important for information systems in the coming years.

Terminology

There are many books about information systems, but very few attempt to define information in any depth. Very few attempt to analyze what makes a system. Does it matter? In our opinion it matters a great deal. The term "information system" does not use the words "information" or "system" in the same way they are commonly used, but if an information systems text fails to distinguish their special use the reader may not realize this.

We have another reason for a detailed examination of terms. There is much practical insight to be gained for the design and construction of corporate and global information systems. An understanding of the differences between the common and technical meanings of the terms leads to an understanding of the problems that have hindered the successful use of IT.

We have chosen not to single out references to particular books for criticism, because we would rather concentrate on positive comments and references to good books which do help with a deeper understanding of these key terms. We suggest that readers examine books about information systems for reasonable discussions about the meanings of the terms information and system, and come to their own conclusions.

Many excellent texts on information and systems are highly technical, and a few, for good reason, present an underlying mathematical basis. We do not treat mathematically based concepts, but, instead, suggest ways in which the essential concepts can be of value.

Like "information" and "system", "architecture" is a semantically overloaded term in the computing and information science literature. We outline some of its uses and explore an architectural analogy. Ours is more than an academic discussion; taking analogies to the limits—*ad absurdum*—can sometimes lead to very interesting insights. It certainly did for us.

"Strictly speaking, metaphor occurs as often as we take a word out of its original sphere and apply it to new circumstances" (Fowler and Fowler, 1931). In this way, expressions such as "information architecture", "building systems", and "growing applications", are part of a process by which metaphors evolve. Eventually many metaphors become part of ordinary language, but until then, there is no consensus about the metaphorical usage. This is how words become semantically overloaded, at least for a certain period of time. We are in such a period now, seeing great differences in the ways the words "information", "system", and "architecture" are used.

Analogies and Comparisons

Many practices in the development and deployment of information systems are still very young and for that reason are not always well executed. They include:

- Planning an enterprise-wide collection of interrelated and interdependent information systems
- Choosing appropriate models to support analysis, simulation, decision making, and so forth, that can be demonstrated to be "good" representations of the real world
- Matching information systems to management and organization styles
- Coping with continual change
- Identifying and using appropriate engineering skills
- Constructing appropriate organizational units
- Finding the best teams and organizing their work
- Selecting and implementing methods

The skills required to define and implement an Enterprise Information Management Model are not yet mature. Analogies provide a good deal of intuitive assistance, but they can be dangerous even though they may be only partially applicable; they can be used over-zealously well beyond their reasonable scope[1].

In order for an analogy to be useful, one must understand the "essence" of the analog. We focus on "essence" rather than detail.

Many analogies exist for the enterprise-wide planning and deployment of information technology and information systems[2]. As we have seen, architecture is one of the most common. Biology (particularly for the development of changing complex structures) and engineering are also useful. An analogy can be a metaphor or a simile, or some other kind of logical correspondence, or it can be a formal identity such as a homomorphic or isomorphic correspondence (Miller 1955).

People use analogies either because the analogies provide a different level of understanding or because they believe the analogies yield some insight. Users of analogy tend to be optimistic and focus on the similarities. However, systematic application of an analogy may also reveal differences, and these, like the similarities, can be helpful even if the analogy is eventually thrown away[3].

Many people who use analogy may be using their intuition just as much, regardless of any lack of theoretical foundation or empirical data from which to construct scientific models. According to Sorokin (1948):

> "Intuitions, often untranslatable into words or concepts . . . are the foundation of the ultimate postulates and axioms of science, religion, ethics, and the arts. . . . the creators of science, philosophy, religion, and moral codes, as well as the foremost artists and poets, are at the same time discoverers of an aspect of reality hitherto unknown."

Enterprises are highly complex systems, and corporate and global information systems can be considered subsystems within them. Scientific models do not yet exist that will improve the practices of system design we have mentioned. Therefore, we must rely on weaker methods of analysis like analogy and hope that they will lead to homomorphisms and eventually isomorphisms.

The discipline that claims responsibility for the translation of

---

1 In fact, von Bertalanffy (1968) considers analogies "scientifically worthless"; they are "superficial similarities of phenomena which correspond neither in their causal factors nor in their relevant laws". Despite this damning criticism, though, he sees three levels of description of phenomena: first, analogies; second, homologies; and third, explanation. Beer (1984) is more forgiving in his view of analogy. He sees a path from insight through analogy (where conceptual models are formed) and isomorphism (which requires rigorous formulation) to a scientific model.

2 See Teichroew (1989), who discusses briefly several categories of analogy such as biological models, manmade human-based systems, physical systems, and production systems.

3 Indeed, during the evolution of this book out of many papers and ideas over a period of years, we found an architectural analogy, including its dissimilarities, particularly helpful. In some respects the architectural analogy is definitely weakening, but we can still use architecture as a metaphor.

requirements into computer based systems is software engineering, but this discipline also does not yet possess the necessary scientific models to deliver its promises; it remains overly prescriptive and heavily dependent on intuition and inspired designers for its successes.

We have noticed a tendency in management and computing literature to apply "hard" analysis techniques to higher levels of enterprise strategy. These techniques have evolved at the computer-application level within software engineering. What we have yet to see, however, is much effort at the overall enterprise level to deal more systematically with knowledge and rules. Like government decision making, enterprise decision making is notoriously difficult. Robertson et al. (1991) look carefully at the difficulties in constructing simulation models, which attempt to represent parts of the real world, and discuss how to use these models to support decision making. They observe:

> "To operate correctly, this procedure must rely on several fundamental assumptions: 1. The simulation model contains all the appropriate components. 2. The parameters of the model can be measured accurately. 3. The decision makers are aware of any doubts about assumptions 1 and 2 and understand the possible discrepancies which these irregularities could cause. All of these assumptions are likely to be false."

They also state:

> "The nub of the problem is that techniques which work well for clearly defined problems are not well suited to the poorly structured domains of, for example, the environment or macro-economic analysis. In these domains the modellers may not know if their model is correct or reliable and, worse, the decision makers may not know that the modellers don't know."

Robertson et al. propose a set of standards they present as expectations from forms of argument. We see the difficulties in using different models to deal with such very practical questions as "Which is the most suitable form of organization for what we want to do?" or "Which is the best method for solving the kinds of problems we face?".

The legal world offers a set of analogies to help enterprises capture their experience, apply objectives and policies, comply with customs and legislative requirements, and reconcile historical experience with new problems. According to Ashley (1990), "Legal argument is interesting as an example of a highly developed system for reasoning from past experiences, cases, as a supplement to deductive reasoning. By modeling this kind of reasoning in a domain where it is a refined art, one can learn how to approach modeling more informal kinds of reasoning from past experiences in everyday life". Nevertheless, as Ashley points out, the legal domain is harder to model than mathematical domains.

It is clear from all this that the challenge facing the serious enterprise modeler is in assembling a comprehensive toolkit that extends from an understanding of the structured information available to the enterprise, through to simulation and the handling of experience and approaches to problems that may be radically different or inconsistent but all potentially "correct" in some way.

Figure 9.1 presents a very simplified schematic of the progress from idea or intuition to reasoned application of a "scientific" model. It is based on some of the ideas from von Bertalanffy, Beer, and Sorokin, although Beer (1987) offers a different representation.

Analogies and Information Systems

Hints of analogies that have been applied to information systems come from expressions such as "information architecture", "software factory", "information engineering", and "software chip". However, few analogies have been explored in detail as a systematic method for gaining insight into the development of information systems. Shortly we will look at the architecture and biology analogies in more detail and at one of the ways they have been used to illuminate information systems development, but first we look at what production and manufacturing can tell us.

Production and Manufacturing Analogies

Production and manufacturing analogies help clear away the confusion that sometimes surrounds the relative economics of hardware and soft-ware production, particularly the frequent assertion that hardware productivity has increased far more substantially than software productivity (often made in conjunction with the promotion of CASE tools or methods)[4].

Computers are usually mass produced after the basic designs have been committed, but software can be either mass produced (for example, operating systems, word processing, spreadsheet packages, and so forth) or one of a kind (such as a bespoke application for an enterprise).

4 For example, Newport (1986) states: "Since 1970 the processing power of computers per dollar spent on them has risen a remarkable 30% a year on average ... software has not kept up with the stunning improvements in hardware. Software productivity, measured by how quickly developers can churn out useful programs, has increased at only an estimated 4% to 7% annual pace for the past 20 years".

Most general-purpose computer hardware is useless without software, so its use is assisted by software that is also mass produced. Producing computers is still a labor-intensive activity (despite the high level of computer assistance). If, like many applications, computers were designed and built to be one of a kind, the difficulty in comparing hardware and software productivity would perhaps become obvious. Failing that, a manufacturing analogy can certainly help make it more clear.

Figure 9.1 From Idea to Model—The Role of Analogy

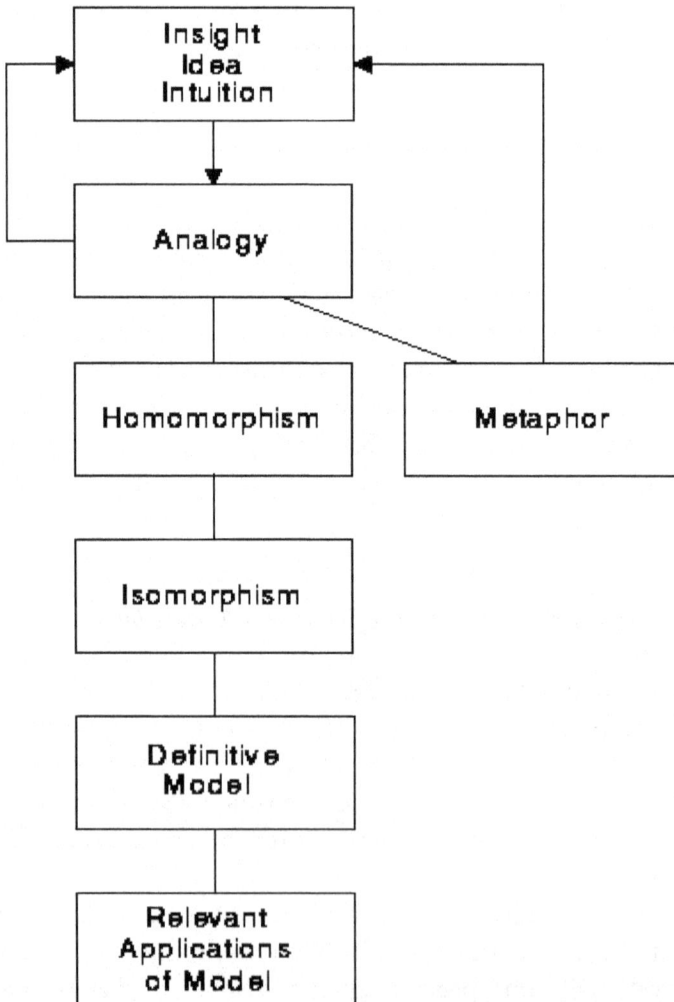

Many kinds of factory are involved in manufacturing processes. Some produce the machine tools used in other factories for the mass production of other products. These tools are one of a kind (or at least the molds and dies used in them may be). True mass production requires that the object produced can be defined precisely, that the manufacturing mechanism can be constructed, and that where necessary the manufactured object can be broken down into a well-defined set of components that can be joined together.

As we shall see, it is by no means clear that a corporate (CIS) or global information system (GIS) can be reduced to a simple set of components. It is likely that parts of a CIS or GIS can be so reduced, and these are the parts most likely to receive computer assistance. We see this in manufacturing, where in the majority of factories people still perform the tasks for which equivalent mechanisms have not yet proved feasible or economical. Since not all manufacturing tasks are automated, by analogy we should not be surprised that not all software production tasks are automated either.

There is a great deal of effort in manufacturing to produce flexible systems. These use flexible machines that can be programmed at short notice to produce different objects or object variants. Flexible systems enable the enterprise to move more rapidly toward just-in-time (JIT) manufacturing. They create savings from substantially reduced inventory levels and reduce the risk of obsolete stock or products. Beyond JIT, we are seeing the emergence of mass customization, resulting from the ability to change some aspect of manufacturing at very short notice. This is the direction car companies are taking when they accept many orders that include options; the assembly lines can produce the options along with regular production on a "mass" scale.

A common software product can be mass produced, but, as in manufacturing, mass software customization is not yet a common reality. So when we talk about a software factory, we need to be sure what we mean. Table 9.1 lists some factory scenarios and how they apply to software production.

Table 9.1 Software Factory

Factory Output	*Software Equivalent*
Specialized one-of-a kind machine tools or product	Tailor-made, bespoke information systems
Low-volume, small batches of output	Software for use in a limited number of installations
Mass-produced product	Software used in many installations
Mass customization	Software libraries, components, and infrastructure available for the rapid generation of new software applications

There is one particularly serious flaw in the manufacturing analogy;

it has to do with responsibility for producing the factory output. Few enterprises construct their own factories to produce the components they need, whereas many construct development departments to produce their software. Presumably, this is because the present software industry is immature and therefore unable to generate sufficient, appropriate mass-produced output. It is also because few enterprises can mass customize software. As with most forms of manufacturing, commissioning one-of-a-kind products is generally very expensive.

Mass customization implies programmable, flexible manufacturing processes and well-defined templates or choices of available options. It also requires a flexible, skillful, and well-informed workforce. All of this could be achieved for software by the development of a large number of components suitable for different problems (such as functionality, low volume, high volume, different computing cultures, different end-user cultures). Some progress has been made in this direction, although mostly in software cultures that employ machine control systems and embedded software.

Very-high-level languages (VHLLs) will help promote software mass customization. With VHLLs an application domain is expressed in a particular structured language, and the available language constructs can be implemented with existing software components that have well-defined interfaces. However, just as there are limits to the possibility for flexibility in manufacturing systems because of differences in required product, there are also limits to VHLLs because of the different problems to be solved and the different cultural environments in which the software must operate.

A VLSI and CAD/CAM Analogy

Consider a software chip: could it be produced in the same way as a hardware chip? CAD/CAM techniques and methods for the design of VLSI (Very-large-scale integration) chips use techniques whereby a graphical representation of requirements can be used as a powerful stage in the production of an actual usable object. With enough precision, software can be developed in a similar way with graphical tools, the output from which can be used to generate programs. Efforts are under way to define the graphical conventions needed to make this approach effective.

As with other analogies, the VLSI analogy is not without problems. At the present time flowcharting and other graphical analysis techniques for software development provide very poor software abstractions[5] According to Brooks (1986), "The VLSI analogy is fundamentally misleading—a chip design is a layered two-dimensional object whose geometry reflects its essence. A software system is not". A VLSI chip results from reducing a very well defined problem to a series of electrical states handled by materials in simple well-defined ways. Most realistic information system requirements cannot be reduced to such simple models.

As an analog to the construction of information systems, VLSI suggests a definition of an information VLSI component as ". . . providing a precise component with an exact function between outputs and inputs and known behavioral characteristics".

Information

Let us explore the uses of the word "information"[6],

Murdick and Munson (1986) say, "Information (in behavioral science) is a sign or set of signs that predispose a person to action. It is distinguished from data, because data are not stimuli to action but merely strings of characters or uninterrupted patterns". According to Davis and Olson (1984), "Information is data that has been processed into a form that is meaningful to the recipient and is of real or perceived value in current or prospective actions or decisions".

Blokdijk and Blokdijk (1987) quote Starreveld's definition of information as "what reaches man's consciousness and contributes to his knowledge", and they see in it two major aspects: "*communication* (reaching the consciousness) and *knowledge.*"

Beer's (1979) definition is more straightforward: "Information: That which changes us. Noise becomes data—when the fact in it is recognized. Data become information—when the fact in them is susceptible to action. How can I possibly know that I am informed?— Only because I have changed my state".

5 Brooks (1986) has an interesting discussion on the problems of the VLSI analogy and software abstractions. The physical characteristics of a chip are amenable to a layered two-dimensional description, but the prior analysis problem is n-dimensional when the semantics and properties of proposed configurations are taken into account.
6 Up to the sixteenth century there were two rather different interpretations of the verb "inform": to describe objects that do not have any particular form, and to impart facts or learning to someone else (its standard interpretation today). In common usage "information" refers to combinations of facts and experience either communicated between two or more people or formed within one person. There are more specialized uses—for example, legal, in the sense of "laying information", and biological, in the sense of genetic code information.

Shannon (1948), in the context of a much more technical definition, says "... the information value of a symbol should be greater the less likely it is ...".

Information appears to be one of those concepts everyone understands initially; it is a metaphor that has passed into ordinary language. As with many words, a precise definition that also conveys the richness of the network of meaning is elusive. Indeed, the *Encyclopedia Britannica Yearbook of Science and the Future*, 1990, concludes: "information phenomena permeate the physical and mental world, and their variety is such that it has defied so far all attempts at a unified definition of information".

Here we offer our definition of information: Information is a meaningful description of something real or abstract, the perception or recognition of which is an event able to trigger some action or decision, or change the way further information is understood or acted upon.

Incorporated in the design of corporate and global information systems must be the recognition that enterprises and organizations do not perceive information; their *people* do, or in some cases their *machines* distinguish a particular state. People or machines act and decide, and the misleading metaphor of an "enterprise" decision can mask the need to consider the psychology and attitudes of the people perceiving the information or the real capability of machines to respond accurately to certain states.

It is difficult to discuss information without reference to communications. The close connection between the two appears in Figure 9.2, presented as a derivative of a model proposed by Shannon (1948)[7].

> *Information is a meaningful description of something real or abstract, the perception or recognition of which is an event able to trigger some action or decision, or change the way further information is understood or acted upon.*

---

7 Shannon as well as Weaver (1949) and Hall (1989) present mathematical explanations of information theory.

Figure 9.2 Ideas, Meaning, and Communication

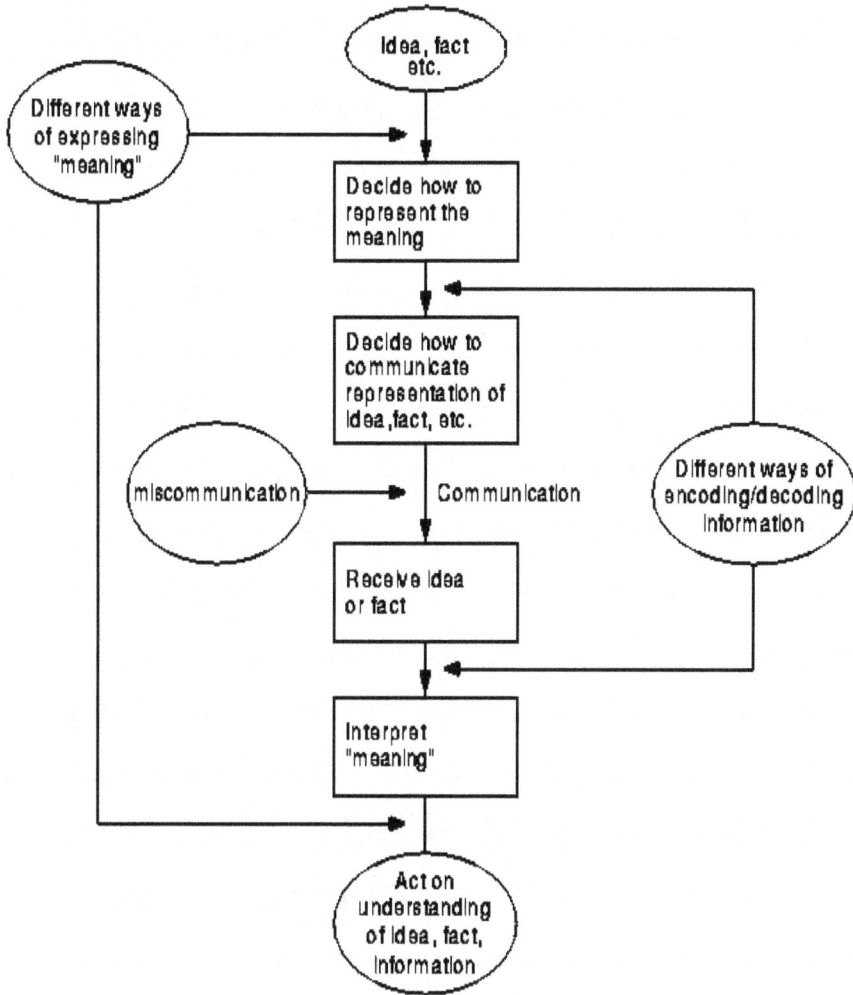

Information has various sources that may be internal or external to an enterprise. A global or corporate information system must be able to recognize and respond to information from appropriate sources and then make it transmittable. It must also extract the information's "meaningfulness" and put it into suitable form. For example, a message presented in French or English or as a graphical image will be encoded in one of several possible ways. It will then be transmitted—perhaps electrically, via optical fiber, or by voice—according to some protocol for transmission and reception. Once received, the message will be decoded, its meaning extracted, and then, usually, some action will be performed as a result.

216

It is time to explore the importance of information theory to CISs and GISs. However, this exploration will not be at the level of individual communications channels within an enterprise, or between computers (this is really the domain of Shannon and Weaver's original work), but rather at the system level, in keeping with our belief that there can be no discussion of the theory of information without reference to systems. To some extent we are using this fundamental view of communications as an analogy, with a glimmer of homomorphism on the horizon.

System

The *Shorter Oxford English Dictionary on Historical Principles* (1933) lists several meanings for the word "system". The first is "an organized or connected group of objects", which corresponds well with common usage.

In recent years "system" has been used in more scientific ways, perhaps the most extensively in the relatively young discipline known as general systems theory. However, its formal use is probably most developed in thermodynamics[8]; indeed, Lee and Sears (1962) point out that two fundamental laws of thermodynamics have been applied extensively to phenomena outside the discipline itself: "Communications, information theory, and even certain biological processes are examples of the broad areas in which the thermodynamic mode of reasoning is applicable".

The investigation of biological and other systems has contributed extensions to the basic system concepts of thermodynamics[9]. Together

8 According to Lee and Sears (1962), "the term *system* as used in thermodynamics refers to a definite quantity of matter bounded by some closed surface which is impervious to the flow of matter". They also introduce some more fundamental concepts of a system:
- A boundary—the closed surface referred to above
- A control surface—a boundary to a control volume across which matter may flow. This is the concept of an open system.
- The state of a system—the system condition usually identified by quantitative properties
- Extensive properties—those that make the total system value equal to the sum of the values of the parts of the system
- Intensive properties—those that do not make the total system value equal to the sum of the values of the parts of the system
- Specific value—a value obtained by a system property
- Process—what the system undergoes when any system property changes (the system state changes)
- Equilibrium—the state in which there are no changes taking place in a system
- Measurement—definitions of the different ways of measuring system state
- Equations of state—those describing relations between system properties

9 The key extensions:
- Purpose—it is difficult to assert that a thermodynamic system displays purpose, but many other kinds of system, including enterprises, can be stated to behave as though they have purposes.
- Viability—the system can survive in its environment.
- Homeostasis—thermodynamics is primarily concerned with closed systems that reach equilibrium and, as pointed out by Lee and Sears, may be described more correctly as thermostatics. Living systems and enterprises maintain a dynamic equilibrium by keeping

these system concepts and their extensions form some fundamental principles that are of profound importance to the definition of CISs and GISs.

The second law of thermodynamics refers to a quantity known as entropy. A closed system whose initial state is not in equilibrium will become less organized or ordered and eventually reach a state of thermodynamic equilibrium known as *entropy*. Entropy is at a maximum when the system is in a state of equilibrium, but decreases as the system becomes more ordered or organized. To become more ordered, the system must be open and receive energy. It is then in a state of *negative entropy*.

Defining a system's boundaries can be an arbitrary process, in part, because a system can consist of other systems at a "lower" level or be part of another system at a "higher" level.

In communications theory, information is equivalent to negative entropy. In other words, what accounts for a system becoming more ordered or organized can be equated to information. It is debatable whether the information in CIS and GIS can similarly be considered negative entropy. In any case, to consider it as such certainly leads to valuable insights.

Another area of systems theory that is important to information systems is the law of requisite variety. Put simply, this law says that to survive, a system must be able to handle the variety it is likely to encounter in its environment. In other words, it must display as much variety as it will encounter. Ashby (1956), who formulated the law, states, "Only variety can destroy variety", and Beer (1979) describes managers as "variety engineers" and considers ignorance the strongest of all variety reducers.

The law of requisite variety leads to some key principles for system design[10]. It is easy to see (one hopes it is intuitively obvious) that for a complex system the total number of combinations of inputs and states with which it must cope in complying with the law of requisite variety can be huge or potentially infinite. Imagine the problem of designing a CIS that could respond to all circumstances both in its environment and within itself. To manage the world would require a system at least as complex as the world. Clearly, such a system is not realistic.

The system designer must have some tricks that make the task

---

       system properties within certain limits.
- Adaptation—the system is able to adapt to changes in its environment.
- Equifinality—the system can reach its objectives in several possible ways.
- Inputs and outputs—everything that crosses the system boundary.

10 Table 5.1 examines the key information principles in more detail.

manageable. The first is called *attenuation*. A system is made of subsystems that communicate; each subsystem must attenuate the information it passes on so that the next recipient does not receive all of it, but only the portion that is relevant. At the operational level in an enterprise, the operational units respond to many details that affect them, but the totality of information is attenuated—summarized—before passing to the next level of aggregated activity. The counterpart to attenuation is *amplification*, another design trick. This is the replication or expansion of information when necessary.

Many enterprises have trouble coping with variety attenuation and information amplification. On the one hand, electronic mail systems in an open environment have an enormous capacity for amplifying information. In this way they can be responsible for what is perhaps the ultimate in information pollution—all members of an enterprise receiving and having to deal with all available information regardless of need. The dream is an automated mail filter that attenuates the available information. On the other hand, the objectives and policies set by the enterprise must be amplified throughout the enterprise so that all the business units can make the necessary commitments and behavioral changes in pursuance of those objectives. Too much centralized policy, when amplified, reduces variety in the lower business units and hence may damage adaptability (although in some cases, such as the implementation of ethical systems, this is desired).

At a superficial level at least, one can see how ideas of system theory apply to an enterprise. An enterprise can be considered a system, and as such exhibits system characteristics: it has purpose; it exercises control and is self-adjusting to maintain stable states as well as adapt to the environment (that is, it displays homeostasis); it becomes more ordered while it survives; and, because it achieves its goals in many ways, it demonstrates equifinality.

The expression "The system is more than the sum of the parts" applies to the system's intensive properties (those that do not make the total value of the system the sum of its parts) but not to its extensive properties (those that *do* make the value of the total system the sum of the values of its parts). Writers on general systems theory have discussed hierarchies of systems and expounded the idea of emergent system properties. Put simply, a system is the sum of all its subsystems plus the effects of interaction between those subsystems. This is obvious in biology, where an animal as a viable system is more than a mere sum of all its constituent parts. It is also true in human behavior, where the actions of a group are not easy to predict on the basis of the behavior of each individual. A group of people illustrates the difference between intensive and extensive system properties: size (that is, number of people) is an extensive property because it is the sum of the individuals or smaller groups; attitude (that is, the propensity to behave in a particular way in a given situation) is an intensive property because it is not the sum of all the individual attitudes.

The point here is the extent to which the individual properties of a CIS or GIS can be considered extensive and intensive. Enterprise revenue, for example, is likely to be extensive, but entrepreneurial ability is likely to be intensive. Similarly, enterprise goals at the board or stockholder level are usually intensive, not being the sum of those at the business unit level. The extensive properties of a CIS or GIS can probably be handled by mechanisms of aggregation and reporting, but the intensive properties, such as control of the strategy, overall organization, or enterprise objectives will need separate treatment and cannot be handled by simple aggregation or feeders between systems.

General systems theory and cybernetics are often confused with each other, but as von Bertalanffy (1968) points out,

> "Systems theory also is frequently identified with cybernetics and control theory. This again is incorrect. Cybernetics, as the theory of control mechanisms in technology and nature and founded on the concepts of information and feedback, is but a part of a general theory of systems; cybernetic systems are a special case, however important, of systems showing self-regulation."

If one views the overall control of an enterprise as an important component of a CIS or GIS, then clearly cybernetic principles are likely to play a major part in system design.

The term "Viable System Model" (VSM) was introduced by Beer[11]. Essentially, it means a system that is capable of maintaining its own existence. A viable system exists in an environment and, indeed, may be dependent on that environment as a precondition for its viability. An animal cannot survive without food. An enterprise cannot exist without cash, or some cash proxy, or without customer orders.

Beer's discussion of a trinity of environment, organization, and management is particularly relevant to corporate and global information systems. His first principle of organization is that the sum of varieties throughout the trinity must equate and that they can do so by ignorance, in which case management can lose control, or by

---

11 See Beer (1979, 1981) and Espejo and Harnden (1989).

220

the design of effective control systems. Espejo and Harnden (1989) refined this principle, pointing out that some parts of the organization will deal with much of the variety and that other parts will deal with the residual variety. Hence, the less variety handled by the enterprise as a whole, the more handled by employees, management, or the environment; the less handled by management, the more handled by the enterprise, or employees, or environment; and so on. This suggests a powerful framework for the design of CISs and GISs. Informal information networks arise in part because the enterprise as managed or organized is unable to handle the variety it encounters with available institutionalized mechanisms.

Architecture

Architecture has been an established profession and occupation for the last few thousand years in many cultures at different times and places.

In reality there are several kinds of "architect", such as building, town, naval, and landscape, where the word is used in conventional ways. In this discussion, the focus will be on the architecture of buildings and their context. The architecture of buildings is a popular analogy in the design of information systems. Let us take a "top-down" look at architectural and planning activity.

The first step in the architectural process is the decision to locate a community in a particular place. In antiquity this decision involved such important considerations as access to resources, along with a habitable and defensible environment. Next comes the planning of basic infrastructure, such as streets and town walls; the balance between living, recreational, and undeveloped space; communication with other groups; food and water; type and location of activities; and the size of facilities. Overall infrastructure planning takes place on the regional and town level, and architects are involved in it to varying degrees.

After infrastructure and regional and town planning come the buildings themselves. Many conventions surround the various kinds of buildings, which are often governed by regulation and custom covering the provision of facilities and the nature of the buildings in relation to the services they must provide. What are some of the architect's tasks with respect to buildings? A client may give a general idea of what is required for a building. The architect must also take into consideration the proposed environment and any of its special features to avoid or take advantage of, cultural constraints, planning requirements and regulations, costs, and feasibility. The architect will also be expected to understand any general principles related to the planned facility.

The architect produces sketches from which the client chooses a final design. These sketches also allow the client to see and decide on particular features. Next come detailed drawings of the chosen design indicating materials and construction techniques, which are subject to building regulations and known properties of the components to be used. At this point it is understood that certain non-explicit requirements will be met (for example, that the roof will not leak).

In developing professionally[12], the architect becomes familiar with various building styles and their specific requirements and also learns how to prepare specifications that surveyors and builders can follow in site preparation and construction. The architect may have a very good working knowledge of how the building will be constructed, but will expect various contractors such as plumbers, electricians, bricklayers, and carpenters to understand how they exercise their own professions.

Benefiting from principles and experience that have evolved over several hundred years, an architect also understands the building types needed to meet client requirements. These requirements might be for bus terminals, factories, farm structures, stores, government buildings, hospitals, restaurants, theaters, schools, museums, houses, hotels, or any of a numbers of others facility types.

There are several essential categories of information and practice an architect will deal with somewhat independently of the type of building to be put up. These include materials, units of measure, design conventions and representations, dimensional coordination, anthropometrics and ergonomics, internal circulation (people and materials inside), external circulation (vehicles outside), heating, ventilation, light, sound, structure, security, cleaning, and landscape. An essential feature of these categories is the standards that have been established to control them. Such standards represent our experience and, in some cases, our tragedies.

The types of building, basic materials, and design principles are conditioned very much by culture and environment. For example, the Kayapo people build their huts in a large circle with a large space in the middle. In the center of the large space is a large, open-sided but that serves as a gathering place for the male members of the tribe.

Finally come the specific tools, materials, and practices the various building trades use in actual construction. These tend to evolve more

12 Information about building types, techniques, and practices can be obtained from books such as Tuft and Adler's *New Metric Handbook: Planning and Design Data* (1979).

quickly than do the underlying design principles.

Our top-down look at the architectural profession makes clear that at a high level architects have three principal concerns:

- Planning—the environmental context in which a building will be designed and located
- Infrastructure—the interdependencies of a building, its occupants, and any infrastructure required for the building to "succeed"
- Buildings—the types, styles, and properties of various buildings and how these match client needs

Additionally, these concerns require the architect to have knowledge of the following areas:

- Materials to implement architectural designs
- Applicable standards, rules, and laws
- Tools (both architectural and construction)
- Architectural principles, practices, and procedures
- Related trades and professions (for example, engineering, construction and legal)
- Methods of representation and communication (such as plans, sketches, units of measure, and specifications)
- Cultural and aesthetic constraints
- The activities an architect engages in include:
- Planning interrelated buildings and infrastructure
- Constructing an environment from discrete components
- Working with the underlying values of the customer
- Proceeding from a rough sketch, via a set of plans, to a working system
- Constructing a communications and operational infrastructure within which people can interact
- Meeting local needs within an overall plan
- Providing a framework of principles of design and construction These activities are governed by certain principles:
- Architects are specialists who have been trained extensively and intensively.
- Different environments fulfill various behavioral needs.
- Only a small proportion of new buildings use "leading-edge" technology.
- Once planned, buildings normally change slowly.
- Most buildings are based on standard tried and tested designs and components.

Architecture and the IT World

The discussion given above may appear to be detailed to the point of tedium but is provided to give the reader a feel for what is needed before information system architects can have the same degree of confidence and accuracy as an architect of buildings.

Certainly, there is a great deal that goes into the planning and construction of a building, all of which the architect must understand completely; but there is also a body of established knowledge the architect can rely on for guidance. No equivalent set of principles and practices exists as yet for the systems architect building an information system, and therefore an information architect cannot have the same degree of confidence the building architect has about the correctness of the final product.

The word "architecture" is becoming more and more common in computer environments and literature. Although its use in this context is as yet neither stable nor precise, we accept it because of its broad use, because it is evolving as a metaphor, and because it does convey meaning. However, we also use some helpful terms from biology and other disciplines within our architectural framework.

Within the information systems world the word "architecture", in its most sophisticated use, probably represents the wish for a set of well-established principles and practices capable of delivering a solution to a set of requirements with a great deal of precision and predictability. In its most basic and ill-defined use, it probably represents a wish for, or intuitive recognition of, some collection or interaction between a set of objects where the pattern of interconnection or interaction may be known but generally has not been specified. At any one time the word "architecture" can be used as a heuristic, as a metaphor, or as an homonym[13].

Analogs are valuable because they point to possible deficiencies

---

13 Computer professionals use "architecture" in very different ways. For example:

- Allen (1989) claims that architecture is an important way for the future: "Architecture is more than just the policy and rules governing IT in the enterprise. It is both the actual and the planned arrangements of the firm's data collections, computers, and communications facilities and programs. It is the plan for the transition from here to there".
- Best (1990) discusses the key concepts of large-scale application architecture as human factors, how applications should support enterprises, and the way in which the functions of a large-scale application should be constructed.
- Inmon (1986) states that the heart of information systems architecture is the modeling of a company's data and processes and how that model relates to the company's business.
- Licker (1987) defines system architecture as "the way that units or subsystems are interrelated to cope with environments . . .".
- Pressman (1987) states that "*architectural design* defines the relationship among major structural elements of the program" and that its objective is "to develop a modular program structure and present the control relationship between modules . . .".
- Willis and Kerridge (1983) do not define architecture, but the scope of their book is computer components and how they relate to each other.

The computing literature has very little about other terms that express accompanying architectural principles.

in the thing to which they are compared. Thus, using the analogy of the design and construction of buildings, one can find a few things information systems requirers, specifiers, and builders generally do not do very well, although the effort is clearly there. (These may be added to the list given earlier.)

- Planning a set of related information systems and predicting required resources
- Creating information systems that can adapt to continually changing environments (growing systems rather than building them)
- Creating an agreed set of business and organization principles for the future
- Identifying and assembling the key building blocks needed to construct information systems
- Finding and stating requirements to establish and deliver "real" user needs
- Predicting the performance of a piece of software before construction
- Designing information systems to take account of both the computerized and non-computerized parts of the information systems
- Contributing to the development of a profession somewhat like building architecture, which is capable of evolving a required set of principles and practices based on a systematic synthesis and analysis of previous experience
- Developing a generally accepted taxonomy of information system or application types, which does not yet exist (except in a very broad sense)

An Architectural Analogy for Information Systems

The building aspect of the architectural analogy has received the greatest attention from information system designers. Zachman[14] identifies three fundamental representations, one for each of the key players in the creation of a building—the owner, the designer, and the builder—and extends this functional division to the creation of information systems. Such an analogy provides some heuristics for constructing information systems, but it is important to remember that an architect is not a builder, and that most people who want a building are not architects.

In focusing on building, it is easy to lose sight of the planning and

---

14 Zachman (1987) offers a detailed exposition of the architectural and building analogy.

infrastructure aspects of the architectural analogy, but these must be in place to support building construction and use. Buildings most certainly can be isolated from other buildings or centers of human activity, and could even be isolated from roads and services. Information systems, too, need planning and must make use of available infrastructure. As Vincent (1990) points out, a complete building may require n person-years, but the important point is that some of those person-years will need an architect, some a builder, some a plumber, and so on. By analogy, the assertion that a software development project requires n person-years misses the point because there will be so many person-years for analysis activity, so many for design, so many for prototyping, benchmarking and testing, and so on.

The appropriate use of information technology requires overall planning of an enterprise's information processing needs, along with the provision of an infrastructure that facilitates the interdependence of and communication between individual information systems.

In the architectural world there there are many different ways to view a structure: satellite views, three-dimensional designs, descriptions of physical properties, blueprints. Similarly, a city can be seen from a satellite, described statistically, or examined according to its street layout. In the biological world the human body can be viewed as a collection of systems: nervous, circulatory, musculoskeletal, and so forth.

Enterprise information is also open to interpretation depending on how it is to be viewed. For example, some people have a data view, some a process view, and some an organizational behavior view. More-over, information may be viewed on the basis of how it is used or how different people react to it. These different views of information are the reason for the different "kinds" of architecture in an architectural analogy. Each represents a different point of view.

Information Architecture

The architectural analogy suggests the following definition of an information architecture: An information architecture is a framework for agreement that provides the art and science of identifying, planning, and implementing integrated information systems and their related infrastructure, and that provides a cost-effective overall application of IT to appropriate activities of an organization or enterprise having certain desirable properties.

226

The desirable properties of an information system are that it is acceptable to users, correct, and efficient; that it provides flexible support to the enterprise; and that it is quickly reconfigurable, interoperable, interconnectable, distributable, and reusable. More specifically, an information architecture:

- Establishes the general principles of applications to support a business
- Defines an infrastructure for the information systems and applications
- Represents a set of cultural preferences
- Ensures that new applications are really needed and fit into an overall business vision that is understood
- Codifies the uses, properties, strengths, and applicability of different kinds of application and appropriate technology for implementation

In summary, an information architecture exists to ensure the integration of the individual applications that use knowledge and information and to provide the essential infrastructure for the easy evolution of the business and its information systems, *regardless of whether those systems are computerized.*

> *An information architecture is a framework for agreement that provides the art and science of identifying, planning, and implementing integrated information systems and their related infrastructure, and that provides a cost-effective overall application of IT to appropriate activities of an organization or enterprise having certain desirable properties.*

Information Biology

At a simple level architecture concerns *building*, whereas biology concerns *growing*. Both building and growing apply to the information world, and for this reason a biological analogy is relevant to the development of information systems in terms of both a life cycle and homeostasis. The use of biological analogies for enterprises and computer systems has quite a long history in the literature. Two early examples are Beer's *The Brain of the Firm* (1979) and *The Heart of Enterprise* (1981)[15].

Among other things, biologists study:

- Biological "objects", such as birds, animals, and plants
- Ecological viability, or the limits of the environment within which biological objects can survive
- The evolution of biological objects
- Fundamental biological principles such as growth, reproduction, respiration, feeding, communication, and survival

There are some clear analogies to be drawn from the biological model:

- Biologists are specialists who have been trained extensively and intensively—information systems planners, analysts, and designers should be trained intensively and extensively.
- Biological systems evolve very slowly, but they do (generally) adapt to change—information systems continually adapt to change.
- Many biological systems are highly complex interdependent networks of specialized functions—highly complex information networks contain complex patterns of information and control flow.
- Biological objects are "grown", not built—information systems require continual development and evolution beyond initial design and construction.
- Biological responses and interactions with the environment may be considered either automatic or voluntary—information technology can be used for the automation of many tasks and can provide support for many manual tasks or decisions.

Given these analogies, we can define an information biology as follows: Information biology is the study of how information systems are grown, continually adapt to a dynamic, changing environment and set of survival factors, work automatically to implement predetermined

15 Other examples are Brooks (1986) and Nolan (1988).

business processes, and respond to specific external stimuli like orders and requests for information.

Generally, it is reasonable to assert that an animal or plant is a viable system because it displays adaptable, purposeful behavior, but that its internal systems—its brain, nervous system, and the like—are not in themselves viable because they cannot display such behavior. Similarly, the enterprise displays adaptable, purposeful behavior and so can be considered a viable system; but its information systems, which correspond to something like the brain and nervous system in an animal, cannot.

> *Information biology is the study of how information systems are grown, continually adapt to dynamic, changing environment and set of survival factors, work automatically to implement predetermined business processes, and respond to specific external stimuli like orders and requests for information.*

Another way to see the enterprise's information systems is as a genetic code that provides some form of immunity against invasion or merger.

"Intelligence" is another common word in the computer world; yet its origin, meaning, and scope are not understood, nor is there general agreement about the nature of intelligence itself[16]. Therefore, because its analog is unclear, the term "artificial intelligence" is also unclear (although we can perhaps understand it as a metaphor) and thus it may be more appropriate to talk of expert systems as a way to enhance human intelligence rather than simulate it. Someday, when there is enough computing power available, it will be possible to support controlling mechanisms by supplementary processes such as conceptualization and dreaming.

Information as an Enterprise Asset

In traditional economic texts assets were given as land, labor, and capital. Capital remains an asset, of course, but over the past hundred years or so, automation has reduced the need for physical space and labor per unit of output. More recently time has become more significant

---

16 We can, for now, consider intelligence as the ability to learn from experience and apply that experience appropriately in dealing with similar problems.

to the enterprise. The optimization of activities within available time definitely contributes to future cash flow[17]. Although time may not yet be a recognized asset according to strict definition requirements, there is no doubt that an enterprise should behave as though time is an asset.

The value of information to the enterprise has begun to be recognized only in the past few years. It has now become one of an enterprise's essential assets, along with cash, time, people, and resources. These four are well understood, but we need to explore information in more detail.

Let us start with Horngren and Sunden's (1987) definition of assets as "economic resources that are expected to benefit future activities". It is traditional for accountants to distinguish tangible from intangible assets, a distinction Horngren and Sunden explain as:

> "*Tangible assets* can be physically observed. In contrast *intangible assets* are a class of *long-lived assets* that are not physical in nature. They are rights to expected future benefits deriving from their acquisition and continued possession. Examples are goodwill, franchises, patents, trademarks, and copyrights."

The essence of intangible assets is their likely contribution to future cash flow, but they are difficult to measure, and in general there is much debate in the accounting profession over how to treat them[18].

Vincent (1990) explains the principle of an asset laid down by the Financial Accounting Standards Board as including probable future benefit directly or indirectly to future cash flow, the ability to control access to the asset, and that the investment in the asset has already occurred. He defines four physical properties of information: it is not consumable, it can be copied, it is indivisible, and it is accumulative.

According to the OECD, the trend of enterprises separating their service activity from their manufacturing activity has created the illusion of a shift from a manufacturing to an information economy. The illusion notwithstanding, there has been an increase in the number of enterprises dealing substantially with information, and Vincent identifies these as banking and finance, insurance and security, most government agencies, marketing and sales, accounting and auditing, software development, and investment. He calls these information-driven companies. An outstanding example is *the replacement of cash by*

---

17 Davis (1987) states that "We are talking about *instantaneous* products and services, those that are offered within the blink of an eye of their conception. If you can imagine this occurring, then the product is in research, in development, in manufacture, and being consumed *virtually* all at the same time. This is a truly holistic conception of the product." Keen (1988) gives many examples of organizing enterprise activities that would probably not be possible without the telecommunications part of IT platforms, and he illustrates the significance of using time to obtain competitive advantage.

18 For example, in the United States the Financial Accounting Standards Board has been wrestling with this issue.

information about cash.

In many enterprises information handling accounts for a significant proportion of total cost. The problem for the accountant is to separate total cost into current expenditure, which should be written off immediately, and expenditure on information, which is a true asset that can be valued and reported as such.

The significance of one of our main themes, that an information infrastructure is far broader than an IT infrastructure, is illustrated by Vincent, who offers the results of a study showing the ratio of average information investment to IT annual expense as 18 to 1 in information-driven industries and 36 to 1 in manufacturing industries. He also points to other studies that show similar ratios of 88 to 1 and 53 to 1.

These ratios do not reconcile easily with the Datamation data in Davis (1989), but that does not alter the fundamental observation that *enterprises spend more on information than they do on IT*. For this reason the enterprise must establish clear responsibilities for information investment, expenditure, and asset management, or, as Vincent says, "The business community must recognize information, not the data-processing hardware and software used to make it available, as its major resource". In the opinion of Strassman et al. (1988), "Perhaps the most imaginative of all taxonomies for identifying the value of information is the Critical Success Factors (CSF) method". He then continues with a critique of an Executive Planning for Data Processing (EPDP) method, which he says ". . . implies a view of the world in which: all gains are attributable to computer technology; all value is calculated based on the costs of the most obsolete technology available, that is, manual methods". He draws the amusing analogy that such a method would "price all existing automobiles in terms of the equivalent market cost of horses", so that the owner of a truck could report a payback on the investment in only 20 days.

Meyer and Boone (1987) report returns on investment from IT that are so high they deserve careful attention. For example, when they attribute an 830,000 percent return substantially to database search results, Strassman, in a review (1988), asks "does it make any sense to assign almost all of the total value gained to a few computerized database searches? . . . this does not allow much for the providers of capital, the sources of technology, the employee teams . . . ".

From out own observations and those of the researchers we have quoted, we conclude that information is an intangible asset, represented strictly by the difference in the value of an enterprise with it and without it.

The Application Of Information Theory

We have discussed many facets of information and information theory. At some risk of being over-simplistic, we offer a minimum set of principles for applying information theory to the construction of corporate and global information systems. We hope the list in Figure 9.3 will be of assistance to the practitioner.

Figure 9.3 Information System Principles

- Information should be supplied only if it must be supplied (because of some law or rule) or it is capable of affecting some decision.
- The cost of providing information should not exceed its possible value.
- An information system must contain necessary information attenuation mechanisms.
- An information system must contain necessary information amplification mechanisms.
- An information system should provide the enterprise with the necessary control mechanisms to implement appropriate homeostasis.
- Information systems must help an enterprise achieve sufficient variety to deal with the variety it will encounter externally or internally.
- Relevant transducers should be deployed for all interactions between the enterprise and its environment.
- An enterprise should not generate or receive more information than it is able to deal with.

Implications of Information Infrastructure

Infrastructure consists of functionality and resources that are available for more than one purpose[19]. It is a concept that is being implemented in increasingly diverse ways. The idea of infrastructure is young with respect to IT (although it is old in relation to many other areas of

---

19 An infrastructure is a structure that is below, underneath, or beneath something else; semantically it is the opposite of supra or superstructure. An infrastructure is something that can be "assumed" in the construction of a superstructure or is something whose properties are considered to be present.

human endeavor). That is, it is not as widely discussed in the literature at the moment, but there is an increasing number of references in the past couple of years or so.

As we will demonstrate, infrastructure is vitally important for an information-integrated enterprise (which is a far broader concept than that of a "computer-integrated company"). Almost all information and computer environments use infrastructure whether or not it is recognized as such.

Much of the current literature on infrastructure (for example, Cash 1988, Gunton 1989, McKay and Brockway 1989, and Winfield 1991) is concerned mostly with IT infrastructure. However, the distinction between *information infrastructure* and *IT infrastructure* is very important.

Some researchers hold a very broad view of infrastructure. Vincent (1990) defines it as "the arrangement of plant, facilities, human organizations, distribution mechanisms, and information and telecommunications", which makes clear his position that both information and IT infrastructures are but parts of the overall infrastructure of the enterprise.

Much is hoped from infrastructure, but infrastructure per se conveys no specific advantages or disadvantages. A highly centralized approach to providing computing capability does itself offer a particular kind of infrastructure. However, the hope is for more than merely a preexisting set of capabilities; what is wanted is a way of handling certain kinds of problems. To put this another way, "what is the difference between a computing environment with infrastructure and one without it?"

There is great danger in the notion that infrastructure ipso facto conveys flexibility; it may not, and whether or not it does is probably heavily dependent on the way it is identified and implemented. (This is very much how Strassman (1990) talks about computers and profitability.)

A computing environment without infrastructure is one where all computing applications are separate, stand-alone, and self-sufficient. An information environment without infrastructure is one where all information applications are separate, stand-alone, and self-sufficient. Conversely, an information or IT environment that is based on infrastructure is one where common facilities result in the interdependence of information and IT applications.

Infrastructure exists at several different levels in an enterprise whenever it is meaningful to separate functionality into layers. In traditional office buildings, for example, separate offices, corridors, and the like, provided the building infrastructure. Now, however, the advent of open offices has left the service infrastructure, such as electric cables, with the structure of the building—but has moved the rest of the infrastructure to the desk and surrounding partitions. In a similar way, workstations, which are networked or clustered together as a replacement for dumb terminals, have taken some of the infrastructure from mainframes while providing some additional infrastructure of its own. Modularity often has the effect of transferring some infrastructure from the encompassing shell to the components; modular components add to the pool of available infrastructure.

At the extreme of infrastructure, each application is simply the use of a particular configuration of available and pre-existing infrastructure components. This is the nature of many enterprise-wide services (among them electronic mail).

One of the economic goals of infrastructure growth is more effective economies of scale and higher returns on investment, gained from the greater reuse that results from effective modularity. Another goal is a reduction in the "investment gap" illustrated in Chapter 7.

The recognition of, and pressure for, infrastructure has arisen because of the emergence of more complex information and IT environments. Most significant environments are very mixed, and hence infrastructure is seen as a way to handle the complexity and improve interconnectivity and interoperability.

Elsewhere we discuss the principles that underlie our approach to information architecture. Here we present some of the principles behind information and IT infrastructures. These principles are shown in Table 9.2.

One may think that because of open systems and standards, there is no more need to plan for infrastructure. On the contrary, the easier it is to acquire plug-compatible systems, and the easier and cheaper it is to buy information power, the more planning becomes essential. Think of the need for planning and managing a country's road system: even if all cars drive on the same side of the road and are built similarly enough so that their drivers are interchangeable, it is still the case that the greater the number of cars, the greater the need for infrastructure. Similar analogies can be brought out of the computer world. In the past the focus was on planning for computing capacity; now the focus is shifting toward planning for communication capacity, interoperability, and related factors like security.

234

Table 9.2 Information and IT Infrastructure Principles

Principle	Explanation
Interoperability	Infrastructure enables the interconnection and interoperability of applications in more complex environments than would be achievable without it.
Organizational complexity	Infrastructure supports levels of organization that would be otherwise unachievable for reasons of economic cost or technical feasibility.
Integration of different cultures	Infrastructure embodies certain common cultural approaches and can provide for interconnectivity between different cultural approaches.
Implement standards	Infrastructure provides mechanisms for the implementation of standards, both statically and dynamically.
Resource sharing	Infrastructure provides a set of mechanisms to optimize resource sharing.
Interdependence	Infrastructure implements interdependence between applications.
Application time to market	The greater the number of available infrastructure components, the shorter the time to market for new applications that are consistent with other applications.
Maximum reusability	A goal is to implement as much functionality as possible in infrastructure rather than in self-sufficient applications in order to maximize reusability.

Information infrastructure comprises the information resources available to the enterprise for multiple purposes. IT infrastructure, at its most simple, is a communication network with the standards for connecting any workstation or other computing platform. Infrastructure complexity increases as time goes by. In practice a number of common services make up infrastructure, including electronic mail, both within and across enterprises, research and library services, and directory services (indicating who and what are where). Video conferencing, video text, and any basic communication services can become part of infrastructure, planned and managed statistically just as an electricity grid for power is planned and managed. We believe the value added provided by infrastructure will increase in the coming years.

The IM&T Executive, or a similar role, owns responsibility for the infrastructure. This is because if computing and entrepreneurial activities become more decentralized, and responsibility for business systems is dispersed, the need grows for very strong, central, strategic and tactical control of the infrastructure. Without such control we will find ourselves back in the early eighties, when technical limitations prevented departments, divisions, and computers from talking to each other. With the adoption of standards, the technical limitations may go away, but that is not sufficient if there is no accurate plan for capacity and if information is not standardized. As time goes by, many representations and semantics of information and data become part of infrastructure.

We summarize the implications of infrastructure as follows:

- Ideally, an IT infrastructure provides multi-vendor inter-operability (to represent the reality of most IT environments); the creation of a corporate or global information infrastructure implies the likelihood of very diverse requirements.
- The client/server model is emerging as a major candidate to help in the creation of modular, flexible, and distributable IT infrastructure components.
- Effective infrastructure evolution is tied to business strategy.
- A greater proportion of the information infrastructure is becoming IT-based or IT-assisted.
- Open systems are a prerequisite for a widely based infrastructure.
- The proliferation of computing boxes, often from many different vendors, makes IT infrastructure more essential.
- The greater the number of cars, the greater the need for transport infrastructure; likewise, the greater the computing power, the greater the need for infrastructure such as communications capacity and accessible security mechanisms.
- Infrastructure can be planned and managed on a statistical basis.
- The more dispersed the computing power, the greater the need for infrastructure.
- Infrastructures evolve in many ways, expanding functionality avail-able from an infrastructure to dispersing infrastructure functionality more widely.

The Enterprise as a Purposeful System

Several new techniques support different views of enterprise strategy. Most tend to be descriptive or prescriptive rather than analytical, largely because traditional strategy studies do not use formal 'techniques of analysis even though there may be a profound understanding of a given enterprise and others similar to it. Many business or strategy consultants do not use formal analysis techniques either, and those who do are frequently unable to simplify concepts or communicate them to the level of management that must make the decisions. To compound these difficulties, some of the literature about enterprise modeling is based on software development analysis techniques that have simply been adapted.

A strategy study brings together many of the key concepts of system, information, and infrastructure. It sets the purposeful directions of the enterprise. We believe enterprises must have the strategic capability to underpin their traditional strategy studies with more formal analysis and checking methods. This requires a mix of skills and people who can "translate" for the various parties involved.

A large part of the input to the construction of a CIS or GIS is likely to be based on personal representations of experience and intuitive techniques, rather than on more formal approaches. Formal approaches are not necessarily "better", but we believe that intuitive approaches to strategizing exercises should be more rigorous. Nevertheless, there is no doubt that many of the available techniques, although they lack a solid empirical foundation, provide enterprise modelers with a great deal of assistance.

In the sections that follow we discuss several common approaches to conducting a strategy study that we consider an essential starting point for building a business architecture. However, we repeat our earlier caveat that a strategy study should be accompanied by systematic efforts to understand the enterprise's overall information needs and the specific ways in which the enterprise can obtain maximum benefit from information and IT. It should not be restricted to the elements described here.

Mission

A *mission* is usually embodied in a mission statement. This is intended to convey the reason for the existence of the enterprise.

Enterprises may be profit-oriented or objective-oriented, but the essence of a mission statement remains the same[20]. Often it contains many good-sounding words to convey a high-level view of what an enterprise is going to do. Such a statement is frequently locked into what the enterprise is doing at the moment.

Profit-oriented enterprises usually have at least an unspoken mission

---

20 Kotler and Roberto (1989) discuss social products in terms of ideas and practice; they give examples such as Amnesty International, human rights, literacy, antismoking, energy conservation practices, rehabilitation, World Health Organization, UNICEF, and so on. This is what we mean by objective-oriented, or not-for-profit, enterprises.

statement, which is something like "The mission of this enterprise is to survive as a viable system and provide maximum benefit to an identified group of people". The spoken mission statement, if there is one, is more likely to refer to a particular kind of enterprise that represents the interests or entrepreneurial vision of the people behind it. Very few businesses start with a group of people saying "we are going to do business" and then making a rational assessment of markets and opportunities to identify the activity with the highest potential for maximum profit—it is more subtle than that. Someone is interested in something and perceives a business opportunity. In this sense entrepreneurial activity is very difficult to separate from creativity. Oil companies exist because certain people looked at oil and perceived a business opportunity; some of those people probably also have some inherent interest in oil.

For an enterprise to work, someone must understand how the vision can be realized; that is the essence of the entrepreneur.

One of the strongest statements about profit making comes from someone with a deep sense of creativity, Salvador Dali. He described himself (during an interview for television) as "a soft cybernetic machine for making money", although we assume he saw money as part of the reward for his art. A tobacco company may have a mission of providing tobacco products, but as public sentiments and markets turn against smoking, their real mission, survival, will become apparent and they will diversify. An airline may have the mission of being the recognized national air carrier, but if teleconferencing and other communications methods pose a threat to business travel, it may take a position in competitive communications methods. This reveals its broader mission of providing services to facilitate communications, which lies between the mission providing air transport and that of merely surviving in any kind of viable business.

An *objective oriented* enterprise is not set up for making a profit and, indeed, probably has an explicit statement of objectives. It may exist for aiding developing countries or for making grants to children with specific needs. It may achieve its purpose by establishing a certain kind of trust, such as one that accepts public donations for a specific purpose. A broader objective-oriented enterprise may be a cooperative society set up simply for the benefit of its members. As such it will have a much more general mission statement.

Objectives and Goals

The *objectives,* or *goals,* of an enterprise (either profit- or objective-oriented) are detailed statements of what it wants to achieve or how it wants to behave. Typical enterprise objectives include:

- Relative size in an industry (being the largest, the second largest, and so forth)
- Market share (achieving, say, a 10 percent share of a particular market)
- Public perception (being perceived as the foremost provider of widget services)
- Service level (providing the fastest response in the industry to special customer requests)
- Service depth (providing support to a particular group of people)

Statements about objectives are often derived from a vision of a desired future state. Some writers distinguish objectives and goals[21], but what is more important for the enterprise is an agreed-upon definition that can be used both for understanding and for directing strategizing activity.

Strategy

Strategy means different things to different people[22]. It is interesting to look at some of these meanings and then at how we use the word for the purposes of this book.

Martin and Leben (1989) call strategy in an enterprise "a pattern of policies and plans that specifies how an organization should function over a given period". Byars (1984) says it is "concerned with deciding which option is going to be used. Strategy includes the determination and evaluation of alternative paths to achieve an organization's objectives and mission and, eventually, a choice of the alternative that is to be adopted". Pascale and Athos (1981) use an operational definition of strategy as a "plan or course of action leading to the allocation of

---

21 For example, Martin and Leben (1989) define an objective as a "general statement about the direction a firm intends to take in a particular area without stating a specific target to be reached by particular points in time", and a goal as "a specific target that is intended to be reached by a given point in time. A goal is thus an operational transform of one or more objectives".

22 *The Shorter Oxford English Dictionary of Historical Principles* (1933) says the word derives from the Greek for the office or command of a general and defines it as "A government or province under a strategus", and "The art of a commander-in-chief; the art of projecting and directing the larger military movements and operations of a campaign". Clearly, these definitions are not strong analogs to the use of "strategy" applied to enterprises. The meaning of the word has been extended substantially in recent years.

a firm's scarce resources, over time, to reach identified goals". Porter (1980) explains competitive strategy as a "combination of the ends (goals) for which the firm is striving and the means (policies) by which it is seeking to get there". Wilson, in Taylor and Sparkes (1977), defines strategy as carried out in General Electric as "that activity which specifies for a business a course of action that is designed to achieve desired long-term objectives in the light of all major external and internal factors, present and future". Finally, Taylor, in Taylor and Sparkes, sees strategy as determining "what products or services are to be offered to which markets, and how resources are to be acquired and allocated".

From these definitions strategy can mean:

- A static definition of various decisions about the general direction of the enterprise
- A static decision about what to offer or produce
- A dynamic process for selecting between alternatives and deciding the direction to take
- A study of the alternatives available to an enterprise

Here is our definition of strategy, which will aid the construction of a model that can be checked for consistency:

> *A strategy is a determined course of action either to take advantage of opportunities or strengths or to overcome critical factors, risks, and constraints in the pursuit of a set of determined objectives.*

Critical Success, Existence, and Failure Factors

Critical success factors (CSFs) are "those few critical areas where things must go right for the business to flourish" (Rockart 1979). Rockart is usually credited with originating the term, which appears with varying frequency in management literature. The obvious corollary to CSFs are critical failure factors (CFFs), which can be defined as, perhaps, "those few critical areas where, if things go wrong, the business will fail to survive". An enterprise can, of course, remain static as well as flourish or decline. Hence, between critical success and failure factors, there must exist critical existence factors (CEFs), which are "the few critical

areas where things must go right for the business merely to exist".
Figure 9.4 shows the relative positions of CSFs, CFFs, and CEFs.

Figure 9.4 Critical Success, Existence, and Failure Factors

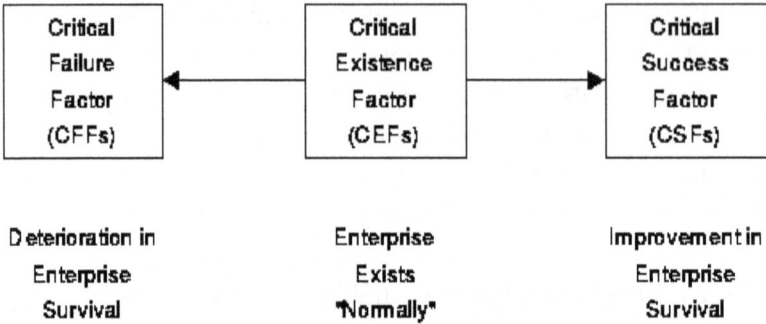

Critical Failure Factor (CFFs)	← Critical Existence Factor (CEFs) →	Critical Success Factor (CSFs)
Deterioration in Enterprise Survival	Enterprise Exists "Normally"	Improvement in Enterprise Survival

Constructing a corporate or global information based solely
on CSFs emphasizes flourishing only, and that may be sufficient if
the enterprise can ensure that it will flourish, which remains to be
demonstrated. It may not be flourishing but will still want to know if
it is surviving, albeit statically, or is actually in decline. We cannot be
sure that the combination of circumstances that make an enterprise
flourish might not also cause its decline. Thus, we cannot presume that
CFFs are simply negative variants of CSFs.

For an enterprise to continue to exist, it will need to interact
successfully with its environment in several dimensions. It may
continue to function within certain limits, which means that it retains
its overall viability because various homeostatic mechanisms are at
work. Thus, if we relate CFFs, CEFs, and CSFs to retail stores, here is
what we are looking at:

- Which factors contribute to the "steady" continued existence of
  the shop—CEFs?
- Which factors combine to make the shop flourish and become a
  chain store—CSFs?
- Which factors combine to make the shop decline and eventually
  go out of business—CFFs?

By definition a CIS or GIS must be able to provide information
about critical factors in support of the enterprise objectives. The
information must also be available to support decisions based on the
state of any of the critical factors.

Enterprise managers should use information to make decisions that will maintain the viability of the enterprise—in other words, keep it in approximately stable and static equilibrium. They may be driving the enterprise to achieve set goals, and if so, they will use information to keep on target. This state may be considered as stable dynamic equilibrium.

With respect to cash and critical success factors, while an enterprise is in equilibrium, cash flow will be within certain predefined limits. It may fluctuate from negative to positive flow (for example, during a holiday season), but over time the limits of fluctuation will remain stable. If the enterprise is flourishing, cash flow will be in unstable equilibrium because after a period of success a new equilibrium will establish itself at a much higher level. It is not possible to generalize about how this unstable equilibrium comes about. One enterprise may attempt rapid expansion in response to available orders, but as a result it suffers a seriously negative cash flow that it must rectify through higher borrowing or equity investment. Another enterprise may be able to expand because it realizes windfall profits that create a sudden positive cash flow. An enterprise in decline has a cash flow that has become unstable and too negative.

We can explore the different roles of enterprise manager and consultant by looking at cash flow in more detail.

A strategizing exercise for the design of a CIS will almost certainly identify adequate cash flow as a CSF. Interpreting this involves some highly technical questions. For example, is a high negative cash flow a problem? Well, yes it is, technically. Does it matter? Well, in some circumstances an initial negative cash flow is associated with a CSF, whereas in others it is associated with a CFF. Hence, the designer of a CIS ust associate cash flow with a complex set of additional factors to know if the enterprise is flourishing or declining. The challenge is to engineer a system to detect the various possibilities and alert the right people—automatically, of course.

To remain in stable static or dynamic equilibrium, an enterprise needs information about suppliers, customers, products, markets, competition, legislation, and so forth. Indeed, many enterprises go out of business after a fire because the one asset they were not able to replace through cash from the insurance company was information about accounts receivable. Competitive and strategic information may also have been lost, making recovery difficult if not impossible.

Financial analysts often take the extreme reductionist view that everything is replaceable with cash, but this is not so with information and knowledge assets. It is also almost inconceivable that an enterprise will flourish without both appropriate information and the models for interpreting that information. In many cases where an enterprise veers out of control, the right kinds of information are not available to rectify the position, although in some cases the information may be available but is another critical failure factor. Clearly, information as an asset is just as likely as other assets such as cash and people to be implicated in critical factors. The difficulty for the strategist is to identify the critical information assets and determine how they combine with other assets to form CFFs, CEFs, and CSFs. Initially, such identification must be independent of organization and technology.

Strengths, Weaknesses, Opportunities, and Threats

Part of the repertoire of the enterprise strategist is the identification of the enterprise's strengths and weaknesses as well as any opportunities and threats it faces. This is often referred to as a SWOT analysis.

Strengths and weaknesses are essentially internal enterprise characteristics, although they are likely to refer to either the external environment or to some perceived normative assessment. Opportunities and threats generally originate in the external environment.

A SWOT analysis is usually a subjective technique; it is a powerful means of achieving consensus within a group of experienced or knowledgeable people in order to identify the required perceptions.

A strategizing study frequently takes SWOT statements at face value, and subsequent strategizing activity concentrates on checking the internal consistency of everything that has been made available, such as critical factors, strategies, objectives, and so forth.

CISs and GISs should support SWOT studies by providing a platform against which to test perceptions. A SWOT study taps belief, intuition, and experience, which, when combined with empirical reality, can establish solid foundation for further work. Many statements made in SWOT workshops can be tested, and should be tested as far as possible, because it is likely that SWOT participants will not represent all the classes of experience available to the enterprise.

The Evolution of Data and Information Models

The thinking about enterprise data or information models has proceeded in step with the evolution of data and information storage technology. This strong link has developed in part because of the increasing separation between an enterprise's *computerized systems* and *total information needs*. Such separation is an unfortunate side effect of traditional organizational design, which has usually delegated responsibility for information modeling to the enterprise department also responsible for the computerized systems. Not surprisingly, the computerized systems have received the major emphasis, and this is reflected in the literature primarily because the writers are very enthusiastic about the technology. It is exceedingly difficult to find good literature about the modeling of enterprise needs that does not look almost exclusively at the computerized systems[23].

Modeling the data and information in computerized systems is, of course, vital, and enterprises should make significant effort to do it. However, the other information needs must not be ignored in the process. The gulf between computerized systems and overall information needs is one of the major drivers of demand for new applications and infrastructure (and new technology adds to that demand).

Many problems of ignorance and inconsistency surrounding enterprise data are a consequence of the application of IT in traditional organizational structures. Enterprises are paying a high price to sort out these problems.

Figure 9.5 presents a simplified history of data and information modeling.

The first level of independence between a computer program and the data it manipulates was achieved by the placement of files on some kind of mass storage device so that more than one program could access them. This led to the development of many file management systems that support file use, sharing, and manipulation. In this way data files were early contributors to IT infrastructure, along with the operating system facilities that supported file access.

---

23 For example, in many enterprises forecasting can be a critical success factor. IT can clearly play a part in forecasting, but it cannot meet all forecasting requirements. Hall (1989) identifies the techniques for environmental forecasting and impact assessment as life-cycle forecasting, historical analogy, multiple scenarios, checklists and their variations, interaction matrices, graphs and cross-impact analysis, trend extrapolations, heuristic methods, theory of consumer's choice, sampling survey methods, failure analysis, and success analysis. There are clear roles for both IT-based and non-IT-based approaches in support of these techniques.

244

Figure 9.5 The Evolution of Data and Information Modeling

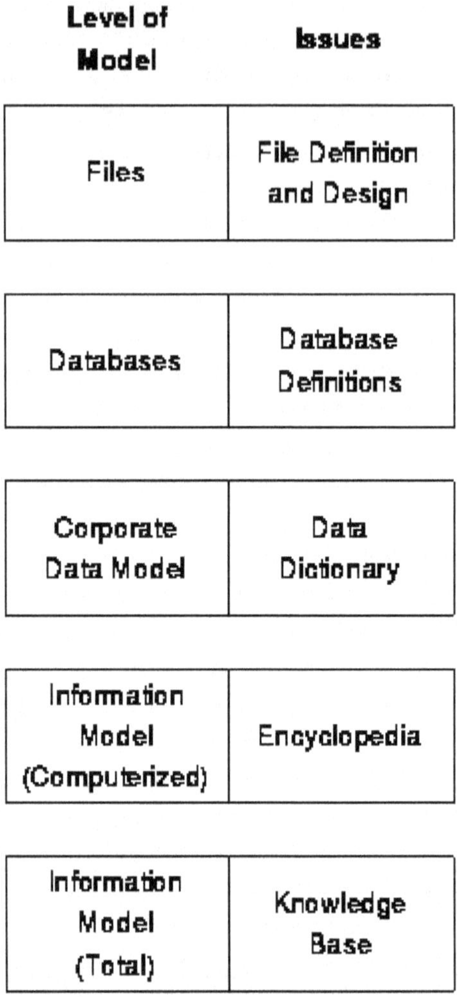

Level of Model	Issues
Files	File Definition and Design
Databases	Database Definitions
Corporate Data Model	Data Dictionary
Information Model (Computerized)	Encyclopedia
Information Model (Total)	Knowledge Base

File sharing by many applications led to too much interdependence between applications and file structures. Therefore, database management systems were created to provide some degree of independence between data storage and application programs.

The rapid application of IT to many enterprise activities created a demand for corporate data models supported by data dictionaries. Database management systems were provided with utilities to define data and the different ways of seeing the data; that is, these systems contained primitive data dictionaries that could evolve quite easily into more sophisticated versions. As data were defined for database management systems, it became relatively easy to incorporate these same definitions in a dictionary used by computer programs, terminal

screen displays, and reports.

Data Management is evolving into information management, but a major difference between the two still lies in how each uses data. A data dictionary usually contains static definitions—not how the data are used but perhaps where they are used—whereas an information model deals with how the data are used as well as, at least, the basic operations performed on them. This requires more than just a data dictionary—it requires something akin to an encyclopedia that contains more information about the computerized processes of the enterprise.

We need a greater understanding of the total information needs of an enterprise, and for this we need information models that cover more than just computerized systems. The result will be an enterprise knowledge base.

We have seen an evolution with respect to the way data in a database are used. This is shown in Figure 9.6.

Figure 9.6 Data and Independence

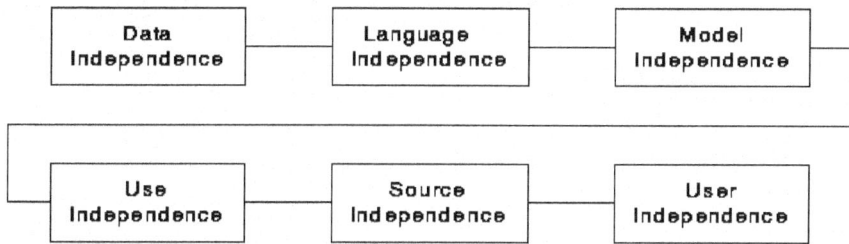

The evolution of file and database management systems produced a greater degree of independence between applications and the data used. This enabled many applications to share the same data structures. It also supported the development of end-user tools that enabled greater ad hoc data access. However, the applications still needed to use a particular data manipulation language to access the database. Database definitions refer to data structures and ways of viewing those structures, not to using the data (other than some security controls, perhaps).

In terms of overall market share, the most common database management system is probably hierarchical, but the one most heavily promoted, or that people feel they "ought" to use, is probably relational. For creating a corporate or global information system, the most appropriate database technological platform is likely to be hybrid, with server mechanisms that handle the access operations[24].

There has been some movement toward language independence, the clearest example being the development of SQL. However, SQL

24Roussopoulos et al. (1991) discuss database management systems for engineering information systems.

only provides access to the data, leaving their manipulation and use to the surrounding application programs. There remains the underlying restriction that SQL implementations imply or use a relational database, and the relational model is only suitable for a subset of an enterprise's information processing needs.

We can see, therefore, some future technological developments that will continue this evolution of applications that make use of common data structures:

- Model independence—languages will evolve that are independent of any particular traditional data storage model, for example, relational, network, or hierarchical.
- Use independence—an enterprise encyclopedia will contain information not only about the data but also about how the data are used or should be used; this needs to be specified independently of the application developers who create the applications. We are beginning to see this in some of the emerging object-oriented approaches to application development. Early database management systems have provided facilities such as constraints and security schemas[25].
- Source independence—so far, file and database management systems have generally known the location of the data needed by the applications; there is an increasing trend, particularly with the implementation of client/server models of computing, for an application to request a data service that is performed by some object not explicitly known to or addressed by the application.
- User independence—most data in an enterprise are only available to, or via, the technically sophisticated; the objective of providing everyone with the information they need, when they need it, in the form they need it, requires giving the end user much more assistance about the information available and how to get it.

Summary

In this chapter, we have looked at some of the deeper meanings behind terms such as "information", "system", "architecture", and "infrastructure". We hope we have demonstrated the value of a more formal and rigorous application of analogy and related approaches. Many of the points made should provide useful checklists to those responsible for creating and maintaining systems of information.

In the next and final chapter we will outline visions for information and IT infrastructures that present a clear view of implementation.

---

25 Security schemas are available in VAX DBMS and are an extension to the CODASYL database management system model.

Information and IT Infrastructures

In this chapter we present a brief general summary of both information and IT infrastructure components. We also offer some principles that might govern the definition of these infrastructures.

What is an Information Infrastructure?

We have demonstrated in several places the need for an enterprise to consider its business, organization, and information strategies together. Doing so enables it to determine which of its information needs can be met by IT and which cannot.

Information is one essential part of the lifeblood of an enterprise. Without it, the enterprise cannot become more ordered or organized; and without organization it cannot develop, flex, and change to provide the variety necessary to set and achieve its objectives and respond to the variety it encounters. It is probably reasonable to assert that an information infrastructure is a necessary, but not sufficient, condition for enterprise success.

Figure 10.1 shows one possible taxonomy of the components of an information infrastructure (remembering that an infrastructure provides a basis for multiple applications of information).

As with spending on IT, it is not the deployment, per se, or money spent on information that makes an enterprise more efficient or competitive; it is way the information resources are managed and deployed. The acquisition of expertise and constructing competency can be significant investments, but they will not have demonstrable returns on investment unless they are applied specifically.

An information infrastructure will include the provision of mechanisms for performing many basic operations on information:

- Origination and collection
- Organization

- Attenuation
- Amplification
- Storage
- Processing
- Interpretation
- Application
- Retrieval
- Communication and dissemination
- Homeostasis and control

Figure 10.1 Information Infrastructure Components

- Knowledge
- A vision of what may be desirable or possible
- Intuition of what will, may, or can happen
- Expertise (the efficient application of skills and knowledge to tasks)
- Competence (the application of expertise and knowledge to achieve objectives or solve problems)
- Facts and information to provide descriptions of objects and situations
- Processes and practices identifying information-handling mechanisms
- Models to provide alternative interpretations of facts and information
- Policies representing preferences and norms
- Standards to specify common and consistent ways of achieving similar effects
- Contracts to embody agreements and commitments
- Cultural preferences, prejudices, and aesthetics

In Chapter 1 we offered suggestions for computer-based and noncomputer-based technology to support these operations. It is a matter for enterprise and organization strategies to determine how such an infrastructure will be defined and implemented.

Figure 10.2 lists what we have identified as key principles behind an information infrastructure. Figure 10.3 depicts a schematic of information infrastructure components, including a "bus" connecting them all to indicate that an information infrastructure should be capable of sup-porting various organizational structures.

The absence of an explicitly designed and implemented infrastructure will mean that arbitrary variants of these components will reside in the individual enterprise departments. It also will mean that crossfunctional integration will be difficult, and there is likely to be replication and redundancy in multiple implementations.

The absence of information sharing across enterprises has always caused problems, usually in proportion to enterprise size, geographical and cultural dispersion, and departmental specialization. It is clear that IT can help resolve these problems, but only if management is aware of them and willing to face organizational issues before applying IT.

Figure 10.2 Information Infrastructure Principles

- The information infrastructure should provide mechanisms by which people can know what relevant information exists and how that information can be applied to their tasks.
- The information infrastructure must handle information from many sources and in different forms.
- The information infrastructure should assist in identifying issues arising out of alternative interpretations of facts and information.
- Each person should be provided all relevant information when needed, in a way that is organizationally and economically optimal.
- The cost of providing the information should be lower than the added value obtainable from it, within the policy requirements of the enterprise.
- Information should be supplied only when it can affect a decision or if it is needed for some statutory or policy requirement.
- The information infrastructure can deliver necessary information in a form suitable for the recipient.

Figure 10.3 information Infrastructure

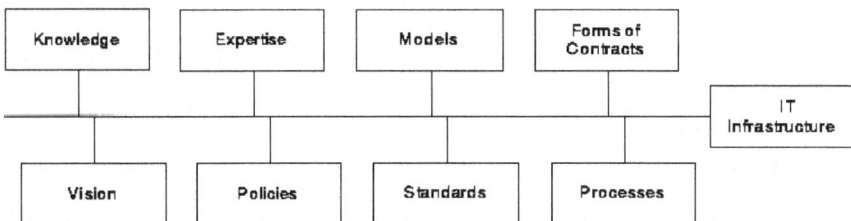

What is an IT Infrastructure?

We define an IT infrastructure as a basic computing and communications platform on which many applications can be based. The following are its major components:

- Hardware platforms
- Base software platforms
- Communications technology
- Clients, servers, and other software (or embedded) components that provide common services to a range of applications
- Enterprise-wide data services such as an employee data directory
- Enterprise-wide applications such as electronic mail and conferencing
- Common handling mechanisms for different data types such as structured data, voice, images, knowledge representations, and graphics
- Methods, standards, and tools

We call such an infrastructure, within the context of the information architecture we identified earlier, a product architecture. A product architecture is the most "physical" manifestation of an information architecture but also embeds some key principles.

It is important to note that *hardware and software products by themselves do not promote business flexibility; it is the way those products are used that can contribute to flexibility or hinder it.*

IT Infrastructure Principles

An IT infrastructure includes a product architecture, which is essentially a set of products, both hardware and software, and other software components, such as tools, clients, servers, and reusable building blocks, for the construction of systems and applications. Figure 10.4 lists the principles that underlie a product architecture.

There is an enormous proliferation of "architectures" in the product space. When we talk about a "product architecture", we mean a collection of products and components that cooperate in providing computing support to the enterprise's information needs.

In order to reduce the cost of a product architecture, it is advisable to use existing software components or packages wherever possible. A technical architecture provides a shopping list of required functionality that can be matched against available products. The gaps in the list identify candidates for investment and development effort, which can be ranked according to maximum value added to the enterprise.

We find that product selection often precedes a rational matching of computing functionality and information needs. This creates much difficulty in that developers and IT strategists sometime select methods and technology before they understand problems and requirements. Indeed, many enterprises must protect themselves against IT strategists who make over-simplistic but enthusiastic decisions about technology based on their view of IS needs rather than on true business needs[1].

Figure 10.4 Product Architecture Principles

- The product architecture identifies a set of products and tools to implement technical architecture principles.
- A common operational infrastructure is required to optimize product architecture functionality, application components, and operational costs.
- Servers to provide access to data and operations on the data should be available as far as possible.
- Available standards should be implemented as effectively as possible in order to provide interoperability.
- Applications should be "distributable".
- A product architecture provides a supportable environment that can evolve with both business needs and technological changes.
- A product architecture implements interconnectivity and interoperability.
- Products should be cost-effective (technically and organizationally).
- Products should support a client/server model of computing.

Dealing with the Proliferation of Computing Resources

The proliferation of computing resources in an enterprise necessitates infrastructure. In fact, the need for infrastructure may well be proportional to the availability and complexity of an enterprise's computing resources.

Personal computers (PCs) provide a very good example of how the proliferation of computing resources can lead to a greater need for computing product infrastructure.

---

1 Alexander (1991) summarizes one of the conclusions of an Index Group survey this way: " . . . senior managers are preoccupied with technologies that are more valuable to the IS organization than to the business at large". He then summarizes the top five emerging technologies with the greatest level of interest among a sample of IS executives as CASE and other software productivity tools, image systems and processing, expert systems, LANs and networking, and database tools and management. This is a clear example of what happens when an essentially IT-focused enterprise department has responsibility for IS and IT strategy.

An enterprise usually introduces a large number of PCs with only a limited available infrastructure. In the worst case each PC will be a stand-alone computing environment. Any sense of a product architecture will be simple, probably consisting of choice of PC, choice of common operating system, and a selection of PC packages. In a more complex environment, there will be communication either through simple networks or by file and data exchange.

Some of the many downsides to PC proliferation are these:

- Software license costs escalate in proportion to the number of PCs.
- Most end users do not want to perform difficult technical operations on the PC, so there must be a support organization to install and maintain PC environments.
- There may be no general understanding of what people are doing with all the PCs; an enterprise data dictionary may be impossible to compile, and meaningless even if it could be compiled.
- The responsibility for ensuring integrity (through mechanisms such as backups) may not be well defined or implemented.
- The greater the number of stand-alone PCs, or networked PCs, the greater the overall security risk to enterprise information assets.
- There may be no clear knowledge or understanding of the underlying models used for enterprise decision making.

These problems, if they arise by virtue of a proliferation of PCs, can only be fixed by the introduction of an infrastructure within which the PCs cooperate. This generally implies the availability of tools for inter-operability, communication, and consistency, along with an operational environment that promotes integrity and security.

The introduction of PCs into traditional mainframe environments has led to discussion and proposals concerning two-tiered and three-tiered computing. In a two-tiered scenario, a mainframe handles central business operations, enterprise-wide database processing, and communications; PCs are used to provide end-user computing capability, which would be prohibitively expensive if handled by the mainframe simultaneously with basic enterprise activity. This kind of problem led to early equivalents of product architectures in the industry. PCs in a two-tiered computing scenario use different subsets of data from the mainframes, which means that end users often try to gain access to the mainframe to obtain the data they need. This led to the idea of a three-tiered computing environment, where initial data extracts from the mainframe are made available to the PCs via intermediate stores of data.

These kinds of product architectures are essentially the consequence of a mainframe and centralized approach to providing computing platforms.

We believe that two- and three-tiered approaches to computing offer very simplistic models of product architectures that are generally incapable of meeting the extensive information needs of an enterprise efficiently and cost-effectively. They are a leftover from the days when data processing was essentially part of the finance department and are probably only suitable for that kind of scenario.

Multivendor Platforms

The proliferation of computing platforms occurs not only vertically in terms of machine size, but also horizontally across different enterprise departments. This means that anyone charged with defining and implementing a CIS or GIS is bound to encounter multivendor platforms. In establishing information systems in conjunction with trading partners, enterprises must be able to handle communications and cooperating functionality between equipment and software from very diverse sources.

The general nature of the problem, and a high level statement of the goals is expressed in a recent Digital publication (Digital 1990), which states

> Solving departmental and end-user problems by acquiring a variety of incompatible hardware and software from multiple vendors has created a new and pressing business problem . . . information sharing is increasingly critical to the success of the enterprise and to its component organizations . . . enterprises need systems that offer more than just wire connections and file sharing. They need applications that work together, throughout a global network of hardware and operating systems from many different vendors. Enterprises want to be able to incorporate new technologies into their computing environments, without discarding existing investments and disrupting users. They want the flexibility to change in the future, and the freedom to make their own choices, with the security of knowing that any new elements they introduce will work with existing components. They want their applications to be available on all the systems they use. Toward that end, they want to be able to move applications easily from one system to another, and to have systems inter-operate, or co-operate together, to run applications.

This represents a significant charter for product architectures that offers considerable interoperability, flexibility and extensibility—all at a justifiable cost.

There are many ways to characterize a computing platform. We know that an essential problem can be created by using a two-dimensional representation of an n-dimensional reality, because whichever characterization is selected will have potential semantic problems. Figure 10.5 is our characterization of a computing platform that brings together several essential building blocks for IT-based applications (which may be distributed in practice). Several facts emerge from this:

- As soon as two or more computers are linked both computing and communications hardware are involved.
- Most applications require hardware peripherals such as printers, magnetic storage, robots, bank teller machines, sensing devices, and control mechanisms.
- Most applications, packages, and system utilities are insulated from the hardware by an operating system.
- Most complex integrated applications involve application systems, packages, and software produced in house. They use various non-procedural software products (such as database management systems and screen management systems).
- End users often have access to more than one application, and they may need access to an application, a package, a piece of in-house software, or some operating system facilities.
- An application system offers end-user access and may be made up from packages, nonprocedural products, or in-house software.

The characterization in Figure 10.5 is layered, not only in conceptual terms, but also in the way the computing platforms have been implemented. Such layering produces greater reusability and portability[2].

Portability involves creating applications and functionality that can operate on computing platforms from different vendors. The very simple layering in Figure 10.6 indicates how an application written as a set of common services can be portable across systems able to implement that set of services.

---

2 This trend in layering received its first major push with the unbundling of computer hardware and operating systems. A very widely used layering concept and implementation is the ISO Reference Model of Open Systems Interconnection (OSI), for a sample explanation of which see Tanenbaum (1981).

Figure 10.5 Autonomous Computing Platform

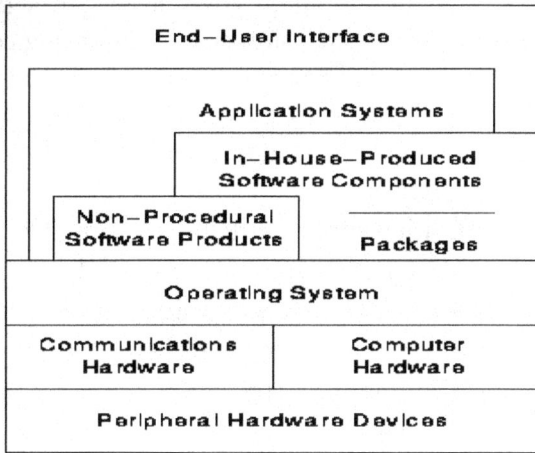

```
┌─────────────────────────────────────────────┐
│              End–User Interface               │
│  ┌─────────────────────────────────────────┐ │
│  │           Application Systems            │ │
│  │     ┌───────────────────────────────────┤ │
│  │     │      In–House–Produced            │ │
│  │     │     Software Components           │ │
│  │  ┌──┴──────────────────┐                │ │
│  │  │  Non–Procedural     │                │ │
│  │  │ Software Products   │   Packages     │ │
│  ├──┴─────────────────────┴────────────────┤ │
│  │            Operating System              │ │
│  ├──────────────────────┬───────────────────┤ │
│  │   Communications     │    Computer       │ │
│  │     Hardware         │    Hardware       │ │
│  ├──────────────────────┴───────────────────┤ │
│  │      Peripheral Hardware Devices         │ │
│  └─────────────────────────────────────────┘ │
└─────────────────────────────────────────────┘
```

Figure 10.6 Portability Layering

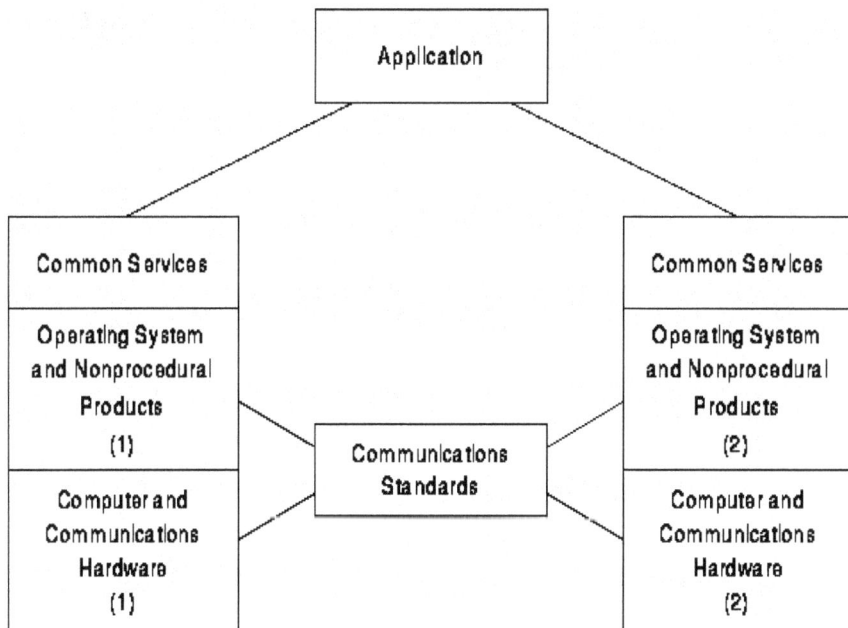

Client/Server Models

Another major issue for a product architecture is the extent to which enterprise functionality and data are to be distributed. Resolving it involves complex optimization problems. For example, whether to have one centralized price database, or to replicate and distribute parts of it, depends on factors such as development costs, losses through down-time, network switching and transmission costs, computing costs, and organizational efficiency and effectiveness. In some cases a distributed system is optimal, but in others a centralized system is best. For these reasons, applications should be designed to be *distributable rather than distributed*[3].

A distributable application implies that the actual location of functionality and data in a network is determined by a particular configuration, which may itself change as business needs, technology, and environment evolve. The ability to reconfigure an application's hardware, software, and communications components has led to the emergence of the idea of client/server computing, which can also be considered an implementation of some object-oriented ideas.

There are various definitions of clients and servers. The ones we offer below are intended to clarify what we mean. Readers who are familiar with software engineering will recognize some key principles.

Clients are infrastructure components that:

- Receive requests for some service to be performed
- Provide appropriate assistance in the formulation a request
- Verify and validate the syntax of a request
- Verify and validate the semantics of a request
- Translate a syntactically and semantically correct request into a series of operations to be performed by servers
- Transmit or make available to servers the operations they are to perform
- Provide the user of a system or application with an appropriate reply or response to each request

Servers are infrastructure components that

- Receive requests for some service from a client, in a standard form that has already been checked for correct syntax and semantics
- Perform the services requested by a client
- Where appropriate, formulate and propagate requests for services to other servers

---

3 Designers of distributable applications must deal with a substantial deficiency in many present-day methods of analysis and design for computer systems. Most methods originated some 15 to 20 years ago, essentially from monolithic MIS-type cultures, and they do not assist the production of distributability. Some of the traditional techniques, such as data-flow diagrams and normalization, if used as the only or main techniques, may well hinder the design of distributability and certainly do not train the adherents to collect information needed to take optimal distribution decisions. (For example, traditional data analysis does not train analysts to capture information about consistency constraints that apply to replicated or distributed data.)

- Coordinate and synchronize the completion of the requested service
- Depending on the protocol of communication between the clients and servers, send or make available to the requesting client any appropriate acknowledgements, responses, and messages
- Receive delegated requests from other servers

Alternative definitions of clients and servers exist, and we are not asserting correctness for ours. However, ours do provide developers with operational definitions that aid client/server analysis and design. By separating the functionality as we suggest, systems usually display high flexibility and distributability.

There are some key additional points to be made about our definitions:

- We make no assumptions about any hierarchical relationships between clients and servers or servers and servers. Client/server infrastructures are of undetermined network morphology.
- Client/server models stretch many traditional analysis approaches beyond breaking point[4] and in doing so expose the weakness of traditional modeling, rather than expose any weakness in the client/server approach.
- When a client passes a request to a server, the service may in fact be performed by some network or hierarchy of servers.
- In some circumstances a system component may be either a client or a server, the difference being the behavior of the component rather than some formal restriction.
- Client/server models may be developed either by structured methods that apply certain software engineering principles carefully or by object-oriented methods.

A client/server implementation offers a flexible and reconfigurable set of hardware and software components. It frequently results in clients that make a request for a service to be performed but never know which server actually performs the service. Similarly, a server can provide a service without knowing the originating client or server that generated the request or received the service.

It is not advisable to separate the development of a product architecture from the overall enterprise and information strategies. This is because the approach to the design and implementation of applications will be heavily dependent on strategic decisions such as the

---

4 For example, there may be server A and server B; in some circumstances A executes before B, but in other circumstances B executes before A. Where both cases exist for one system traditional hierarchical de-composition techniques will fail.

need for portability, flexibility, distributability, and interconnectivity.

No enterprise uses all available products because of cost considerations and the need for a common operational infrastructure. The particular collection of components in a product architecture is a statement of consistency and completeness and is not necessarily a statement about the goodness of products included or the inadequacies of those left out. Sometimes the best technical products are not selected, and the least effective are not always rejected. It is impossible to make use of all very good products, and there may be commitments to use certain products that still need enhancement.

Portability

Digital uses a specific architectural approach, known as Network Application Support (NAS), to provide application portability and interoperability in a multivendor environment. The concept behind NAS is that common services are provided to an application developer to be run on different platforms. This set of services provides a layer between the application and other applications, application users, data, and the underlying system. Figure 10.7 illustrates the NAS model. The *NAS Handbook* provides a more detailed explanation.

Figure 10.7 Network Application Support (NAS) Basic Model

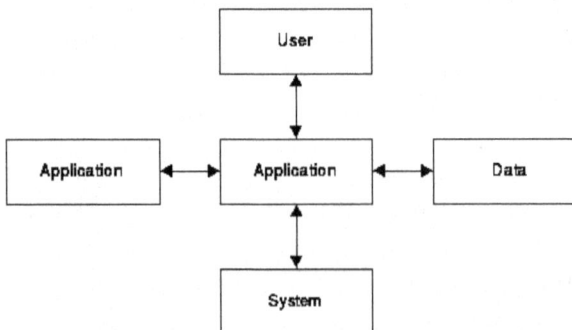

NAS is one clear example of the implementation of a multivendor open architecture. Many large corporations and governments are now establishing their own IT procurement criteria whereby they define the open standards with which their suppliers must comply. The Multi-Vendor Integration Architecture (MIA) introduced in January 1991 is one example[5]. The MIA requirements made use of existing

5 MIA was developed by a consortium that includes Nippon Telegraph and Telephone (NTT), NTT

international standards (such as SQL, OSI, and MOTIF). Where international standards did not exist or were not mature enough, the MIA Consortium adopted de facto standards or developed new technology.

Standards

Standards are the cause of much activity at present (their relationship to technical challenges was introduced in Chapter 8). Every enterprise needs to ensure that its strategy addresses standards, even if the decision is to ignore those that already exist.

An enterprise can choose from a number of different kinds of standards, among them.

*   Scientific—these arise as a result of well-founded theory under-pinned by sufficient empirical evidence and lead to applicable scientific theory that has demonstrable predictive value.
*   Industry accredited, or *de jure*—these are established by a major international, national, or industry enterprise that sees standards definition as a major activity; they may be supported by international treaty, national legislation, government or public authority mandate, or major buyer specification.
*   Consortium—these are defined by a consortium of enterprises that sets out to define standards.
*   *De facto*—within an industry or activity, these emerge generally as a result of the popularity or significant market share created by a particular approach.
*   Pseudo-standards—these are promoted as "standard", and many people repeat the belief or hope that there is a standard. In reality, however, the term "standard" is another word for a "wish", the reality being that there are so many implementations and variations of the "standard" that it does not deserve the name.
*   *Ad hoc*—these are produced as one-off standards with either single or multiple enterprise sponsorship and promotion.
*   Proprietary—these are defined and implemented by some enterprise (or combination of enterprises) that can exercise intellectual, implementation, and market control over them. (Some "public" standards are actually subject to intellectual property rights because the standards body does not license their free use for any purpose.)
*   Enterprise standards—these are defined by the enterprise itself because established standards from other sources are not acceptable for some reason, or there are gaps in available standards, or the culture of the enterprise is always to define

standards for itself.

Most of the standards discussed in the literature are of particular use to the IT infrastructure components of CISs and GISs rather than to the broader information infrastructure. For example, Gray (1991) identifies the market forces driving standards for open systems as follows:

- Hardware manufacturers (Open standards promotion with respect to IT is highly variable between manufacturers.)
- Software authors
- Innovative researchers and developers
- Software distributors
- Hardware resellers
- Commercial users
- Government agencies
- Academic institutions

An enterprise's approach to standards can range from minimum awareness of emerging standards efforts (along with associated market shares and application domain penetration) to substantial participation in standards setting activities. However, every large enterprise is likely to become multivendor, so standards will become important. Even so, regardless of the care taken, a portfolio of standards may include inconsistencies the enterprise will have to deal with.

Table 10.1 shows the application of standards to IT infrastructure and illustrates the emerging extensive nature of standards. It is not meant to be complete, although it does include both defined and emerging standards. This is a very rapidly changing area, and it is essential for the interested reader to obtain up-to-date information.

Table 10.1 Standards for IT Infrastructure

Standard domain	Applicability	Example standards
Operating system	POSIX	ANSI/IEEE 1003.1 ISO 9945-1
Application access	Windowing Forms Terminal Application control Graphics	X Window System OSF/Motif ANSI X3113 IEEE 1201
Data access	Data access language Data manipulation language	SQL CODASYL

Standard domain	Applicability	Example standards
Communications and networking	Data communications interfaces Transmission error detection and correction Network communication protocols Messaging Electronic data interchange Integrated services digital network (ISDN)	ISO Reference Model of Open Systems Interconnection (OSI) CCITT X.400 ASC X12 EDIFACT
System development	Software design descriptions Software requirements specifications Software life cycles	ANSI/IEEE 830-1984 ANSI/IEEE 1016-1987 IEEE P1074 US DoD 2167A SSADM
Document handling and presentation	Compound document services Dictionary services Information interchange services Character and symbol services Internationalization Print services	ISO 8613 ANS X3.143 ISO 8824-5 ASCII and extended ASCII ISO 8859, ISO 10646, JIS C 6299 ECMA/ISO Distributed Print Architecture PostScript DDIF (Digital Document Interchange Format) and DTIF (Digital Table Interchange Format)
Quality systems	Quality management and quality assurance systems	ISO 9000 ISO 9001 ISO 9002 ISO 9003 ISO 9004

An infrastructure based on an appropriate range of standards is the best way to provide interoperability in multivendor environments; it also provides a framework for the cooperation of many applications in a cross-functional infrastructure. Tools are increasingly available to implement particular standards on and between different computing platforms; these tools are essential components of an enterprise's product architecture.

So far we have only discussed the technical aspects of infrastructure. It is important to note that there are many non-technical standards that an infrastructure should incorporate. Here are some sources of non-technical standards that have a profound impact on CISs and

GISs:

- Audit requirements, to demonstrate the economic activity of an enterprise or report on aspects such as profitability
- Freedom of information provisions, which allow access to information either inside or outside the enterprise
- Security requirements to prevent unauthorized access and unauthorized disclosure by those with access to those who should not have the disclosed information
- Accounting and other professional standards, which must be incorporated in or supported by the information systems
- Data protection requirements limiting access to personal information
- Treaty or convention requirements controlling the trans-border flow of information
- National legislation covering matters such as requirements or provisions for information encryption
- Treaty, convention, or national legislation controlling trading and information exchange between countries

IT Infrastructure Components

These are the essential points an enterprise must know to construct the computer-related pieces of a CIS or GIS:

- The computing platforms and applications that must be integrated *within* the enterprise
- The *external* computing platforms with which the enterprise will wish to deal, as trading partners or otherwise

In many cases, emerging standards will be available to be applied to the technical issues of communication and application cooperation, but additional standards will be needed to handle the nontechnical matters.

Table 10.2 lists several IT infrastructure components for an enterprise CIS/GIS, along with principles and examples that apply to each.

Roles and Responsibilities

As discussed in Chapter 8, we advocate an information management and technology (IM&T) executive role at the enterprise level. This person must be accountable for the information and IT infrastructure. If such a position does not exist, it is at least necessary to have an IT executive with responsibility for the IT infrastructure.

The IT infrastructure implies significant capital investment and ongoing expense, so there must be in place an appropriate budgeting and control mechanism. The IT infrastructure budget should not be subjected to painful individual negotiations with the different business and department managers. Rather, top management must allocate a certain percentage of revenue to it as they do to R&D, corporate advertising, or finance. The IT executive must be empowered to manage the allocated budget and to drive optimization across the enterprise. Appropriate measurements must be established in terms of cost per unit of power, cost per unit of transmission, service level, and so on, so that the performance can be measured.

One way top management can assess IT infrastructure efficiency is through competitive analysis and comparison of different enterprises with respect to IT infrastructure cost. (There are independent consultants who provide this service.) It is also possible for the IM&T or IT executive to outsource the IT infrastructure operation completely while retaining responsibility for direction setting and accountability to management. Such an option is now being considered by more and more companies that wish to focus their resources on core competencies and have increasing difficulty maintaining the necessary in-house IT expertise[6]. The recent trend toward more outsourcing has arisen precisely because of the identification of infrastructure and, hence, services that can be outsourced without the enterprise losing responsibility for the use of information[7].

****

Table 10.2 Principles of IT Infrastructure Components

Component	Principles and Examples
Computing platforms	The client/server model provides the greatest flexibility; other models are variants of client/server processing. All computers and related operating systems should be able to operate within the context of wide interconnectivity and interoperability standards. The two- and three-tiered models are special cases of client/server models. The centralized versus distributed debate is essentially irrelevant, insofar as applications and IT components are distributable. Every large company is multivendor, so a CIS or GIS will require mechanisms for interoperability and inter-connectivity.

6 Krass (1990) discusses outsourcing. Other examples of subcontracted infrastructure services are building maintenance, catering, and component manufacturing.
7 This confirms the general industrial trends identified by OECD

Component	Principles and Examples
Communications infrastructure	It is necessary to integrate data, voice, and image, and it is necessary to provide a common transport infrastructure. PABX technology should be the responsibility of the IT manager. The infrastructure is built and managed as a company resource across all departments. The network must extend to customers, suppliers, and partners.
Enterprise-wide applications	These represent the functionality with the broadest reuse. The pervasiveness of IT provides opportunities for common task automation. Electronic mail is one of the most common enterprise-wide applications. Conferencing can support virtual teams and eliminate some costs from travel and meetings. Videotex services provide opportunities for the broadcast of information needed in multiple destinations. These applications include: — Electronic approval — Word and document processing — Access to common data — Access to common tools for manipulating data — Data integrity operations (such as backups)
Enterprise-wide clients	Enterprise-wide client standards provide end users with consistent interfaces to all available applications. They direct end users to the available functionality. They help end users in the use of applications. Videotex access provides an entry point to broadcast information. Office automation collects under some umbrella all the office functionality available. Transaction processing system front-ends provide the support for transactions throughout their entire life cycle. Executive system interfaces provide an umbrella for decision making and access to relevant expert systems. Management reporting systems present data and information to users that match their information needs. Information-handling services obtain and structure requests to handle, process, and present information in particular ways.
Enterprise-wide servers	Servers are implemented for common services needed by the enterprise. They are designed and treated like "black boxes" to provide a high degree of insulation between logical application requirements and the technology used for implementations. Access to servers is provided by appropriate client mechanisms. Servers make it easier to support information needs with hybrid technology and should eliminate pressure for inappropriate strategic decisions about technology such as database management system products. Enterprise data warehouses should be established for all major enterprise data subjects (for example, directories of people in the enterprise, price and product information, expertise centers, policies and procedures, customer reference information, training information and materials, job descriptions, and bulletins).

Epilogue

This book has outlined a long journey and provided many explorations. In the coming years, computers, information processing, and information use will be more pervasive, not less. If we are truly entering an information revolution, with the consequences that will entail, it is inevitable that information and IT infrastructures will become more extensive. Hopefully that will be a managed process, rather than one that continually takes people by surprise. The growing needs for inter-connectivity and interdependence will require that the core of any infrastructure that is put in place will need to be well architected.

One of the greatest challenges of the 1990s will be to handle total information needs, not just those that are computer-based. Power bases are shifting, patterns of management and organization are altering radically, and the nature of work is undergoing fundamental changes. To add to this, the next few years are likely to see greater emphasis on matters of principle and ethics, with a deeper concern for the human impact of applying technology.

This book has explored many issues, objectives, and practical steps to be taken in defining and implementing information infrastructures. We hope our readers have enjoyed this journey with us.

Appendix A:
Acronyms and Abbreviations

4GL	Fourth Generation Language
ADP	Automated Data Processing
ANSI	American National Standards Institute
ASCII	American Standard Code for Information Interchange
CAD	Computer Assisted Design
CAM	Computer Assisted Manufacturing
CASE	Computer Aided/ Assisted Software/System Engineering/ Environment
CCITT	Consultative Committee on International Telephony & Telegraphy
CDROM	Compact Disk Read-Only Memory
CEF	Critical Existence Factor
CFF	Critical Failure Factor
CEO	Chief Executive Officer
CIC	Computer Integrated Company
CIO	Chief Information Officer
CIS	Corporate Information System
CODASYL	Conference on Data Systems Languages
CSF	Critical Success Factor
DDIF	Digital Document Interchanging Format
DTIF	Digital Table Interchange Format
DP	Data Processing
ECMA	European Computer Manufacturers' Association
EDI	Electronic Data Interchange
EDP	Electronic Data Processing
EKI	Electronic Knowledge Interchange
GIS	Global Information System
HRO	Human Resources Officer/Organization

IEEE	Institute of Electrical and Electronics Engineers
IFIP	International Federation for Information Processing
IM&T	Information Management and Technology
IIS	Individual Information System
IS	Information System/Services
ISDN	Integrated Services Delivery Network
ISO	International Standards Organization
ISSP	Information Systems Strategic Planning
IT	metaphor for information technology artifacts
IVIS	Interactive Video Instructional System
JIS	Japanese Institute for Standards
JIT	Just-In-Time
LAN	Local Area Network
LDM	Language Definition Manager
MIPS	Million Instructions Per Second
MIS	Management Information System
MRP	Manufacturing Requirements Planning
NAS	Network Application Support
OSF	Open Software Foundation
PABX	Private Automated Branch Exchange
SQL	Structured Query Language
SSADM	Structured Systems Analysis and Design Methodology
SWOT	Strength Weakness Opportunity Threat
VAX	Virtual Address eXtension
VAX DBMS	VAX DataBase Management System
VHLL	Very High-Level Language
VMS	Virtual Memory Management System
VSM	Viable Systems Model
VLSI	Very Large-Scale Integration
VTX	Videotex

References

Alexander, Michael (1991) "Survey looks at critical issues in technology", *Computerworld*, 14th January, 1991.

Allen, Brandt (1989) *Building an IT Architecture for a Changing Organization*, International Center for Information Technologies.

Anderla, G. and Dunning, A. (1987) *Computer Strategies 1990-9*, John Wiley & Sons.

Anthony, R. N. (1965) *Planning and Control Systems: A Framework for Analysis*, Harvard University Press.

Archier, Georges and Serieyx, Herve (1984) *L'Entreprise du 3e Type*, Seuil.

Ashby, W. R. (1956) *An Introduction to Cybernetics*, Chapman and Hall.

Ashley, D. (1990) *Modeling Legal Argument*, MIT Press.

Avison, D. E. and Wood-Harper, A. T. (1990) *Multiview: An Exploration in Information Systems Development*, Blackwell Scientific Publications.

Bailey, N. T. J. (1957) *The Mathematical Theory of Epidemics*, Charles Griffin and Company.

Beer, Stafford (1972) *The Brain of the Firm*, John Wiley & Sons.

Beer, Stafford (1979) *The Heart of Enterprise*, John Wiley & Sons

Beer, Stafford (1981) *The Brain of the Firm*, John Wiley & Sons.

Beer, Stafford (1984) "The Viable System Model: Its Provenance, Development, Methodology and Pathology", *Journal of Operations Research* Vol. 35, (and included in Espejo and Harnden 1989).

Belbin, R. Meredith (1981) *Management Teams: Why They Succeed or Fail*, Heinemann Professional Publishing.

Best, Laurence J. (1990) *Application Architecture—Modem Large-Scale Information Processing*, John Wiley & Sons.

Blokdijk, A. and Blokdijk, P. (1987) *Planning and Design of Information Systems*, Academic Press.

Boehm, Barry W. (1981) *Software Engineering Economics*, Prentice-Hall.

Brooks, E.P. (1986) "No Silver Bullet: Essence and Accidents of Software Engineer¬ing", in *Information Processing '86*.

Butler Cox (1987) *The Impact of Information Technology on Corporate Organisation Structure*, Butler Cox & Partners Ltd.

Byars, Lloyd L. (1984) *Strategic Management: Planning and Implementation*, Harper & Row.

Cash, James I. , McFarlan, F. Warren and McKenney James L. (1983) *Corporate Information Systems Management: Text and Cases*, Richard D. Irwin.

Cash, James I. , McFarlan, F. Warren and McKenney James L. (1988) *Corporate Information Systems Management*, (2nd. ed.) Dow Jones-Irwin.

Checkland, Peter (1981) *Systems Thinking, Systems Practice,* John Wiley & Sons.

Checkland, Peter (1990) *Soft Systems Methodology in Action* John Wiley & Sons.

Child, John (1984) *Organization: A Guide to Problems and Practice,* Harper & Row.

Clemons, Eric K. (1991) "Evaluation of Strategic Investments in Information Technology", *Communications of the ACM,* Vol. 34 No. 1, January 1991.

Cutaia, Al (1990) *Technology Projection Modeling of Future Computer Systems,* Prentice-Hall.

Davenport, Thomas H. and Short, James E. (1990) "The New Industrial Engineering: Information Technology and Business Process Redesign", *Sloan Management Review,* Vol. 31 No. 4, 1990.

Davis, G. B., and Olson, M. H. (1984) *Management Information Systems: Conceptual Foundation, Structure and Development,* (2nd. ed.) McGraw-Hill.

Davis, Stanley M. (1987) *Future Perfect,* Addison Wesley.

Davis, Dwight (1989) "U.S. Giants Run a $50 Billion IS Tab", *Datamation,* 15th November 1989.

Dickson, G.W., and Wetherbe, J.C. (1985) *The Management of Information Systems,* McGraw-Hill.

Digital (1990) *NAS Handbook: Developing Applications in a Multivendor Environment,* Digital Equipment Corporation.

Drucker, Peter F. (1986) *The Frontiers of Management,* Heinemann.

Drucker, Peter F. (1988) "The Coming of the New Organization", *Harvard Business Review* January-February 1988.

Dumaine, Brian (1991) "The Bureaucracy Busters", *Fortune International,* Vol. 123, No. 1.

Espejo, R., and Watt, J. (1978) *Management Information Systems: A System for Design,* University of Aston Management Centre.

Espejo, R., and Harnden, R. (eds.) (1989) *The viable systems model: Interpretation and Application of Stafford Beer's VSM,* John Wiley & Sons.

Fowler, H.W., and Fowler, E.G. (1931) *The King's English,* Oxford University Press.

Freeman, C., and Soete, L. (1985) *Information Technology and Employment: An Assessment,* Science Policy Research Unit, University of Sussex.

Friedman, Andrew L., and Cornford, Dominic S. (1989) *Computer Systems Development: History, Organization and Implementation,* John Wiley & Sons.

Gerelle, Eric G. R., and Stark, John (1988) *Integrated Manufacturing Strategy Planning and Implementation,* McGraw-Hill.

Gray, Pamela (1991) *Open Systems: A Business Strategy for the 1990s,* McGraw-Hill.

Grenier, Ray and Metes, George (1992) *Enterprise Networking: Working Together Apart*, Digital Press.

Gunton, T. (1989) *Infrastructure*, Prentice-Hall.

Gurbaxani, Vijay and Whang, Seungjin (1991) "The Impact of Information Systems on Organizations and Markets", *Communications of the ACM*. Vol. 34, No. 1, January 1991.

Hall. Arthur D. (1989) *Metasystems Methodology*, Pergamon Press.

Hammer, Michael (1990) "Reengineering Work: Don't Automate, Obliterate", *Harvard Business Review*, Vol. 68, No. 4.

Horngren, Charles T. and Sunden, Gary L. (1987) *Introduction to Management Accounting*, (7th ed.) Prentice-Hall.

Inmon, W. H. (1986) *Information System Architecture: A System Developer's Primer*, Prentice-Hall.

Johansen, Robert (1988) *Groupware: Computer Support for Business Teams*, Free Press.

Johnson, Tim and Chappell, Caroline (1990) *The Computer Integrated Company: Market Driver for the 1990s*, Ovum Ltd.

Kearney, A. T. (1990) *Barriers to the Successful Application of Information Technology*, A. T. Kearney Management Consultants.

Keen, Peter G. W. (1988) *Competing in Time*, Ballinger.

Keen, Peter G. W. (1991) *Shaping the Future: Business Design through Information Technology*, Harvard Business School Press.

Kotler, Philip and Roberto, Eduardo L. (1989) *Social Marketing*, The Free Press.

Krass, Peter (1990) "The Dollars and Sense of Outsourcing", *Information Week*, 26th February, 1990.

Lee, John F. and Sears, Francis Weston (1962) *Thermodynamics*, (2nd. ed.) Addison-Wesley.

Licker, Paul S. (1987) *Fundamentals of Systems Analysis with Application Design*, Boyd and Fraser.

Loveman, Gary W. (1988) *An Assessment of the Productivity Impact of Information Technologies*, in the *Working Papers for Management in the 1990s*, Massachusetts Institute of Technology.

Lucas, H. C. (1986) *Information Systems Concepts for Management*, McGraw-Hill.

Maddison, Richard N. (ed.); Baldock, Robert; Bhabuta, Love; Darnton, Geoffrey; Feldman, Paul; Fitzgerald, Guy; Hindle, Keith; Kovacs, Almos; Lane, Aden; Mansell, Gilbert; and, Wood, Bob (1989) *Information System Development for Managers*, Paradigm in association with the Open University.

Martin, J., with Leben, J. (1989) *Strategic Information Planning Methodologies*, Prentice-Hall.

McFarlan, F. Warren (1981) "Portfolio Approach to Information Systems", *Harvard Business Review*, September/October 1981.

McKay, David T., and Brockway, Douglas W. (1989) Building I/T Infrastructure for the 1990s, *Stage by Stage*, Vol. 9, No. 3.

Meyer, N. Dean and Boone, Mary E. (1987) *The Information Edge*, McGraw-Hill.

Miller, J. G. (1955) "Toward a General Theory for the Behavioral Sciences", *American Psychologist*, Vol. 10.

MIT (1989) *Management in the 1990s Research Program Final Report*, Massachusetts Institute of Technology.

Murdick, Robert G. with Munson, John C. (1986) *MIS Concepts & Design*, (2nd. ed.) Prentice-Hall.

Newport, John Paul Jr. (1986) "A Growing Gap in Software", *Fortune*, 28th April 1986.

Nolan, Richard L. (1973) "Managing the Computer Resource: A Stage Hypothesis", *Communications of the ACM*, Vol. 16.

Nolan, Richard L. (1979) "Managing the Crisis in Data Processing", *Harvard Business Review*.

Nolan, Richard L. (1988) "Top-Down-Driven Architecture Design", *Stage by Stage*, Vol. 8, No. 1.

Nolan, Richard L., Pollack, Alex J., and Ware, James P. (1989) "Toward the Design of Network Organizations", *Stage by Stage*, Vol. 9, No. 1.

Nolan, Richard L. (1990) "The Knowledge Work Mandate", *Stage by Stage*, Vol. 10, No. 2.

Norton, David P. (1989) "Whatever Happened to the Systems Approach?" *Stage by Stage*, Vol. 9, No. 2.

OECD (1986) *Trends in the Information Economy*, OECD,

OECD (1987) "Information Technology and Economic Prospects", OECD.

OECD (1989a) "The Internationalization of Software and Computer Services", OECD.

OECD (1989b) "Information Technology and New Growth Opportunities", OECD.

OECD (1989c) "Major R&D Programmes for Information Technology", OECD.

Olle, T. W. (ed.) (1982) *Information Systems Design Methodologies: A Comparative Review*, North-Holland.

Olle, T. W. (ed.) (1983) *Information Systems Design Methodologies: A Feature Analysis*, North-Holland.

Olle, T. W. (ed.) (1986) *Information Systems Design Methodologies: Improving the Practice*, North-Holland.

Olle, T. W. (ed.) (1988) *Computerized Assistance During the Information Systems Life Cycle*, North-Holland.

Onions, C. T. (1933) *The Shorter Oxford English Dictionary on Historical Principles* (revised and edited) Oxford University Press.

PA Consulting (1990) *Information Technology: The Catalyst for Change*,

Mercury Books.

Pascale, Richard Tanner and Athos, Anthony G. (1981) *The Art of Japanese Management*, Simon and Schuster.

Porter, M. E. (1980) *Competitive Strategy*, Free Press.

Porter, M. E. (1985) *Competitive Advantage*, Free Press.

Pressman, Roger S. (1987) *Software Engineering: A practitioner's approach*, McGraw-Hill.

QED (1989) *Information Systems Planning for Competitive Advantage*, QED Information Series.

Remenyi, Dan R. S. (1991) *Introducing Strategic Information Systems Planning* NCC Blackwell.

Roach, S. (1988) "The Business Week Newsletter for Information Executives", *Business Week Newsletter*.

Robertson, David (1991) *Eco-Logic: Logic-Based Approaches to Ecological Modelling*, MIT Press.

Rockart, John F., and Short, James E. (1988) *Information Technology and the New Organization: Toward More Effective Management of Interdependence*, Center for Information Systems Research, Sloan School of Management, Massachusetts Institute of Technology.

Rockart, John F., and Short, James E. (1989) "IT in the 1990s: Managing Organizational Interdependence", *Sloan Management Review*.

Rogers, Everett M. (1989) *The Critical Mass in the Diffusion of Interactive Technologies*, Annenberg School of Communications, University of Southern California.

Rothman, Andrea with Grover, Ronald and Neff, Robert (1991) "Media Colossus", *Business Week*, March 25th, 1991.

Roussopoulos, N., Mark, L., Sellis, T., and Faloutsos, C.(1991), "An Architecture for High Performance Engineering Information Systems," *IEEE Transactions on Software Engineering*, Volume 17, number 1, pp. 22-33.

Savage, Charles M. (1990) *Fifth Generation Management*, Digital Press.

Scheer, A.-W. (1989) *Enterprise-Wide Data Modelling*, Springer-Verlag.

Schlender, Brenton R. (1991) "A High-Tech Bird for a Ground War," *Fortune International*, Vol 123 No. 4.

Schutte, H. (1988) *Strategic Issues in Information Technology*, Pergamon Infotech Ltd.

Shannon, Claude (1948) "The Mathematical Theory of Communication", *Bell Systems Technical Journal*, Vol. 2.

Sorokin, Pitirim A. (1943) *Sociocultural Causality, Space, Time*, Duke University Press.

Stewart, Thomas A. (1991) "Brainpower", *Fortune International*, Vol. 123, No. 11.

Strassman, Paul A. (1988) *Measuring Business Value of Information Technologies*, International Center for Information Technologies.

Strassman, Paul A. (1990) *The Business Value of Computers*, Information Economics Press.

Synott, William R. and Gruber, W. H. (1981) *Information Resource Management*, John Wiley & Sons.

Synott, William R. (1987) *The Information Weapon: Winning Customers and Markets with Technology*, John Wiley & Sons.

Tanenbaum, Andrew S. (1981) *Computer Networks*, Prentice-Hall.

Taylor, F. W. (1911) *Principles of Scientific Management*, Harper and Row.

Taylor, B., and Sparkes, J.R. (1977) *Corporate Strategy and Planning*, Heinemann.

Teichroew, Daniel (1989) "Software Engineering and CASE in the 1990's", at the Symposium *Taking CASE into the 1990's*, Geneva: Digital Equipment Corporation April 1989.

Teichroew, Daniel and Darnton, Geoffrey (1992) *Software Production into the Twenty First Century* forthcoming.

Toffler, Alvin (1990) *Powershift: Knowledge, Wealth and Violence at the Edge of the 21st Century*, Bantam Books.

Tuft, Patricia and Adler, David (1979) *New Metric Handbook: Planning and Design Data*, Architectural Press.

Vincent, David R. (1990) *The Information Based Corporation*, Dow Jones Irwin.

von Bertalanffy, Ludwig (1968) *General System Theory*, George Braziller Inc.

Waterman Robert H., Peters, Thomas J., and Phillips, Julien R. (1980) "Structure is Not Organization", *Business Horizons*, June 1980 pp 14-26

Weaver, Warren (1949) "Recent Contributions to the Mathematical Theory of Communication", *Scientific American*, July 1949.

Wood-Harper, A. T. , Antill, Lyn, and Avison, D. E. (1985) *Information Systems Definition: The Multiview Approach*, Blackwell Scientific Publications.

Willis, Neil and Kerridge, Jon (1983) *Introduction to Computer Architecture*, Pitman.

Winfield, Ian (1991) *Organisations and Information Technology: Systems, Power and Job Design*, Blackwell Scientific Publications.

Zachman, John A. (1987) "A Framework for Information Systems Architecture", *IBM Systems Journal* Vol. 26, No. 3.

Zuboff, Shoshana (1988) *In The Age of The Smart Machine*, Heinemann Professional Publishing.

Index

Symbols

5 Zeros Concept 41–42
    and Information Architecture 42

A

Actuality
    of enterprise 64
Adaptation
    system 217
Ad hoc standards 259
Adler, David 221, 274
Administration
    as enterprise-wide business process
        96
Aesthetics
    component of infrastructure 248
Alexander, Michael 251, 269
Allen, Brandt 223, 269
ALL-IN-1 45
American Airlines 200
American Hospital Supply 145
AMIS 135
Amplification 106, 218
    helped by IT 128
Analoges and comparisons
    used in this book's topics 206
Analogy 209
    architectural 69
    biological 155
    from idea to model 210
    legal 208
    production and manufacturing 209
    role of 210
    software chip 209
    transport 235
    VLSI and CAD/CAM 212–213
Anderla, G. 105, 269
Anthony, R. N. 70, 161, 269
Antill, Lyn 274
Application and Infrastructure Balance 187
Application integration and distribu-

tion 46–47
Applications portfolio management
    30–31
Archier, Georges 41, 269
Architectural Analogy for Information
    Systems 224
Architectural facilitators 84
Architecture
    and infrastructure 2
    and the IT world 223
    concepts and definitions 220
Artificial intelligence 66
Ashby, W. R. 200, 217, 269
Ashley, D. 208, 269
Asset management
    of information 152
Assets
    enterprise 202
    information 152, 172
    intangible 229
Athos, Anthony G. 42, 238, 273
Attenuation 106, 218
    helped by IT 128
Authority
    do not lead by 192
Automotive industry
    IT systems in the product 89
Autonomous computing platform 255
Avison, D. E. 110, 269, 274

B

Bailey, N. T. J. 185, 269
Baldock, Robert 271
Beer, Stafford 18, 64, 104, 155, 166,
        200, 209, 213, 219, 227, 269
Belbin, R. Meredith 132, 269
Beliefs
    significance of for IT 150
Berkes, Leslie xv
Best, Laurence J. 223, 269
Bhabuta, Love 271
Blokdijk, A 63, 213, 269
Blokdijk, P. 63, 213, 269
Boehm, Barry W. 132, 269
Boone, Mary E. 230, 272
Bottom-up approaches 95, 145

282

Land, labor, capital, enterprise
   plus information - as economic fac-
      tors of production 228
Lane, Aden 271
Latency 65
Law of requisite variety 217
Leben, J. 95, 176, 238, 271
Lee, John F. 216, 271
Legal argument 208
Libraries 45
Licker, Paul S. 223, 271
Linkage analysis planning 61
Localized exploitation 115
Logical requirements 177
Logistics
   as enterprise-wide business process
      96
Loveman, Gary W. 117, 271
Lucas, H. C. 271

M

Machines
   pure IT, IT-based, IT-assistend, non-
      IT 144
Maddison, Richard N. 63, 271
Mail filters 128
Mainframes 190
Management
   strategic actions for top 27
Management Information Systems
      (MISs) 161–164
Management recommendations
      25–32
   application portfolio management
      30
   infrastructure 31
   models and architecture 29–30
   organizational recommendations
      28–29
   strategic actions 26–28
   top-down 25
Management reporting processing
      environment 50
Management styles
   evolving 134
Managing Knowledge in the Enter-

   prise 173
Mansell, Gilbert 271
Manufacturing and Selling
   as enterprise-wide business pro-
      cesses 96
Marginal effectiveness of information
      158
Mark, L. 273
Martin, J. 61, 65, 95, 176, 238, 271
Massachusetts Institute of Technology
      272
Mass customization 7, 212
Matrix management
   for organization 21
matrix structures 36
McFarlan, F. Warren 62, 70, 198, 269,
      271
McKay, David T. 232, 272
McKenney James L. 62, 269
Mechanization 18, 121
Mediatex 169
Mergers 7
Meta-data 9
Metes, George 133, 271
Methods engineers 84
Meyer, N. Dean 230, 272
Middle management
   decrease in need for 128
Miller, J. G. 207, 272
Minitel 153
MIS
   conceptual, logical, and physical 163
   cycle 164
Mission 26, 88, 236–237
MIT 141, 272
   five levels of business reconfigura-
      tion 114
Models
   alternative interpretations of facts
      and information 248
Moving into new markets 7
Moving work to the people 129–130
Multi-Vendor Integration Architecture
      (MIA) 258
Multivendor Platforms 253–254
Munson, John C. 213, 272
Murdick, Robert G. 213, 272

Servers 256
  common services needed by the
    enterprise 264
  component of IT infrastructure 250
  defined 256
Service delivery and resource acquisi-
  tion
  as enterprise-wide business process
    96
Shannon, Claude 214, 273
Shared decision making 115
Shared experience 115
Shared goals 115
Shared recognition and reward 115
Shared responsibility, accountability,
  and trust 115
Shared work 115
Shift from obtaining power by control-
  ling information, to obtaining
  power by providing it 192
Short, James E. 94, 116, 270, 273
Simulation models 208
Skills
  component of organization 124
  interaction with organization and
    tasks 114
  principles 127
Social paradigms
  shift in 3
Socio-technical system 183
  IT a component in 159
  IT as 159, 183
Socio-technical systems 66
Soete, L. 270
Software chip
  also as analogy 209
Software development
  types of activity 225
Software Factory 211
Software platforms
  component of IT infrastructure 250
Sony 90
Sorokin, Pitirim A. 207, 209, 273
Sparkes, J.R. 239, 274
Specialization 18, 120
Spider-webs 28
Standard of living

dependent on many IT applications
  153
Standards 181, 221, 259–263
  component of infrastructure 248
  for IT infrastructure 260–261
  market forces driving 260
Stark, John 165, 270
Starreveld, R.W. 213
Stewart, Thomas A. 19, 273
Stock market crash 160
Stone, David xv
Strassman, Paul A. 3, 230, 232, 273
Strategizing elements 91
Strategy 26, 88, 238–239
  definition 239
  origin of the term 238
Strengths, Weaknesses, Opportunities, and Threats 242
Suchan, Kathleen xv
Sunden, Gary L. 229, 271
SWOT. *See* Strengths, Weaknesses,
  Opportunities, and Threats
Synott, William R. 201, 274
System
  concepts and definitions 216–220
  emergent properties 218
  extensive properties 218
  intensive properties 219
System is more than the sum of the
  parts 218
Systems Architecture xii, 14, 47, 53, 67
  components 66, 75–76
  creation 79
  cross-functional 77
  definition maintenance 80
  linkages 75
  objectives 72
  principles 71
  processes 78
Systems operations
  as enterprise-wide business process
    96
Systems thinking
  vs functional thinking 63

286

T

Tanenbaum, Andrew S. 254, 274
Tasks
 component of organization 124
 interaction with organization and
  skills 114
 principles 126
Taylor, B. 239, 274
Taylor, F. W. 94, 119, 274
Taylorism 119
Technical Architecture 14, 47, 50–51
 as a statement of fundamental design
  principles 51
 several for each enterprise 49
 taxonomy 50
 unique to each enterprise 51
Technical challenges 171, 179–187
Technocentrism 150
Technological paradigms
 shift in 3
Technology
 cultural differences in extent of
  dependence 148
 meaning of the term 142
Technology impact analysis 61
Technology stability 177
Teichroew, Daniel 190, 207, 274
Teleconferencing 36
Thermodynamics
 second law of 217
Thermostatics 216–217
The system is more than the sum of
  the parts 218
Threats. See Information technology
  threats and SWOTs
Time-sharing operating systems 40
Time to market
 improving 7
Toffler, Alvin 2, 17, 19, 174, 274
Top-down 95, 145
TOP Mapping 110
 example 111
Traditional responsibility for DP 195
Training
 IT as enabler of 118
Transactional integration 46

Transactional processing environment
 50
Transaction processing systems 162
Transport
 analogy 235
Tuft, Patricia 221, 274

U

Ubiquity 5
Unstructured vs structured information
 more unstructured information 172

V

Value
 of information 11, 158
 of information infrastructure 36
Values
 significance of for IT 150
Variety attenuation. See also Law of
  requisite variety
VAX DBMS 246
VAX (with VMS) architecture 45
Vertical integration 39, 40, 46, 178
Very-High-Level Languages (VHLLs)
 212
Viable System Model (VSM) 219, 237
 viability 216
Videotex 169
Vincent, David R. 62, 117, 225, 229,
 232, 274
Virtual teams xiii, 6, 36
 forming 132
 self-coordinated 131
Vision 26, 193
 component of infrastructure 248
 organization 21
VLSI and CAD/CAM Analogy
 212–213, 213
Volvo 119
von Bertalanffy, Ludwig 104, 200, 207,
 209, 219, 274

W

Ward, Norman xv
Ware, James P. 272
Waterman Robert H. 42, 274
Watt, J. 65, 270
Weaknesses. *See* SWOTs
Weaver, Warren 214, 274
Wetherbe, J.C. 270
Whang, Seungjin 271
Which comes first?
    enterprise strategy or IT strategy?
        100
Willis, Neil 223, 274
Winfield, Ian 232, 274
Wood, Bob 271
Wood-Harper, A. T. 110, 269, 274
Working styles
    evolving 134
    impact of IT on 122

Z

Zachman, John A. 224, 274
Zuboff, Shoshana 2, 15, 19, 174, 274

[page left blank intentionally]

www.ingramcontent.com/pod-product-compliance
Lightning Source LLC
Chambersburg PA
CBHW060542200326

41521CB00007B/451